Bride of the Revolution

Krupskaya as a young woman

Bride of the Revolution

Krupskaya and Lenin

by Robert H. McNeal

Ann Arbor
The University of Michigan Press

For
J. F. McN.

Acknowledgements

Any merits that this book may have owe a great deal to the numerous persons who have helped its author in one way or another. A special word of thanks must go to Sheila Fitzpatrick for sharing so generously her unique material from Soviet archives and to Bertram D. Wolfe for offering so freely of his large store of information and encouragement. Other scholars, who helped in ways too varied to itemize, are: Oswald Backus, Bohdan Bociurkiw, Anna Burgina, Stephen Cohen, Richard Day, Ralph Carter Elwood, Lewis Feuer, Leonhard Haas, Basil Harasymiw, David Joravsky, Thomas Martin, Jack Miller, Stephanie Miller, Alexander Rabinowich, T. H. Rigby, Charles Sampson, Leonard Schapiro, Alfred Senn, Harold Shukman, Robert Tucker, Boris Souvarine, Gleb Struve, Marina Utechin, and Tova Yedlin.

I am also indebted to the University of Toronto for granting me leave during 1967–1968, and especially to J. M. S. Careless, then head of the Department of History. During that year I enjoyed the hospitality of St. Antony's College, for which I am grateful to the Governing Body and to the Warden at that time, F. W. Deakin.

The Harvard University Library has kindly permitted me to quote from the Trotsky archives, and the library of the Hoover Institution has been equally generous with respect to the archives of the Paris office of the *okhrana*.

Contents

CHAPTER I

Nadezhda Means Hope

The vocation of revolution took shape in Russia around the middle of the nineteenth century. Appalled by the degradation of most of their countrymen, a few Russian noblemen who had absorbed the democratic values of the European enlightenment were the first recruits to this calling. In time they were joined by men of miscellaneous social background who had been educated somehow and shared the noble radicals' alienation from the existing order in the empire of the tsars. By mid-century there was a small cluster of men — landowners, civil servants, military officers, teachers, and writers — who formed a world apart in their own country. They had no organization, although they generally read the same magazines and often belonged to some small discussion circle, but they had a clear sense of their own identity, defined by moral rejection of the existing society and a devotion to its thoroughgoing alteration.

The word "devotion" is perhaps the key to the spirit of the radical intelligentsia of Russia. Self-sacrifice for the cause was the supreme value for them, and with reason, for they had little else but their devotion with which to oppose the might of the tsars. In the prophecy of Nicholas Cherny-shevsky, the struggle required, and would produce, "new men," who were to be distinguished precisely by their devotion.

The vocation of revolution, then, was less a specific career than a moral commitment in search of a career. Early experiments in such practical activities as mass propaganda and terrorism were not very promising, and there was profound concern for the question posed by the title of Chernyshevsky's most influential work, the novel *What Is to Be Done?* Nevertheless, the revolutionary calling was a well established option for educated Russians by the eighteen-sixties.

The largest class of humans to be liberated in Russia was clearly the peasantry, before *and* after the legal end of serfdom in 1861. For most radicals the "peasant question" necessarily was the central issue until nearly the close of the century. But it was a frustrating problem. Although many peasants hated the landlord, policeman, and bureaucrat, they were separated from the educated intellectuals by an enormous cultural gap. Efforts to bridge this gap in the early eighteen-seventies by "going to the people" — that is, by attempting to assimilate members of the radical intelligentsia into peasant culture — were on the whole a depressing failure.

Alexander Herzen and Nicholas Chernyshevsky were the two most eminent intellectual figures in Russian radicalism before the coming of Marxism toward the end of the century. Before all others they established the spirit of moral commitment that distinguished the vocation of revolution. Each man wrote one and only one novel to propagate his beliefs, and these two novels remain their principal ideological tracts. The very titles, *Who Is to Blame?* and *What Is to Be Done?* bear witness to the moral intensity of the writers. One might have expected that the chief issue in these books would have been the plight of the peasants, but it is not. Both novels are primarily

about the bondage of another large category of humankind
— women.

In the consciousness of the Russian radicals the
"woman question" (*zhenskii vopros*), as it came to be
called, was established almost as soon as the intelligentsia
itself took form, and it vied with the peasant question for
the concern of the radicals. This was a reasonable proposi-
tion morally. Women in Russia were at least as firmly
bound by law and custom as in other European countries
in the mid-nineteenth century. On the very highest aristocratic level there had been a few bluestockings since the
age of Catherine the Great, but the average noble or mer-
chant-class woman, not to speak of the peasants, was subject
to a more oppressively patriarchal society than prevailed
in the West. Compared to the peasant question, the lot of
women also posed some practical possibilities. Women in
the more privileged social orders shared something of the
western cultural values of their brothers, they could be
reached through missionary efforts, and they responded
readily to the idea that they were humans, too. Moreover,
it was not necessary to achieve the overthrow of the government and the whole economic system to establish some
measure of equality, within the intelligentsia, between
men and women.

So it was that by the eighteen-sixties a small but
noticeable stream of Russian women began to mingle with
the radical intelligentsia. They were usually from the
privileged social orders (about 60% of noble rank according to a survey of 379 cases) and were well educated compared to most Russian women (about a third had a secondary education, which was rarely available to females
until the last decade of the century). Thanks to the propaganda of Herzen and Chernyshevsky, it was absolutely forbidden for male members of the intelligentsia to doubt the
innate equality of the women or to exclude them as comrades. There was a theoretical repudiation of marriage, as
a form of slavery. Fictitious marriage to free women from

the legal domination of their fathers was approved and sometimes practiced, but with the assumption that actual sexual relations would be carried on elsewhere in a free relationship. Cohabitation without sexual relations was idealized, and sometimes practiced, by couples or communal groups of young men and women. The ideal of male sexual self-denial as a sign of the new moral elite is stressed by Chernyshevsky.

In practice, however, there were difficulties. Cohabitation without sex had its drawbacks. On the other hand, sexual activity meant children, who were hard to take care of except in a family, given the existing social and economic surroundings. Although bent on the liberation of man, the intelligentsia was largely composed of people with a real sense of responsibility to others. Legal marriages, leading to stable family units, predominated in the real life of the intelligentsia, and not just because the law often made this the line of least resistance.

It is not clear that the majority of the women who joined the intelligentsia really wanted liberation from marriage, and it is very doubtful that the men were ready to cede their traditional dominance in practice. Gesya Gelfman, who was condemned for her part in the assassination of Tsar Alexander II in 1881, had availed herself of the right to multiple lovers, and Chernyshevsky approved of his wife's affairs, by way of doing penance for centuries of the double standard. But for most men and women of the Russian intelligentsia the pattern that emerged from all the talk about the "woman question" was merely a liberalized form of the traditional family. The male was the leader in the unit, while maintaining more humane and reciprocal relations with his spouse than his forefathers had. There was a fairly traditional division of labor, with the female specializing in child-rearing. This male leadership within the family was carried over into political life. Women were welcome in the various attempts at radical organization, but men predominated in numbers and authority.

The myth of equality of the sexes in the movement persisted, but it served mainly to prevent the radical women from seceding to form some kind of female liberation movement of their own. The dominance of the male began with his nearly complete monopoly in the realm of ideas, which was so vital to the Russian intelligentsia. Women might smuggle handbills, teach the peasantry, shoot generals, and die on the scaffold, but they very rarely wrote theoretical articles. One of the first Russian radical women, Catherine Breshko-Breshkovskaya, recalled in later years the atmosphere of shock that she produced in her discussion circle, around 1870, by speaking out against the opinion of a male comrade. She was told after the meeting that it had been the first time that any woman in the group had spoken in a discussion. The important intellectual figures of this age of Russian radicalism were all men: Herzen, Chernyshevsky, Bakunin, Lavrov, Pisarev, Dobroliubov, Tkachev, Mikhailovsky.[1]

It was into this social setting that Nadezhda Konstantinovna Krupskaya was born in 1869. At the time of her birth the vocation of revolution was already a clearly defined option in Russian life, and it was open to women on terms of quasi-equality. She was virtually born to this vocation, the only child of a radical man and an emancipated woman. If Krupskaya's life entitles her to be called the bride of the revolution, her birth entitles her to be called a daughter of the revolution.

The tragic life of Konstantin Ignat'evich Krupsky, was intimately bound to Russian-occupied Poland. He was first ordered there in 1858, after graduating from the Konstantinovsky Cadet Corps in Petersburg. This was a reasonably auspicious start for the career of a member of the hereditary nobility of Russia, especially considering that Krupsky's family owned no property and that both parents died in 1847 when Konstantin was nine years old. The tsar's government took over the care of the orphan, taking him from his native Kazan province, on the central reaches of the Volga, to the capital, the Cadet Corps, and the promise of a career at least partly open to talent. When and how disaffection with the service of the tsar first began with young Krupsky is not clear.

After the failure of the Decembrist uprising in 1825 the officer corps was not generally a hotbed of radicalism, although a few members of the dissident intelligentsia were recruited from the army. Very likely moral distaste for the life of an infantry officer, especially on duty in an army of occupation, had something to do with it. In December 1862, on the eve of the Polish uprising, Krupsky petitioned his regimental commander for transfer to his native province of Kazan. Even with allowances for changing fashions in epistolary style, Konstantin's letter (his only surviving writing, it appears) seems highly unmilitary, smacking more of the poet Nekrasov than of the Cadet Corps: ". . . a kind of unbearable yearning weighs on my soul — on my entire being (*organizm*) ; and the wish to serve in my native land possesses my soul more strongly day by day, it paralyses all my thoughts."[2] The Soviet archivist who turned up this modest find may be correct in suggesting that the whole affair was inspired by the commander, who did endorse the petition, and might have been seeking an easy way to dispose of an officer whose loyalty he distrusted. It is possible that Krupsky had jeopardized his situation by consorting with some embryonic subversive organization among the officers. Soviet historians proudly point to the appearance of Krupsky's name along with two others from his regiment, in a list of officers belonging to an alleged "revolutionary organization." This list was compiled in London by Herzen's collaborator, Ogarev, who wrote and wished revolution, but never organized a clandestine party. Years later Krupskaya recollected that her father had been a reader of Herzen's newspaper *The Bell*, which was smuggled into Russia in this period. If true, this might have explained how Krupsky's name appeared on Ogarev's list, and why the commander suspected him (if he did) .[3]

6   Bride of the Revolution

But there is no solid evidence that Krupsky did anything to tarnish his record during the bitter war of pacification in which his unit was involved in 1863, wrecking his hopes for transfer east. Nothing has been published by Soviet historians concerning his personal role in this campaign, but he must have satisfied his superiors, for they soon afterwards sent him to the Military-Juridical Academy in Petersburg, one of the top-level professional institutions in the army. If, as Nadezhda Krupskaya said many years later, he had helped Polish insurgents to escape during the fighting and had maneuvered his company out of combat, he must have skillfully avoided detection.[4]

Krupsky studied law, while on government service, from the mid-sixties until 1870, marrying and becoming the father of Nadezhda ("Hope") along the way. Upon graduation he passed into the civil service with the title of "Collegiate Assessor" in the quaint, irrelevant terminology of Peter the Great's Table of Ranks (Krupsky belonged to no college and did not assess anything).

His superiors evidently did not suspect him of softness towards Poland, for they assigned the fledging administrator as *nachal'nik* (chief, commander) of the Grojec *poviat* or district in Warsaw province—the heart of pacified, but hardly reconciled, Poland. Konstantin Krupsky was now a personage, a near-dictator in a not inconsiderable domain, and the road to promotion, by keeping his subjects in line, or to wealth, by taking bribes, lay open.

But Krupsky seems to have determined to use his authority in an enlightened way. In the same years that Lenin's father was energetically attempting to build up the educational system in Simbirsk province on the Volga, Krupsky was opening a hospital, combatting persecution of the Jews, and establishing a system of regulation of hired labor, in which employers were obliged to issue some kind of record book for each man hired.[5] Lenin's father was promoted for his zeal, while Krupskaya's was called before the highest court of Warsaw province, in 1874, to answer government charges concerning his administration. This disparity in rewards is partly a matter of different official attitudes towards the proper treatment of Russians and of Poles, but there must have been something more specific.

In 1937 Krupskaya recollected something that she had not thought to mention previously: that her father had contacts with Marx's International Workingmen's Association, which had called for a statistical survey of the state of the working class at its first congress in 1871. Supposedly Krupsky's system of labor registration was an attempt to fulfill this resolution. She also said that, after her father's death, she and her mother received an unexpected call from N. Utin, an active Russian radical organizer and participant in the congress of the International. Supposedly he was the contact man between the International and Krupsky.[6]

What Krupsky's persecutors thought he had done is not at all clear, and the records of his trial were destroyed by the Second World War. Clearly they did not indict him for some crime of overt political subversion, for he was never in jail and was not deported to Siberia. Apparently he did not conform sufficiently to the ultra-patriotic standard that was expected of bureaucrats in his position. Among the twenty-odd charges originally laid against him, it was alleged that he "danced the mazurka" (a *Polish* dance, which, however, had once been popular in the tsar's own ballroom) and that his "daughter [age four] spoke Polish." This was probably true. Krupskaya later recollected having had a nurse in those days, and this kind of help would have been hired from the local people. Moreover, her mother evidently knew Polish well, for she was the author of a small children's book, *The Child's Day. A Gift to Children in Poetry with Twelve Pictures,* which was published in Polish not long before her husband's trial.[7] This was, no doubt, an un-Russian activity for the wife of a responsible bureaucrat in occupied Poland, but as a crime it evidently would not stand up in court. Of all the charges against Krupsky, the only one that was not quashed was that he had "exceeded his authority" in the matter of ordering employers to register their workers. For this he was sentenced to pay court costs, reprimanded, and ejected from the government service. He appealed the decision and six years later, in 1880, the highest court of the land reversed this decision, a triumph of justice that never impressed Nadezhda. Her father recovered his court costs and resumed the right to be called "collegiate assessor," even though he was no longer in the service. Years later the police reports on Nadezhda decorously referred to her as "daughter of a collegiate assessor," her legal title. After Krupsky died his widow received a small pension. One odd feature of the hearing of his appeal, which he conducted personally at the final stage, was that the prosecutor sought to show that he had been trying to help the Polish *nobility*, who were indeed the main object of official Russian oppression at this time. This argument is indeed implausible, if one can believe anything about Krupsky's democratic outlook, but it does imply the absence of any really serious police reports concerning ties with Marx's International or Utin. If the trial of Konstantin Krupsky was muddled by imperial prosecutors, its place in the life of Nadezhda Krupskaya is amply clear. Her father, when she was five, was deprived of his privileged, reasonably well-paid position and became a wandering, disturbed failure. In place of a prosperous, stable home, Nadezhda grew up in financially and emotionally precarious circumstances.

If the injustices in society had formerly moved Krupsky, he had, after his dismissal, personal reasons for bitterness toward the established order. Soviet writers assert that he was either a member of *Narodnaia volia* (The People's Will), the underground organization that killed Alexander II, or a sympathizer with it. When she was nearing seventy Krupskaya even went so far as to tell an old friend that her father had known of the assassination of Alexander II on the eve of its occurrence.[8] This is not impossible. The terrorist organization was clandestine, and the absence of surviving documentary evidence of

Krupsky's connection with it proves nothing. On the other hand, it is possible that this dramatic claim is a bit of embellishment or speculation on the part of Krupskaya or Krizhanovskaya, her friend. In her published writings relating to her father Krupskaya never went this far, and it would seem a bit perverse that she should have omitted the most dramatic of all her memories about him. What she did recall, writing in 1925, was that various adherents of the radical movement had visited her father, but that she had always been sent off on errands when they were in the house.[9]

If Krupsky was an active member of the revolutionary underground around 1880, it was quite brash of him to call attention to his previous troubles with the government by pressing the appeal of his case with the Senate. Or perhaps he no longer cared, for he had contracted tuberculosis, which ended his life in 1883 at the age of 45.

What are we to make of Nadezhda Krupskaya's paternal legacy of radicalism? Soviet historians press the evidence rather hard, but there is good reason to see in Krupsky a man of radical sentiment, and *possibly* a revolutionary activist, repelled by the regime of serfdom in which he grew up, troubled by Russian oppression in Poland, and disappointed by the crushing rebuff that the government dealt to his efforts to rule justly. In Krupskaya's own recollections of her childhood, however, her father's inspirational role in the cause of radicalism is limited to a few particular incidents, which are fairly low-key. Shortly after his discharge from the service, he went off to seek work, leaving his wife, with Nadezhda, to serve as a governess on a rural estate. The next winter, having picked up his family in a sleigh, they encountered some hostile peasants (this would be about 1875) who beat up their driver and threatened to shove him through a hole in the ice of a nearby stream. No doubt Nadezhda was terrified, but her father supposedly reassured her by explaining how long the peasants had been abused by the nobility — hardly a consoling thought if you are swimming under the ice. On another occasion Krupsky, who evidently was an atheist, chided his daughter's bedtime prayers (but without shaking her religious faith, Krupskaya recollected later). Such memories of childhood do not suggest much specific revolutionary indoctrination. Instead, one senses only a generalized feeling of moral outrage at the state of Russia and an acceptance of personal sacrifice in the interests of some vague idea of human betterment.

In this spirit Krupskaya's mother, born Elizaveta Vasilevna Tistrova, may have had at least as great a role in shaping her daughter's destiny, even though nobody has suggested that this Orthodox Christian, modest woman was a revolutionary conspirator. Born in 1841, Elizaveta Tistrova grew up in much the same circumstances as her future husband. Her father was a landless member of the hereditary nobility, who had retired from the army as a major and had gone to Siberia as a mining engineer. Here in 1844 his wife died, leaving him with nine children, the youngest of whom was Elizaveta. Their father took them to Petersburg and apparently died there a few years later, probably in 1850. In this year his two youngest daughters were enrolled in the Pavlovsky Institute, a government-sponsored educational institution for young gentlewomen in distress.

The Institute provided about the most advanced formal education available to a woman in Russia at the time, and in 1858 Elizaveta graduated with a diploma that qualified her as a governess. There followed a cheerless decade working for wealthy families, and then marriage in about 1867. Elizaveta Krupskaya was a devoted wife, with sufficient interest in the intellectual concerns of the day to sympathize with her husband's disaffected outlook. Nadezhda recalled her mother telling her about the wickedness of the serf-owning nobility she had worked for. On the other hand, Elizaveta was an Orthodox believer, who not only kept an icon in each room, as custom dictated, but — at one time after her husband's death — frequently kept a candle burning before each icon, a greater than normal display of piety. Nadezhda recalls that she grew up with an icon over her bed, but says that her mother was not a great church-goer, even though she sometimes took her daughter to evening services.

As already noted, Elizaveta Krupskaya was not only a teacher but the author of children's poetry. How she came to write her poems in Polish is unexplained, but this suggests an unusual breadth of cultural outlook in a Russian noblewoman. She herself undertook the primary education of her daughter, and was evidently resented by Nadezhda for many years as an over-protective mother.[10] Yet there is reason to see Elizaveta Krupskaya as a model for much in her daughter's life. Elizaveta displayed stoic wifely devotion to a radical, persecuted by the autocracy. She was a dedicated teacher, giving lessons for a living until after Nadezhda had grown up. And in her whole being she suggested the idea of educated, emancipated womanhood — not in a radical sense, politically or sexually, but as an independent human being, morally equal to men.

Elizaveta Krupskaya was in some ways very like Lenin's mother. Neither woman was politically-minded, but they encouraged in their children an intellectual ambition and a sense of obligation to society which, in Russia, was likely to lead to active radicalism. When this happened, both mothers seemed to accept it as a fitting result of their labors, even though they did not understand the ideologies that so possessed their children. They diligently helped them in prison, pleaded with the authorities on their behalf, and gave them financial assistance after they had become "professional revolutionaries" who showed no signs of ever supporting themselves. Lenin's mother, having several children to look after, in or out of jail, could not see her son often in his adult years, but Elizaveta Krupskaya chose to follow her daughter's (and son-in-law's) fortunes from Siberia to London. She is supposed to have cheerfully packed illegal publications in false-bottom trunks and to have written harmless letters to members of the underground, so that Nadezhda could write secret messages between the lines in invisible ink. She took up cigarette smoking somewhere along the line. She even expressed disbelief in God shortly before she died in 1915. She never announced herself a socialist, still less a Bolshevik, but she seems to have kept on good terms with her volatile son-in-law, over many years, a feat that few Bolsheviks could boast. It is a great' pity that Elizaveta Vasilevna Krupskaya has not left us some memoir of the fifteen years that she spent in crowded quarters with the most imposing figure in Russian history since Peter the Great.

From her birth on February 26, 1869, until her parents left Poland in 1874, Nadezhda Konstantinovna Krupskaya had a secure, normal childhood in upper-middle-class surroundings. But for the next five years her life was an unsettling mixture of parental affection and protection, and stress, insecurity and constant movement — almost the life of a fugitive. Except for a short period at age 7-8 when the family lived in an apartment in Kiev, she did not attend school in these years. Sometimes she was left in the charge of an indifferent fourteen-year-old girl, the best governess her parents could afford, while her mother was out giving lessons. Sometimes Nadezhda lived as a sour, antagonistic house-guest of wealthy people — in one case a rural family that hired her mother as a governess just after the Krupskayas left Poland. Another time it was a factory-owning family that employed her father as a manager. These people took little Nadya for a summer on their country retreat and were repaid by her lifelong scorn. At one point, her father worked as a factory inspector employed by a factory-owner in Uglich on the Volga. The idea of an inspector was the factory-owner's, and it lasted until Krupsky filed a report on the abuses in the plant.

That winter Nadezhda actually played with neighborhood children her own age. They were working-class children, and from this period comes a tale of exemplary revolutionary ardor. Having learned from her father and playmates a hatred of the class oppressors, Nadya joined the other young militants in ambushing the factory director with a barrage of snowballs.[11] Whether or not this happened, it tells us something about the mature Krupskaya that she seems to have taken this episode seriously. But by and large Nadya seems to have been more of a bookish, serious little girl than a tomboy.

She recalled that the one subject that she enjoyed in the Kiev school was "the law of God" (religious instruction), taught by an Orthodox priest. It seems that she was really stirred by his revelations, particularly concerning the power of prayer. The idea that God "understands all, listens, and does not laugh," made a "colossal impression" on Nadya. She decided to talk to a neighbor's wife about this — her own parents would not understand, she felt, while the neighbor was always fighting with her husband, a dentist, and should therefore know about prayer. So Nadya, age six, asked if it was true, as in the story of Samuel which she had just heard, that God would answer if you said, "Speak, Lord, Thy slave listens." ("*Govori, Gospodi, rab tvoi slushaet.*") Only Nadya had misunderstood "slave" (*rab*) as "crayfish" (*rak*), so it came out, "Speak, Lord, thy crayfish listens," which threw the good woman into fits of laughter.[12]

Neither this incident nor her father's quietly antireligious attitude unsettled Nadya's faith. When she was about ten, according to her recollections, she could still be shocked when a young friend, seeing the icon over her bed, said "Spit on the icon. Mama says there is no God."[13] Her case would not, however, support the thesis of the Russian philosopher Nicholas Berdyaev, that dogmatic Communists are bred from dogmatic Orthodox Christians. Krupskaya says that she rejected mysticism, which is central to Orthodoxy. She probably never went to church on her own, and as a child developed strong anticlerical feelings. As we shall see, she found temporary intellectual and spiritual refuge as a Tolstoyan when she was an adolescent, and the main drift of her religiosity seems to have been more toward deism-humanism than to Orthodoxy.

Krupskaya later considered her piety as a reaction to her loneliness as a child (and she reasoned from this that all Soviet children ought to have a hearty "collective" life). She was lonely and for long periods found her world in books. Some were classics — Pushkin, Lermontov, and Nekrasov in particular. But other books available in her home ranged from *20,000 Leagues under the Sea* and *Little Women* to *Secrets of the Court of Madrid* and other more or less racy pulp literature that her ailing father had bought as a distraction.

Her susceptibility to the realm of imagination must have predated her reading, for she has described herself as a highly sensitive child, rather easily terrified by the mythological. Once, while in Kiev, her fourteen-year-old baby-sitter found a way to keep Nadya busy while she went off to gossip with a friend. If you sit alone in a room and stare into a mirror, Nadya was told, you will eventually see the man you will marry, standing behind you. Nadya stared and stared. At great length she saw a bear standing behind her, screamed and fell to the floor, for she had been told some frightening stories about bears. The mature Krupskaya, who told this story, seems to have lacked the imagination to see that the mirror's prophecy proved to be quite accurate in a symbolic sense.

Later, during a summer when Nadya lived in the country in Pskov province as guest of her father's employers, the Kosyakovskys, she came out of her shell to some extent. She was able to have pets, a rabbit and a mongrel dog named "Carson," and she made friends with an old woodcutter, who let her drive his cart, and with some of the women who sorted rags for the paper factory the Kosyakovskys owned. Best of all, she became the devoted follower of the eighteen-year-old teacher in the rural school, "Timofeika," as the peasants called her. The eleven-year-old Nadya was tremendously impressed by the zeal of the older girl and by the great respect accorded her by the peasants. She, too, would become a rural teacher, Nadya decided. She followed Timofeika like a shadow that summer of 1880, sitting in on her classes and attending the final examinations for the year, which were held on the estate of a neighboring nobleman, whom Krupskaya scorned (he fed soup to his dogs and grew roses).

Most of all she loved listening in on Timofeika's special Sunday gatherings of adult peasants. At these meetings the teacher told her listeners that they didn't need landlords, and she would read aloud from the poems of Nekrasov. Here was a perfect idyl of the Russian *narodnik* (populist) movement, fusing the responsive peasants, an earnest young *intelligentka* and Nekrasov, the sometimes pathetic, sometimes humorous, richly colloquial bard of populism. Nadya already knew his writings. Later, moving to Petersburg, she devoured them in the company of her cousin, Lelya Alexandrovna Krupskaya, their favorites being "Red-nosed Frost" and "Russian Women." This poem glorifies the wives of the Decembrist rebels of 1825, who voluntarily followed their martyr-husbands into Siberia. The adult Krupskaya was to praise Nekrasov again and again, quoting him with greater warmth than Marx. Her first essay in propaganda, for example, opened with a quotation from Nekrasov's longest work, "Who Lives Happily in Russia?"

> *Thy lot is hard, a woman's lot.*
> *A harder lot can scarce be found.*

Quite likely Krupskaya had seen the effectiveness of this folk-poem in reaching simple peasants when Timofeika had read it to them.

Nekrasov never represented any specific political ideology, and to say that Krupskaya was a Nekrasovite at heart rather than a Marxist would be misleading. But it was Nekrasov — and Timofeika — who gave Krupskaya her first clear idea of social protest. She was an admirer of Nekrasov's writings long before she heard of Marx and through her whole life the Russian poet spoke to her more vividly than the German philosopher-economist. In her mature years Krupskaya often recalled the poet's greatness, and on the centennial of his birth she had the pleasure of arranging a nationwide celebration under the auspices of the Soviet government.[14]

The idyl ended badly. Konstantin Krupsky left the employ of the Kosyakovskys toward the end of 1880 and the family moved to Petersburg. Nadya learned that a wolf had eaten "Carson" during the winter and that Timofeika had been arrested. A search of her room produced illegal literature and a portrait of the tsar, bearing some inscription resembling a death sentence. When such a sentence was carried out by the bomb-throwers of The People's Will in March 1881, Krupskaya felt first hope for the future, then disillusionment.

In September of that year Krupskaya's life entered a new phase when she entered the "Prince A. A. Obolensky Female Gymnazium," a distinguished private girls' secondary school in Petersburg. Today this somewhat antique building is the "N. K. Krupskaya Secondary School." It was not Nadezhda's first attempt at secondary school, but the two previous efforts had been far from successful. She had finished a year in the Ekaterinsky Gymnazium, but did poorly and complained that the teachers had favored the rich girls. The next year she started the Liteinyi Gymnazium but withdrew before the year was out, officially because of illness. Yet she recalls no major childhood illness, and one suspects that this was a second case of poor adjustment to school.

In any case the Obolensky Gymnazium at this time seems to have been blessed with intelligent and devoted teachers and lively students — the one real formula for success in education, which no policy or theory can provide. Although Krupskaya spent much of her adult life striving to replace pre-revolutionary Russian schools with something quite different, she never referred to the Obolensky Gymnazium except in praise. She was there as a student from 1881 until 1887 and continued as a part-time teaching assistant until 1891. The curriculum was substantial, including Russian, German, French, geography, history, science, and arithmetic, and Nadezhda for the first time distinguished herself as a student, achieving all "fives" — the equivalent of "A" — in 1882. Like her future husband, she won the gold medal in her class, the premier award for scholarly excellence. Her final year as a student consisted of the "pedagogical class," an optional year for seventeen- to eighteen-year-old girls who were interested in teaching.

Her gymnazium days were darkened by the death of her father in 1883, and both the widow and her daughter were obliged to give lessons and take on part-time clerical work in order to make ends meet. Between her own studies and other work, the teen-age Krupskaya had little time for frivolity, although there were prolonged summer vacations. On the other hand, the death of her invalid father probably relieved some of the financial and nervous strain on the household, and the hardworking survivors were able to take up a relatively settled, comfortable way of life which lasted over ten years. They had a decent three-room apartment on Znamenskaya Ulitsa, and later a similar one on the Staryi Nevsky, both respectable middle-class addresses. A school friend of those years recalls that they employed a cook who slept on a cot in the kitchen, and Krupskaya remembered long summer holidays in rented cottages in the nearby country.

No doubt one of the great attractions that the Obolensky Gymnazium held for Nadezhda was the number of persons there who shared in some measure her vague but very intense feelings of social protest. Soviet writers maintain that the staff of the school included both "progressives" and some former revolutionaries. The principal, A. Ya. Gerd, had a reputation for liberalism, and his daughter, who attended the school, married a pioneer of Russian Marxism, Peter Struve. Certainly many of the girls were budding young recruits to the radical intelligentsia, with whom Nadezhda could easily form warm friendships. Among her friends were the sisters Alexandra and Olga Grigor'eva, whose mother was said to have been a member of The People's Will. Later Alexandra became a provincial actress and committed suicide in 1903, while Olga became a radical, taught school under the Soviet regime, and occasionally corresponded with Krupskaya.

The first service that this family rendered Nadezhda's career as a radical was to loan her books. She recalls reading poems by Ogarev (she could not know that he had listed her father as a radical officer) and Lermontov, loaned by the Grigor'evs. Quite possibly they introduced her to Chernyshevsky's novel *What Is to Be Done?* which was a standard part of the education of any Russian radical in these years. Certainly Krupskaya knew the book before she met Lenin, and in later years she accorded it the reverence that it customarily received. But she left no specific recollection of her first reading of Chernyshevsky's novel, nothing to suggest that it was a major event in her awakening as a radical. Evidently it did not occupy a place beside the works of Nekrasov and Tolstoy in her private pantheon of Russian social literature. Considering the problems of love and marriage that Krupskaya later faced, it is worth noting that she never gave her blessing to Chernyshevsky's radical views on the sexual liberation of women.

Another gymnazium friend was Ariadne Tyrkova, whose brother Arkady had been sent to Siberia in 1881 because he belonged to The People's Will. In her memoirs, written in America years later, Tyrkova recalls Krupskaya with nostalgic affection. She depicts her as a tall, shy, quiet girl, who did not flirt with the boys, moved and thought with deliberation, and had already formed strong convictions. "Earlier than any of us," Tyrkova writes, "more unyieldingly than any of us, she had defined her views, had set her course. She was one of those who are forever committed, once they have been possessed by their thoughts or feelings. . . ."[15] This was a notable comment on Nadezhda's beliefs, for Tyrkova recalls that their whole circle of friends "was astir with criticism of the existing order." Three of them were married to leading Marxist intellectuals during the 1890's: Krupskaya to

Lenin, Nina Gerd to Struve, and one Lidya Davidova to Tugan-Baranovsky, an outstanding economist.

But this does not mean that any of these girls had even heard of Karl Marx when they graduated from the gymnazium around 1887. Krupskaya may have "defined her views" in the sense that she rejected society as it was, but she had some distance to go before settling down with one particular ideology.

Nadezhda seems to have seen education as the key to reform. In the tradition of the "To the People" movement, Krupskaya sought to attack the old order through the peaceful resources of the schoolteacher. In her case the opportunities for subversion were pitifully slight. Some of her teaching was with small groups of pupils at the gymnazium who needed extra drill; most of it was with individual boys or girls from well-to-do homes who needed tutoring outside school. In a worshipful, but essentially plausible memoir, one of her pupils (a younger sister of Krupskaya's school-friend Davidova) recounts her experience with Nadezhda.[16] She went for her lessons to the Krupskaya apartment on the Staryi Nevsky. It consisted of two rooms and a kitchen and was impressively quiet and tidy. The room one first entered served as the dining room and the bedroom for Elizaveta Krupskaya. It was austerely furnished with a table, a few chairs and a wooden-backed sofa, which presumably doubled as a bed. Nadezhda's room was long and narrow, but large enough to contain her bed, a wardrobe, a commode, bookcases, a work-table, and two chairs. A picture of her father hung on the wall (along with an icon, according to Tyrkova, who also visited this apartment).

The pupil had been shifted from school to school, nagged by her mother and governess, and was sorely lacking in self-confidence. Krupskaya supposedly calmed the child by allowing her to plait Nadezhda's waist-length hair and by serving cocoa after the lessons. Davidova recalls that Krupskaya got in a few digs at the class structure, pointing out the falseness in a story about some nice children who gave their used clothing to the poor, for example.

It was through her zeal to develop as a teacher that Krupskaya was drawn to Tolstoyism. The sage of Yasnaya Polyana had conducted a school for peasant children on his estate and had published various essays on pedagogy. Krupskaya was at about this time looking for guidance in this field. She had observed public school classes in Petersburg and had a try at teaching drawing and sewing in a trade school, but did not like the state schools. In this Tolstoy was congenial. His educational theories were epitomized by the inscription over the door of his school: "Enter and Leave Freely." Tolstoy rejected strict discipline and rigid curricula, substituting the ideal of spontaneous interest and adventurous imagination. He was particularly concerned that the teacher maintain close personal ties with pupils, striving above all to help them develop as individuals. This may sound tediously familiar today, but it was definitely experimental and anti-establishment in Russia in the nineteenth century. It was natural that she should find Tolstoy's educational ideas attractive, for she already felt herself to be on the side of liberation and enlightenment, against the imperial system, with its bureaucracy, priesthood and police. Later, when she turned more seriously to the study of pedagogical theory while she was in emigration, Krupskaya continued to value Tolstoy's ideas. Even as a Marxist, she associated herself with an ardent disciple of Tolstoy, the educational theorist and editor I. I. Gorbunov-Posadov, whose wife Krupskaya had known as a teacher in the 1890's. One of the particular attractions of Tolstoyan educational theory was that it could be mingled quite harmoniously with the increasingly influential American ideas on pedagogical liberalization, which Gorbunov-Posadov and Krupskaya both found promising.

Reading Tolstoy's pedagogical essays drew Krupskaya toward his religious-philosophical writings, which were gaining a considerable following among the intelligentsia in the 1880's. In this period the appeal of populism, including its terrorist phase, had faded. Marxist socialism was still almost unheard of. In these circumstances the moralism of the great Russian novelist spoke to many. It had the advantage of wholly rejecting the existing social order without involving activities that were illegal, at a time when the police were ruthlessly vigilant.

No socialist had greater scorn for the rich, whom Tolstoy considered parasites. Unlike socialists, however, he proposed to attack the problem of want and misery mainly through individual moral regeneration, abstention from luxuries, non-dependence on servants, and participation in the manual work of the world. At the time when Krupskaya was drawn to Tolstoy, he had not fully worked out his rejection of the state or his pacifism, although he had dwelt on the "non-resistance of evil." This teaching had a mixed reception even among intellectuals who admired Tolstoy, and Krupskaya, by her account, was one of those who were not convinced by it. Still less was she persuaded by Tolstoy's hostility to the emancipation of women and his rejection of science, both fundamental articles of faith among the intelligentsia.

Krupskaya remembers that she was not much interested in Tolstoy when she first encountered him as the author of required novels in school, but at age fourteen she found his non-fictional works and was greatly moved. From about this time until about age twenty Krupskaya was an ardent Tolstoyan, along with many members of her generation. When she reminisced about this phase in her development, she neglected to refer to the place of religion in her Tolstoyan experience. It is understandable that the militant Bolshevik Krupskaya should be reluctant to discuss freely the extent to which she had been involved as a near-adult in what might be considered an evangelical movement. But she did acknowledge that her religious belief continued until she became a Marxist, and the general drift of her piety would easily fit Tolstoy's un-Orthodox, predominantly ethical faith.

What Krupskaya did recall was her diligent efforts to find satisfaction in Tolstoyan self-denial and labor. She was greatly inspired by Tolstoy's essay on "Luxuries and Labor," which she first read toward the end of her gymnazium days, having received the thirteen-volume works of Tolstoy as a graduation gift. While Nadezhda was not wealthy enough to forgo very much as a mark of her new-found conviction, she abstained from "luxuries" and started doing her own housework. For the rest of her life Krupskaya was something of an ascetic, deliberately maintaining both an austere personal appearance and bare living quarters. This was typical of the radical intelligentsia, including those — like Lenin — who were never Tolstoyans. But if we find in the adult Krupskaya a special contempt for stylish clothes and comfort, it may be fair to think that a bit of the Tolstoyan ascetic endured in her.

Happily, being a Tolstoyan did not require abstention from summers in the country near Petersburg—in one case living in a cottage on an estate owned by a certain Levin, which added a nice touch out of *Anna Karenina*. Here Nadezhda could practice her Tolstoyism by working in the fields along with the peasants. Soviet writers refer to this experience with vague phrases about understanding the peasants' life and learning to speak simply with them, but she recollected no anecdotes or personalities from these months, merely noting that she washed children, worked in kitchen gardens, and cut hay for families that were short-handed. Quite likely this intense, rather shy girl from a stylish gymnazium had difficulty in overcoming the suspicions of the peasants, a common problem among those who tried to "go to the people."

Tolstoy's creed offered intellectual tasks as well. Rather inconsistently, perhaps, he urged that the educated classes put their culture at the service of the dark masses at the same time he was trying to wash off this very culture in the sweat of peasant labor. In addition to his personal experiments in education he tried to encourage the spread of worthwhile reading among those who had at least mastered their letters. One particular project, in which he enlisted the cooperation of the publisher Sytin, was the inexpensive reissue of popular books in good editorial form. Existing cheap editions were said to contain numerous errors, confusing to the reader. This may seem to be a pretty modest project, but in Russia at this time reformers were able to develop a lot of enthusiasm for "small deeds," as they were called. Tolstoy's proposal, when it became publically known, elicited a surprisingly vigorous response. It seems that an earnest group of girls in Tiflis read his moral essay "What, Then, Must We Do?" published in 1886, and naïvely wrote to ask just what they *could* do. Tolstoy suggested that they provide volunteer editorial labor to correct the books that were to be published in the new, cheap series. Soon there was a flood of offers to perform such work. Nadezhda read of this in the newspapers in March 1887, and almost at once wrote Tolstoy a letter (dated March 25), which breathes the artless, earnest, modest — yet messianic — spirit of the girl (and happens to be her earliest surviving writing) :

> Esteemed Lev Nikolaevich!
> You, in your reply to the appeal of the young ladies of Tiflis to you, with their request for work, said that you have work for them — the correction of as many as possible of the books published for the people by Sytin.
>
> It may be that you will give me, too, a chance to take part in this work.
>
> Recently I have felt more and more keenly how much work, strength, health [my well-being] has cost many people, of the fact that up to the present I have benefited by the labor of others. I made use of them and utilized some of the time [that they gave me] for the acquisition of knowledge; I thought that I would then be of some use to them, and now I see that nobody needs at all the knowledge that I have, that I am unable to put it to use in life, even soever slightly to use it to make up for the evil that I all-unintentionally brought — and thus I could not, did not, know how to begin . . .
>
> When I read your letter to the Tiflis young ladies I was so glad!
>
> I know that the work of correcting books which the people will read is serious, that great ability and

knowledge is needed for this, and at eighteen I still know too little . . .

But I appeal to you with this request because, it is thought, perhaps, that through my love for the work I shall succeed somehow in helping my lack of ability and ignorance.

Therefore, if it is possible, Lev Nikolaevich, send me, too, one or two such books, and I shall do all that I can with them. I know history and literature better than other subjects.

Pardon me for having disturbed you with this request, I took you from work . . . but surely it will not occupy you for especially much time.

N. Krupskaya[17]

(Ellipses all in the original. It is hard to convey in English the particular style of this letter — painfully awkward but not uneducated.)

No doubt to Nadezhda's disappointment, she received no reply from the great man, but only from his daughter Tatyana. But Krupskaya did receive a book that was supposedly in need of correction for the new edition — *The Count of Monte Cristo*. On a visit to France some years before, Tolstoy had been impressed with the knowledge of history that common people there supposedly had acquired from Dumas's novel, which Tolstoy valued. So in a way Nadezhda received a major assignment. She evidently threw herself into this hardly revolutionary project with all the ardor she had promised, for on June 4, 1887 — about two months after the earliest date on which she could have received her assignment — Krupskaya wrote to Tolstoy to report the job complete. What became of her work nobody seems to know, but this outlet for her humanitarian zeal was not extended. Although she asked for another book to correct, none was sent.

It is hardly surprising that Krupskaya's attachment to Tolstoyism waned, although it did not collapse at once after the *Count of Monte Cristo* affair. By the time she was twenty she was definitely looking for a more satisfying answer to the perennial question of the intelligentsia, "What is to be done?" In the fall of 1889 she enrolled in the Bestuzhev Courses in Petersburg, the first university-level education for women in Russia. Searching for wisdom in diverse areas, she enrolled in the physical-mathematical faculty, while also attending history lectures. The level of study here was excellent; for example, one of the history lecturers whom she heard was Platonov, a leading figure in his profession. But Krupskaya was quickly disillusioned with higher education. The knowledge that the course imparted did not include an answer to the question "what is to be done?" and Krupskaya dropped out in early 1890.

Much more promising were the horizons offered by the circles (*kruzhki*) which radical youth, especially in the capital, were reviving at this time. The basic idea was old: a group of intellectuals in search of a commitment would meet regularly under a leader to talk about their quest. The circles had gained eminence in the 1830's when the young Herzen had belonged to one guided by Stankevich. Fyodor Dostoevsky had been sentenced to forced labor in 1849 because the police convinced themselves that the circle he attended was subversive. In the seventies Chaikovsky's circle had helped inspire the youth to "go to the people." After the assassination of Alexander II in 1881 the police took a harsh view of almost any form of intelligentsia gathering, and the circles went into temporary decline. When they revived in the latter part of the decade, they were generally very cautious in their discussions, often avoiding a direct approach to the forbidden, vital issues of Russian society.

By the opening of the 1890's, however, some of the bolder youth began to form circles that were specifically concerned with social and political issues. Quite rapidly a variety of radical, underground discussion groups appeared, consisting mainly of young men and women very much like Krupskaya in their background and outlook. In the past, Russian intellectual circles did not have very sharp ideological definition, and were fairly tolerant of diversity, providing that everyone showed proper devotion to the general idea of transforming society. But in the early nineties a distinction between two kinds of socialism began to emerge. Some considered themselves narodniks — advocates of revolution and a new social order based on the Russian peasant masses. Others described themselves as Marxists — socialists who believed that the new society, in Russia as elsewhere, could only come after capitalism had matured and died, at the hands of its most outraged victims, the industrial workers. Both narodnik and Marxist were in a somewhat tentative state of mind in the early nineties in Russia. Most of them were far from sure what their creed should be. The narodniks had inherited a vague jumble of ideas, which might or might not be applicable to the modernizing economy of Russia, while the Marxists had to learn what their major prophets had said and how it might apply to Russia. Neither narodnik nor Marxist was sure yet of their mutual relations. There was plenty of argument between them, but real hostility took a few years to develop.

In the late 1880's Krupskaya had dabbled in the reviving, cautious circles with very little satisfaction. One was Tolstoyan, held at the headquarters of the *Posrednik* (*Intermediary*) publishing enterprise. But she was depressed by the discussion here of the "non-resistance of evil." In another circle they discussed the agrarian situation in Italy and the fate of Ireland — topics no doubt chosen as surrogates for discussion of more or less analogous problems in Russia. Another that she attended was literary, and when the famous radical journalist-philosopher N. K. Mikhailovsky came as a speaker, he actually restricted himself to *Macbeth*.[18]

Around the time she turned twenty-one (in the fall of 1889 or early 1890) Krupskaya's school friend, Olga Grigor'eva, put her in touch with a discussion circle headed by a technology student named Ya. P. Korobko, which was ostensibly devoted to the study of "ethics." Soviet writers maintain that this was a Marxist circle, subordinate to an embryonic underground organization headed by M. I. Brusnev. This is probably more or less true, although Krupskaya's own experience with it showed that the narodnik influence was considerable in the circle. The group assigned her the task of studying P. L. Lavrov's *Historical Letters,* a famous narodnik tract of the seventies. Krupskaya recalled that she was very excited by this work at the time, perhaps simply because it symbolized the world of revolutionary conspiracy, despite its rather arid contents.

The names of Marx and Engels evidently received some mention in the circle, whether or not they were regarded as the main prophets of socialism. This seems to have stirred Krupskaya's interest to learn more about them, and she apparently sought to include their works in her reading.

This was not simple at the time. *The Communist Manifesto* could not be obtained and *Capital,* volume I, was hard to find, even though there had been a legal Russian edition in 1872. She succeeded in obtaining a copy from a man named S. N. Yuzhakov, whom she met through the family of a radical friend — most likely the Grigor'evs again. Yuzhakov was a narodnik who was despised by Lenin and is remembered by Soviet historians as a pernicious anti-Marxist propagandist. Possibly his generosity in loaning Marx to Krupskaya was mixed with a desire to show her its irrelevance to Russia, for he also loaned her a narodnik critique of Marxism, *The Fate of Capitalism in Russia* by V. V. Vorontsov. As if this were not enough for the fledgling student of the social sciences, Yuzhakov also added a specialized narodnik study of peasant landholding in the far north and a more or less Marxist book on primitive society by a Russian professor named Ziber.

Loaded with this peculiar assortment of literature, none of it written for the beginner, Krupskaya retired to the country in the spring of 1890, working for the last time in the fields for the good of her Tolstoyan soul. What would a young woman like Krupskaya make of such a jumble of ideas after a day in the hay-fields? Her formal education was good in its way, but provided almost no background for *Capital* or Vorontsov's book. Her extracurricular reading, ranging from Louisa May Alcott to Chernyshevsky (from *Little Women* to "New Women") , had never included anything that could be called philosophy, economics, or sociology. Although she was an excellent student in the gymnazium, terribly diligent in a conventional way, nothing in her life's work suggests that she had the least talent in these fields of study.[19]

She frankly acknowledged that she found the first two parts of *Capital* difficult going, as well she might, considering that they consist largely of technical economic analysis. But the third part, she recalled, was much easier, and this is highly plausible. Much of it consists of shocking descriptions of labor conditions in nineteenth-century Britain; it appeals more by moral force than by economic argument. The kind of moral sensitivity that could be aroused by Tolstoy's denunciation of the rich could hardly fail to be moved by Marx's picture of child labor. "I literally drank the water of life *(zhivaya voda)* ," recalled Krupskaya, introducing the vocabulary of folklore. Nor is this inappropriate, even for a "scientific socialist." The idea of science has fundamental associations with the realm of the magical, and to one of Krupskaya's unlimited moral ardor and limited intellectual background the very mystery of Marx's economic science could enhance its appeal to the emotions. And unlike Tolstoyism, which could never offer much reason to hope that evil would be overcome, Marx offered the reader diligent enough to work through *Capital,* volume I, a shimmering vision of certain victory for those lucky enough to survive to the revolution: "The knell of capitalist private property sounds. The expropriators are expropriated." When she read these words, Krupskaya wrote, "my heart beat so that it could be heard."[20]

It is entirely plausible that this is a fair picture of Krupskaya's conversion, which she never recanted. No teaching that she had heard before or after could compete with this simple vision of victory over the enemy, who was now clearly identified as the capitalist.

A good deal of painstaking historical scholarship has been devoted to the perception of Marxism by various Russian socialist leaders — Plekhanov, Lenin, Martov, Trotsky, Bogdanov, Struve, and others. This is valuable research, but it should not obscure the probability that most devoted Russian Marxists knew and cared little about theoretical subtleties. The conversion of Krupskaya, whose education and intelligence were not below the average in the movement, probably tells us much more about the intellectually uncomplicated but morally intense reaction of most Russian Marxists to their creed than does the case of a Plekhanov, a Lenin, or a Martov. And without the humble, loyal Krupskayas, the intellectual leaders would have had no movement.

Returning to Petersburg in the fall of 1890, Krupskaya made some further effort to grapple with Marxist theory. She joined another circle, composed mostly of students from the Institute of Technology and headed by a young man named P. E. Klasson. This group was definitely Marxist. In it Krupskaya reviewed the first volume of *Capital* and read two new works: a handwritten copy of part of Engels's *The Origins of Private Property, the Family, and the State* and Plekhanov's speech to the founding congress of the Second International in 1889. She also visited the public library and struggled through its copy of Engels's *Anti-Dühring* in German, which must have been very taxing and left no trace on her later writings. By early 1891 Krupskaya's serious labors in Marxist theory were finished, never to be resumed.

What she wanted at this point was not more theory but a chance to work for the cause, now that she knew its name. Seeking this, she moved to still another Marxist circle, headed by M. I. Brusnev, but the best that they offered her in the way of active assignments was marching in the funeral cortege of N. V. Shelgunov, a liberal journalist, and an invitation to teach some worker's wife her

A B C's. Unfortunately, it turned out that the good woman did not want to read and write. At this point "a school friend" came to the rescue and introduced Nadezhda to a cause that was to occupy her quite fully for five years (1891–1896).[21] This was the "Evening-Sunday School" which lay "beyond the Neva Gate," that is, in the grim industrial suburbs of Petersburg. Such schools had been founded in the 1880's by philanthropic factory owners who wished to provide, at their expense, an elementary education to workers who wished to seek it. The school, whose staff Krupskaya joined on August 29, 1891, offered a solid program in adult education. Its chief sponsor was N. A. Vargunin, a porcelain magnate whom Krupskaya respected then and in later years because of his sincerity and because he closed his eyes to the radicalism of some of the teachers. He was, incidentally, the brother of the man who had hired and fired her father as a factory inspector. The principal was a liberal lady who loved Nekrasov, and the teachers, most of whom taught children in the regular schools during the day, included various narodniks, liberals, and Tolstoyans at the time Krupskaya joined them.

On Sundays and two nights a week Krupskaya taught all-male classes, starting with illiterates and moving up to more advanced pupils. She taught arithmetic, history, and Russian literature. There were problems: drunken absenteeism, the priest who taught an obligatory class in the "law of God," and school inspectors who were displeased with a lesson that went beyond the minimal goals set by the approved curriculum. But Krupskaya clearly loved the work, and in later years looked back on the school as her own "university."

Certainly it was interesting as an experiment in education. The teachers conducted annual excursions to public art exhibits at the Hermitage, through which Krupskaya became slightly acquainted personally with the painter Gay, a celebrated artist and friend-disciple of Tolstoy. Some of the staff, including Krupskaya, helped others organize an exhibit of teaching materials, which became so substantial that it came to have its own building in Petersburg. Special lectures were organized, illustrated with a magic lantern. Best of all, there were the numerous responsive students, tired after a day's work but eager to learn. Much more than the peasants whom Krupskaya had tried to reach, these factory hands were trusting and friendly in their relations with the educated, middle-class women who wanted to help them.

Krupskaya must have been a success as a teacher, because her colleagues first elected her to the principal's advisory committee and later, in 1893, to the directorship of the evening sessions of the school.[22] Years later, when she had become a revered heroine, other, more doubtful achievements were remembered. We have, for example, the memoirs of the former pupil, F. Zhukov, which reads like a Billy Graham success story, upside down:

> I came to the classes a deeply religious person, blindly believing in God and the tsar. In the classes I was reborn. Instead of a fanatical believer I became an atheist, instead of a loyal subject — a revolutionary, a Bolshevik. For all this I am indebted in the first instance to Nadezhda Konstantinovna, who taught the classes.[23]

Since Bolshevism only emerged about ten years after Zhukov's school days, this kind of memoir should not be taken literally. Nevertheless, the school did provide some contact with earnest workmen, and this no doubt was a great attraction to the young Marxist Nadezhda. At a time when there was scarcely any organized socialist movement in Russia, when many of the radical intellectuals were almost wholly cut off from the common folk, her job at the school provided a sense of being in the front lines of the class struggle. The school could not be used for open agitation, but at least one could get some idea of the harsh life of the worker. On one occasion Krupskaya and a colleague went to the trial of a pupil who had knifed a supervisor. The accused supposedly made a flaming speech, which stirred Krupskaya, even though she could do nothing to help him.

After a year or two a number of Marxist teachers joined the narodniks and liberals on the staff. These included Zinaida Nevzorova, who became a friend for life, Alexandra Kalmykova, a well-to-do woman who later financed Lenin's first émigré newspaper, and Lidya Knipovich, a narodnik who became a Marxist around 1895 and later served as one of the underground agents of this newspaper. Still another Marxist teacher, whom Nadezhda met through the exhibit of teaching materials, was Elena Stasova, who in 1917 was to replace Krupskaya as party secretary. The presence of a nucleus of Marxists on the staff gave rise to some efforts to use the school for political ends. In its most modest form this meant such things as a lecture on Nekrasov (of course) by Krupskaya or a series of lectures on the geography of foreign countries, into which some kind of social message was insinuated. More boldly, Marxist teachers at the school formed an underground circle to coordinate their activities, including the recruitment of workers to Marxist indoctrination groups and the dissemination of propaganda concerning strikes that were organized in nearby factories during 1895–1896.

The rise of Marxist activity at the school revived Krupskaya's interest in the intellectual circles. The Brusnev circle had been arrested in 1892, but a new one, led by S. I. Radchenko, was formed, and Krupskaya apparently attended it. In fact, four of the female teachers at the adult school joined this circle, and in a short time all married members of the circle, a good record for any lonely-hearts club. Sometime in 1893 she heard from Radchenko that a learned young Marxist had arrived from the Volga. It was said that he was so devoted to the cause that he had never read a novel in his life. Awesome, perhaps, but for one of Krupskaya's cultured tastes not very appealing.

CHAPTER II

The Copper Ring

Nadezhda Krupskaya met the learned Marxist from the Volga — his name was Vladimir Ilyich Ulyanov — in February 1894, at the Marxist circle, and they were married over four years later. The story of this courtship (if that is the right word) is not easy to unravel. Soviet eulogists of Ulyanov (later called Lenin), led by Krupskaya, have relentlessly tried to stress that he was "the most human of humans," but they have been discreet in dealing with his intimate life, including his loves and marriage. In this they have no doubt respected his wishes, for he was a most reticent man concerning his personal affairs. Even his letters to his mother, to whom he was deeply attached and wrote fairly often as an adult, read like interdepartmental correspondence, although they often close, incongruously, with "Many kisses. . . ." As Krupskaya herself once observed in a letter to his mother, "Volodya is quite unable to write [letters] about the ordinary side of life" (by which she seems to mean any kind of personal matter, unconnected with the Cause).

Granted, Lenin has been the subject of endless, officially approved, vacuous memoirs, and there are numerous

34

museums full of his memorabilia, but the Soviet image of their hero is as poor in human verisimilitude as it is rich in reverence. This happens to be illustrated by the question of Lenin's proposal to Krupskaya. Various Soviet writers, in treating this point in his life, have said that he "called her to him" — an attempt to strike the correct note of Olympian dignity. For the irreverent this may conjure up the image of a bald-pated, goateed Zeus waggling a finger at a passing mortal; it certainly does not convey anything about Lenin as a human being.

Because of the vague, tendentious, and contradictory official picture of Lenin's approach to love, marriage, and Krupskaya, their social democratic romance cannot be as simple a narrative as many love stories. Only by picking over the evidence in some detail, can one come close to reconstructing a part of Lenin's — and Krupskaya's — life that in the past has been too much obscured by his cult.

Although Lenin and his future wife may have been introduced at the meeting in February 1894, which took place at the apartment of Krupskaya's friend Klasson, it does not appear that this introduction had any immediate sequel. The only specific recollection of this first meeting in Krupskaya's generally worshipful memoirs of Lenin is negative: he made a sarcastic remark about a literacy committee (the kind of cultural missionary activity that she generally admired) and laughed. "Something evil and arid sounded in his laugh — I never heard him laugh that way again." Here one may wonder if Lenin's style of laughter changed later (his love of sarcasm certainly did not), or if it was Krupskaya's attitude toward him that changed.[1]

They next met at a meeting of the Radchenko circle at the end of 1894 at which Lenin read his best-known polemic against the narodniks — "What Are the 'Friends of the People' and How Do They Fight Against the Social Democrats?" Krupskaya probably appreciated the lecture because it gave her ammunition to use in her arguments with narodnik friends among the teachers at the adult school, not that she had recourse to Lenin's biting hostility in these debates, judging by later memoirs. In general Lenin's polemic established his reputation as an ideologist to be reckoned with in Petersburg radical circles, and, probably, a man to be looked up to in Krupskaya's eyes. (Figuratively — judging by the few photographs of the pair standing side by side, Krupskaya was at least as tall as Lenin and probably taller.)

She evidently had some opportunity to get acquainted with him in the winter of 1894–1895, when he came to call on her at the apartment she shared with her mother on the Staryi Nevsky, not very far from Lenin's own lodgings. In her memoirs Krupskaya invested these visits with an aura of danger, noting that her apartment building had a court-yard that permitted Lenin to shake off police spies by coming in from one street and leaving by another. True, Lenin was suspect as the brother of an executed terrorist, but at this time he was living legally in Petersburg and was not the object of a manhunt. If Lenin was being watched, one would think that he would have been quite willing to lull the police by letting them know about his visits to a respectable young noblewoman. No spies were actually visible, it seems.

The pretext for these visits was mutual interest in the factory workers of the district beyond the Neva Gate. Krupskaya, of course, was experienced as a teacher of these workers in the adult school. In the fall of 1894 Lenin began giving lessons in Marxism to a few radical workers, some of whom happened to be adult school students as well. This kind of preparation for revolution, indoctrinating a few proletarians at a time on a fairly advanced intellectual level, was usually called "propaganda." It did not appeal much to Lenin, according to his colleague of that day, M. A. Sil'vin, and he devoted very little time to such teaching.[2] Although one over-zealous memoir-writer has Krupskaya actually recruiting Lenin's study-group for him, she cannot recall anything so creditable, and even notes that it was only much later that she or her students ever hinted to one another that they knew Lenin.[3]

It does not appear that the two became personally well acquainted during these visits, which may have been few in number. Both loved Russian literature, yet it was only after they had settled down in Siberia in 1898 that Krupskaya, by her recollection, ever talked to Lenin about "Turgenev, Tolstoy, Chernyshevsky," and learned that he was not really such a monomaniac that he ignored novels.[4] It is hard to imagine Krupskaya having many long chats with anyone about her teaching without getting around to Nekrasov pretty soon. Perhaps these and other matters of personal interest would have come up in their conversations, had Lenin's visits not been interrupted in March 1895 by a bout with pneumonia. During his illness his mother came from Moscow to nurse him. Krupskaya probably came to visit, but after he recovered they seem to have had only one other encounter before the fall. This was a rail trip on Easter Sunday to Tsarskoe Selo, near Petersburg. Here was the palace of Nicholas II and also the humble quarters of the Marxist Sil'vin, who received Lenin, Krupskaya, and two other members of their group, which by this time was often called the "Old Ones" (*stariki*) to distinguish it from a younger, rival group. The whole expedition seems slightly incredible, though it probably did take place. Tsarskoe Selo was a small town adjacent to the royal palace and was probably the most closely watched place in the Empire. Yet this was the site chosen for what amounted to a lesson in security procedures. Each traveler pretended to be alone on the train, only to proceed to the same apartment, which could well have been under surveillance, considering its occupant. There Lenin is supposed to have given a lesson on codes. Krupskaya, who later became the chief Bolshevik cryptographer, professed to be impressed with Lenin's expertise, presumably learned from members of the old People's Will. In general there is no reason to think that Lenin was any kind of professional in the security field. He was always an easy mark for police agents, and in this case he evidently failed to teach his class much about the art of cryptography. They encoded some material, including their confidential address list, for practice, but found afterwards that they could not decode their handiwork. For Krupskaya the most important point in the Easter excursion was that she was designated to succeed Lenin as the guardian of the address-list and code-book (which nobody had mastered) in case of Lenin's arrest. This job never amounted to much in practice, and certainly did not mean that she had become a kind of vice-president, but it must have been flattering to receive some special mark of Lenin's esteem.[5]

About two weeks later their collaboration was interrupted by Lenin's first trip to western Europe, which lasted over four months. Although the pretext on which he had obtained a passport was medical treatment, the real purpose of the trip was to discuss revolutionary strategy with G. V. Plekhanov, "the father of Russian Marxism," and to become better acquainted with west European socialists. Lenin did not try to communicate with Krupskaya from abroad.

While Lenin was abroad, Krupskaya made a considerable change in her personal affairs. After twelve years of giving private lessons, she dropped this livelihood and became a copyist with the accounts section of the state railroad administration. At this point and for several years afterwards her zeal for pedagogy seems to have declined, although she did continue to teach three times a week at the adult school. A few years later, while in Siberia, she summarized her feelings on the matter in a letter to her sister-in-law Maria, who was pursuing her education in Belgium: "If money is needed you can get a job with some railroad, where at least you will be able to work off the necessary number of hours and have no cares, you will be free as a bird; but all this pedagogy, medicine and so on absorbs a person more than it should [for the good of the cause]."[6]

The new job had other advantages, too. The civil servants who worked in this office, while not socialists, were tolerant of Krupskaya's political activities and pretended not to know that she was using her position as a cover for contacts with comrades who came to deliver or receive messages on the pretext of having official business with her. Judging by her later testimony to the police, her work involved issuing some kind of form to people with complaints, so it was not quite as obvious as it might have been that some of her callers were there on false pretenses. The job had another advantage, which could hardly have been foreseen. One of her co-workers was a man named I. N. Chebotarev, a friend of the Ulyanovs, with whom Lenin took his main daily meal in the latter part of 1895. This gave Nadezhda a channel of communication with Lenin which was very helpful when he was jailed. Mrs. Chebotarev, though not an active socialist, was willing to serve as a mail drop for the imprisoned Lenin. Letters could be mailed to her and picked up by Krupskaya without calling the attention of the police to any member of the Marxist group.

Between this full-time job as a copyist, the evening adult classes, and an increasing tempo of socialist underground work, Krupskaya must have been very busy in the latter part of 1895. Partly because of spontaneous labor unrest, partly because of the increased activity of Lenin and other radical intellectuals, there was an upsurge of socialist activity in the last months of 1895. Lenin was enthusiastic about moving beyond the stage of discussion circles by bringing out an occasional underground newspaper, *The Workers' Cause* (*Rabochoe Delo*), which he had discussed with Plekhanov. This fitted in with another effort to increase the impact of the radical intelligentsia, the "agitation" movement. The main advocate of this was Julius Martov (Tsederbaum), whom Lenin met in October, and liked immensely. Martov had just returned from a stay among the Jewish workers of Vilno, where a labor leader named Kremer was proposing and practicing agitation — the encouragement of strikes over immediate practical grievances — in place of "propaganda," the gradual education of advanced workers who understood Marxism. Obviously it was easier to turn out a thousand strikers over something like a pay reduction than by slowly explaining *Capital* in tutorial groups. The pitfall of this short-cut to militancy, as Lenin noted a few years later, was "economism" — the restriction of the workers' protests to matters of short-term welfare at the expense of ultimate revolution. But in the fall of 1895 Lenin, Martov, and their followers were eager to plunge ahead with agitation, particularly through increased publishing activity.

To support this increase in activity the "Old Ones" attempted to replace the formless circle with a more definite organization, which was often referred to as the "Group of Social Democrats." It had no individual head, although Lenin and Martov were the dominant personalities, but did establish an executive ("Interregional Bureau") of four. The size of the whole Group has been put at seventeen, all of them intelligentsia (engineers, students, teachers, physicians). This count probably omitted a few individuals, but it does show how small an elite group was trying to lead the agitation campaign among large numbers of workers, and how badly it needed the services of each devoted member. Krupskaya was such a one, and for the first time in her career as a radical she had plenty to do. She was one of four members of a bureau which was established to direct activities in the Neva district, one of three district bureaus in the capital. This was, of course, the workers' district that she knew best — better than her colleagues in the bureau, (Krizhanovsky, Lyakhovsky, and Malchenko). While it was said that she was in charge of the legal or overt library in the region, this probably was not a major activity.[7] For years she had been lending workers books, which she had borrowed from downtown libraries or private persons, and presumably she simply continued to do this. More to the point in the agitation campaign was her role in gathering information about factory conditions for use in the Group's leaflets and in getting the leaflets distributed. Few of her colleagues had much direct contact with actual workers or entrée to factories. Krupskaya did, and could use her position for gathering intelligence. She could talk to worker-students quite easily through the adult school, and in at least one case she persuaded a worker named Krolikov to collect data on factory conditions, utilizing a form specified by Lenin. She even introduced Krolikov to Lenin for further interrogation. This was more of a step forward than it seemed. The socialist worker Babushkin recalls that at this very time Lenin was rebuffed when he personally tried to obtain information from textile workers. The proletarians were still often suspicious of "white-handed intelligentsia," excepting a few like the adult school teachers, who had gained their confidence.

The same Krolikov, according to his later police interrogation, escorted Krupskaya and her teacher-friend Apollinarya Yakubova to inspect the appalling dormitory of the Thornton Textile Factory. And Krupskaya was able to visit the Maxwell metallurgical plant quite legally, using the pretext that her classroom work required her to know what kind of machines the workers used.[8] Again, such first-hand observation was surprisingly rare at the time.

She also made herself useful in the arrangement of illegal printing. The Group of Social Democrats had no press of their own and could not hire a legal printer. The only possible facility belonged to a branch of the People's Will, which hid it in the Lakhta district on the edge of Petersburg. Despite the ideological differences between the Marxists and adherents of People's Will, the latter agreed to print the social democrats' material. Krupskaya had a link with the operators of the underground press through her friend at the adult school, Lidya Knipovich, and it was probably through this channel that Lenin's negotiations with the press were started. Afterwards Krupskaya appears to have been an intermediary between the Group and Lidya, who dealt directly with the press.

Lenin and Krupskaya were closely associated during the six or eight weeks following the formation of the Group of Social Democrats in October 1895. The various activities just sketched brought them into frequent contact for the first time and gave Lenin a chance to appreciate Krupskaya's vigor and devotion as a co-worker. Nobody, including Krupskaya, has recollected any anecdotes about close personal ties between the two during this time. And indeed both must have been pretty fully absorbed in their work. Even earlier Krupskaya had decided not to waste her time on anything as frivolous as seeing a man just for fun. Shortly after she had started her work at the adult school she seems to have been interested in an engineer, a radical who got cold feet and left the circle. She apparently saw a good deal of him and *even* went to the theater with him, for which the severe Lidya Knipovich "flew at" her: "When you work together, it is sufficiently silly to go to the theater together." At the time Krupskaya flared back, "What business is it of yours?," but, she recalls, soon came to see that Lidya was right.[9] In other words, by the fall of 1895 Krupskaya was so accustomed to the ascetic ways of the radical intelligentsia that she was not interested in having "bourgeois" personal relations with Lenin.

The success of the Group of Social Democrats in fanning strikes at the Thornton and several other factories in November 1895 was their undoing. The police apparently decided after these disturbances that the Group was too dangerous to be left at large. As has been seen, Lenin and his friends had anticipated trouble, and had made some faint efforts to prepare themselves. Members of the Group adopted pseudonymous nicknames for internal communication, though they resided at known addresses under their real names. Some tactics for those arrested seem to have been planned. Apparently it was agreed that they would deny as much as possible as long as possible when arrested. This was not a wholly obvious decision; in the past a number of arrested conspirators had tried to turn arrest to the advantage of the cause by eloquently courting martyrdom. Elementary plans for coded communication to and from prison were prepared, relying merely on marked letters in books and "invisible" milk-ink writing between the lines of innocent letters or books.

But these measures were inadequate and a bit naïve. Nobody was really trying to live under cover, with a false public identity, and nothing was done to persuade workers with whom they had dealings not to talk freely if arrested, as several of them did. In an anecdote intended to dramatize Lenin's skill in conspiratorial technique Krupskaya unwittingly illustrated the vulnerability of the Group. She recounts that a cousin who happened to work in the public address bureau, a completely open directory of persons, told her that two detectives had come in and looked up Vladimir Ulyanov's address, saying "We've trapped an important state criminal . . . . He won't get away now."[10] But this merely establishes that Lenin was living legally, under his real name, at a known address, nor did he do otherwise after Krupskaya tipped him off about the detectives. Any fool could have walked into the address bureau and found his address, which reveals these detectives as utter buffoons if they really took such professional pride in this achievement.

Thus on the night of December 8–9, 1895, the police had no trouble arresting Lenin and most of the members of the Group of Social Democrats. Now, at least, some of the emergency arrangements were useful. Krupskaya was able to determine through her acquaintance Chebotarev that Lenin had not turned up for dinner on the 9th, which implied the worst. Other communications through the Chebotarevs followed. In the first, dated January 2, 1896, Lenin discussed at length his need for reading materials to support the study he hoped to undertake in his cell. To a considerable extent this letter meant what it said, although he did not expect that the Chebotarevs would execute his requests themselves. But this or a similar letter on readings managed to work into the text oblique references to the nicknames of his colleagues, asking if they were "still in the library" (not arrested). To ask after Krupskaya he is supposed to have used a particularly roundabout allusion, one that probably would have been intelligible only to his sister, because it must have been based on some common childhood reading. According to Anna, he asked if the book by Mayne Reid was still available; she notes that one of his stories was called "The Lamprey" (in Russian, *Minoga*), which was another underground nickname for Nadezhda.[11]

Another letter, according to Anna, reached Krupskaya through Chebotarev in invisible ink, telling her to tell his relatives to get rid of his trunk, stored in Moscow, and buy another that looked like it. Lenin had returned from the West with a double-bottomed trunk, which the police knew about. After his first interrogation in early January Lenin knew that they knew and hoped to destroy the incriminating evidence before the police traced it to his mother's apartment. To carry out this instruction safely, Krupskaya had to go in person to Moscow and call on Lenin's mother.[12] The most ambitious of his compositions in milk-ink that was dispatched from jail was a brochure entitled "On Strikes." It apparently came through his sister, and then to Krupskaya, who "developed" it and passed it on to the printers, in vain, for it was captured in a police raid on the press.

Another aspect of the Group's emergency planning did not work at all well, partly because Krupskaya seems to have lost her nerve, at least briefly. The first issue of Lenin's new Marxist newspaper was in proof, and the day before his arrest the executive of the Group approved it for publication. One of the two extant proofs was taken by the police, but the other had been given to Krupskaya for safekeeping. Clearly she was supposed to hand it over to the press if anything happened to the other copy. But, upset by the number of arrests, Krupskaya instead got rid of the incriminating material by giving it to her gymnazium friend Nina Gerd, who was sympathetic to the socialists but not an activist, and therefore safe from the police. In her memoirs she explains this action by saying that she feared further arrests. Her colleagues among the survivors evidently were less cautious. When Krupskaya delivered to them a draft leaflet by the worker Babushkin, who had slipped it to her at the evening school, they decided to publish it. Still more challenging to the police, they decided to sign their future agitational publications "Union of Struggle for the Emancipation of the Working Class."

The police responded by arresting Martov, whom they had missed in the first round, and most of the others who were still at liberty. But the "Union of Struggle" was able to carry on, largely because new forces joined them, particularly the "Young Ones" (molodye), led by K. M. Takhtarev. In a few years he would be anathematized by Lenin for "economism," the excessive emphasis on short-term gains in worker welfare, but in 1896 it was quite acceptable for Krupskaya to give him her support. During May 15–June 15, the new leadership entrusted her with a considerable task: a trip to Kiev and Poltava in the Ukraine to contact Marxist groups there in preparation for the convocation of a congress of social democratic groups, to form a so-called party. She does not seem to have accomplished much in this line, and returned to the capital after she learned that a major wave of strikes had broken out.

Soon afterwards she learned of the arrest of Lidya Knipovich, a serious blow at the publishing arrangements of the "Union of Struggle." Knowing that Lidya had various valuable items in her care, Krupskaya hurried out to her country cottage in the town of Valdaika, some distance southeast. To her horror, she found that there was a large quantity of leaflets that Lidya's friends were supposed to have concealed for her, but which they had dumped in the cottage after her arrest, fearing for themselves. The place was still occupied by servants, whom Krupskaya bribed to go off to a nearby St. Peter's Day fair, and a young student of midwifery, whose aid she enlisted. Though it was midsummer, they stoked the stove and spent quite a while burning the leaflets. The place was being closely watched by police spies, she was certain, though why they had not searched the cottage or questioned visitors to it is quite incomprehensible. There remained a box containing type-faces and some manuscript that Lenin supposedly had left for the press, months before. Krupskaya recounts that she and her helper took advantage of drizzling weather to don raincoats, one concealing a shovel, the other the box. Thus disguised, they supposedly walked right past the police spies, who merely snickered at the sight of two (rather lumpy?) young ladies walking in the rain. The conspirators disappeared into the woods and successfully buried the treasure, which may still be there as far as one can tell.[13]

If Krupskaya really did outwit the police that time, her luck was running out. And she had been lucky, even if one discounts some of her stories about "detectives." Although surviving police archives show that she was listed as a person of "doubtful reliability" sometime in 1894, such people were very numerous, and no special investigation followed. The police agent whose reports led to the arrests of December 1895 was a dentist named Mikhailov, who posed as a socialist and met most members of the Group. But he overlooked Krupskaya, who was identified as a possible revolutionary only around the beginning of May 1896. Her activity as a contact between the radical intelligentsia and workers attending the adult school brought her to the attention of an agent known as "Larionich" (Aleksandr Larionovich Garnovsky), who was posing as an artisan with a small metal-working shop in the factory district. Having met Krupskaya at the home of one of her worker-students, he evidently found her a promising political suspect and attempted to lure her into conducting a secret study-circle for workers. She declined but agreed to furnish a leader, a representative of the intelligentsia, and she did — a man named Sergei Hofman. After this she was placed under surveillance, which she did not detect. This is amusing, considering how prone she was to "see" detectives frequently. On August 10, along with her friend Apollinarya Yakubova, she was reported as a member of the "Union of Struggle," and two nights later was arrested

and placed in the "House of Preliminary Detention."
Lenin was also a resident of this establishment at the time,
but, of course, they could not communicate.[14]

Krupskaya was a tough prisoner, if one may judge by
the published portions of her testimony to the police. They
could not use torture or other physical pressure, especially
on young noblewomen, but there was no right to counsel
or *habeas corpus,* and the prisoners knew that the police
could decide to send them to the least pleasant parts of
the Russian Empire for several years without a trial. After
several months they wore down Krupskaya's friend Zinaida
Nevzorova to the point of giving a pretty full confession
of her activities in the "Union of Struggle," naming her
colleagues quite freely.[15] Nadezhda never retreated that
far. In her first interrogation, on September 2, she deposed,
"I do not consider myself guilty," and went on to deny that
she had been visited by a Konstantin Bauer or even knew
Mikhail Sil'vin, both members of the Union. The police,
for reasons that are not clear, even released her on October
10, whereupon she rashly set out as a solicitor of funds to
help strikers in the city of Kostroma (all strikes were then
illegal in Russia). Arrested again on October 28, she was
confronted with the damaging testimony of a worker-stu-
dent named N. Bugorovkov, who had been a member of
the circle to which she had supplied a leader. Now she
admitted having introduced him to some intellectual, just
some friend of a friend, she claimed, who wanted to meet
a worker for reasons not known to her. She denied knowing
Hofman, the leader whom she had sent, but now admitted
that she had known Sil'vin, Nevzorova, and Yakubova, without being aware that they were engaged in any illegal activities.[16] This was a good try, but the police nevertheless
concluded, on the testimony of two of the workers from
the circle she had helped to start, that she had used her
position as a teacher in the school to further the aims of
the "Union of Struggle."[17] One thing the police did not
discover was that she was acquainted with the accused
Lenin, partly because both of them had been cagey in

their testimony, partly because they had not been inseparable before his arrest.

Krupskaya remained in jail until March 10, 1897, waiting for the police to decide what should be done with her. It was far from the worst of all possible jails. An intellectual named Ivanov-Razumnik who was there a few years after Krupskaya and who later experienced various Soviet prisons wrote, "There was a 'prison' for you." The women inmates had female warders, were served tea hot enough to "develop" milk-ink, and visitors could bring food and books to them. Krupskaya made some efforts to renew her study of English. But it was chilly in jail and Krupskaya was probably overworked and half-ill before her arrest. Her code-name, "The Fish," referred to a bulging of the eyes, a symptom of a thyroid condition which bothered her the rest of her life. Her future sister-in-law referred to her as looking like a herring about a year after she had been released from prison. Presumably it was this ailment that accounted for her mother's alarm concerning her health while she was in jail. Elizaveta Vasilevna repeatedly petitioned for her daughter's release, insisting that any doctor would certify that Nadezhda's very life was in danger. The prison doctor in early March 1897 did in fact confirm that her health was "unsatisfactory."

The authorities remained hard-hearted until a young woman named M. F. Vetrova, imprisoned in the tough Sts. Peter-Paul Fortress Prison, where all the warders were men, poured kerosene on herself and burned to death. Not wanting additional dead female prisoners on their hands, the police released Krupskaya and other ailing women prisoners on March 12, 1897.[18] She then had to wait for a year to have her sentence determined.

In arresting first Lenin and then Krupskaya, the police might appear to be interrupting an incipient romance. In fact, they were unwittingly playing the role of matchmaker and eventually father-with-shotgun. The peculiar conditions of political persecution provided by the Imperial government not only served as a backdrop for the marriage of Lenin and Krupskaya but even brought it about. There are no indications that Lenin was contemplating matrimony, legal or unchurched, before his arrest. His interest in marriage came only gradually while he was in custody, and in stages that made it difficult for him to describe his feelings to his bride-to-be.

And what were the feelings of this revolutionary at the age of twenty-six or seven, concerning marriage and the sexes? First, it is clear that Lenin never believed in "free love," which he considered "bourgeois," and specifically supported the ethic of married love. Of course, he rejected religious marriage rites, being a militant atheist, even though he seems to have remained attached to the kind of traditional family in which he was reared.

Beyond this his outlook is somewhat enigmatic, owing to the depths of his personal reticence which have already been noted. It is at least clear that he could never have been an effusive lover, would never permit his obsessive concern for the cause of revolution to be seriously rivaled by passion for any woman. Krupskaya, who should know, once asserted that Lenin was incapable of loving a woman who did not share his devotion to the cause. But if a woman qualified in this respect, as Krupskaya did, it seems likely that Lenin was capable of loving her in his fashion. It even appears that as a young man he invested his own idea of love, which might seem depressingly cool and utilitarian to some people, with exceptionally noble intensity.

According to Krupskaya, in two entirely separate accounts, thirty years apart, Lenin as an adolescent had become imbued with the ideal of love propounded by Turgenev in a short story entitled "Andrei Kolosov."[19]

This is the rather flat story, published in 1844, of an "exceptional person," who had complete control of his emotions. This was the ideal that Lenin seems to have adopted as his model quite early in life, resembling Chernyshevsky's iron-willed "new people," whom he also admired. Andrei Kolosov proved his exceptional character by immediately breaking off with his girl friend, without a word of farewell or explanation, the moment he realized that his love for her was not quite perfect. There is no particular indication that his love, when in full bloom, was at all sentimental, passionate, or even warm. Its perfection apparently was more or less metaphysical, having little if any connection with sex.

Perhaps the very weakness of the story — Turgenev's failure to provide a convincing picture of Kolosov as a man capable of ever loving — explains Lenin's attraction to the ideal of Andrei Kolosov. Turgenev was attempting to show how such an "exceptional person" was the only kind who could really understand love: "O gentlemen," declaimed Turgenev's narrator, "the person who leaves a woman whom he never loved, in that bitter and great instant when he involuntarily realizes that his heart is not all, not fully imbued with her, that person, believe me, understands better and more fully the sacredness of love than those small-souled people who from boredom, from weakness continue to play on the half-broken strings of their sluggish and sentimental hearts." Lenin wanted to be that kind of imposing person. But perhaps he was aware that this kind of rocklike character, and his own developing personality, were alien to the more conventional notions of love. This being so, how reassuring to learn that his kind were capable of a more profound love than ordinary mortals.

Despite Lenin's own, exalted opinion of it, his love, as it emerged in reality, seems to have been quite ordinary, guided by unexceptional, even depressingly practical considerations. It appears that Lenin liked the convenience and coziness of a conventional domestic establishment, populated with solicitous females. He had grown up in a home of this sort and arranged his adult life to suit this patriarchal yearning, living not only with a wife but also his mother-in-law and, later, his sister. Quite possibly, as he sat in the Petersburg jail or Siberian exile his mind turned back to the favorable impression that the tidy apartment of the two Krupskayas had made on him when he had visited Nadezhda. Surely he was aware that he needed someone to keep house for him, for his admiration of domestic order did not mean that he could do much for himself — he once thought to buy material for a blouse by the pound. And he surely must have been aware that he needed a secretary, especially for the deadly job of producing fair copies of the many books and articles he hoped to write, typing not yet being the standard medium for finished manuscripts.

It just happened that Nadezhda Krupskaya was a professional in this line, spending her days making neat copies of the paperwork of the railroad administration. This was not her only attraction. Physically there was much in her favor. Had she been a princess, involved in stylishly shocking escapades, writers probably would not have called her a rare beauty, but might have referred to her arched eyebrows, fine, high cheekbones and firm jaw — all conveying a sense of feminine challenge. They might have mentioned her slightly over-full lips, presuming them sensuous, and her intense eyes, which are not in fact bulging in the photographs taken about this time, including the mug picture the police took. As it was, Krupskaya wanted to look like the opposite of a frivolous princess, while still retaining an air of middle-class respectability. Judging by her pictures, her dress in these years was invariably a dark, long-sleeved affair, with very little shape except for slightly puffed-out shoulders and upper arms and a collar of the same stuff that pretty well covered her throat. Her luxuriant hair, parted a little off the middle, was drawn straight back, both neat and austere. Far from seeming drab to Lenin, it is fair to guess that Krupskaya's conservative style was just right for his taste. Here was a young woman whose obvious disdain for frivolous display bespoke her devotion to more important things, but did not conceal the fact that she was fundamentally good-looking.

Lenin only told Krupskaya of his admiration for Andrei Kolosov after their marriage, and it seems likely that his premarital overtures to her failed to make it at all clear that he was in love with her, even by lesser standards. Not only were the two cut off from one another by prison walls or great distance between December 1895 and May 1898, but it is likely that Lenin was rather shy in raising such an intimate matter by such crude means of communication as he had. Also, he had little if any romantic experience and may well have been overawed by the sanctity with which he invested his ideal love.

All of this greatly complicated the background of Lenin's courtship of Krupskaya, and the peculiar status of "fiancées" and "wives" in the world of the Russian radicals further confused the situation. The police were remarkably considerate of the romantic attachments of their political prisoners. While in jail awaiting a verdict, the prisoner could be visited not only by relatives but also by his or her betrothed. No evidence of intention to marry was required, so revolutionaries took advantage of the system to provide their incarcerated comrades with fictitious fiancées who could deliver books, coded messages (which could also be received from the prisoner), and encouragement. Since the radical intelligentsia scorned such orthodox customs as betrothal, there rarely were any real fiancées among them. Ivanov-Razumnik recalls that a fellow-prisoner in his time was once visited by three fiancées at once. The warder asked him to choose the real one, but he could not for there was none. In short, it was quite natural for a radical girl to become the fiancée of some prisoner without assuming that there was any romantic attachment between them.

Just this kind of engagement seems to have been suggested while Lenin was in jail and Krupskaya still at large — December 1895 to August 1896. The most plausible version of this story occurs in a memoir by Lenin's sister Anna, who was in Petersburg at the time, visiting Lenin several times a week, and who put down her recollections in the relatively early year 1924. Anna says that Krupskaya proposed herself as a fiancée for Lenin, presumably for the usual conspiratorial reasons, but possibly with some more tender, unspoken idea. Lenin, when his sister told him this, "categorically opposed" the idea, saying that he would have nothing against a "neutral" fiancée, which presumably meant a girl who was less politically involved and therefore less vulnerable to guilt by association. This sounds like Lenin's language — hardly encouraging to sentiment.[20] In a variation on this theme Elena Stasova claims that Krupskaya, not long before her death in 1939, confided that Lenin had sent out a request that he be sent a fiancée, "and I did not know, should I go or someone else? I went and it turned out that Vladimir Ilyich wanted me." It is pretty clear that Krupskaya did not actually visit Lenin in jail, but there is probably some basis for the story — something connected with the discussion of Krupskaya becoming "engaged" to him.[21]

Once Krupskaya herself had been arrested, there was no question of her visiting Lenin in jail. But when Lenin was released in February 1897, with orders to leave shortly for three years' residence in Siberia, he probably reopened the question of an "engagement." We are told that he contacted Krupskaya's mother and had her transmit a secret note in which "he spoke of his love for her." Just what he succeeded in communicating is uncertain. Krupskaya, by her account, was only able to develop milk-ink messages by dipping them in the hot water that was brought for tea, because no flame was permitted in jail. Perhaps a throbbing profession of love could be transmitted in this soggy medium, but one wonders. It would have been easier to leave a letter in plain ink in the custody of Krupskaya's mother, to be delivered when Krupskaya was out of jail, but Lenin's love letter was in "chemical" form.[22] The only thing that may be fairly definitely deduced from available evidence is that he suggested to her that, *if* she were given a term of exile, she might petition for permission to join him as his fiancée. This much is clear from Anna's memoir, in which she recalls how she comforted her mother, when they learned of Vladimir's sentence, by pointing out that "surely Nadezhda Konstantinovna would go to join him after her case had been completed."[23]

This Krupskaya could do only if she were a recognized fiancée.

In passing, Anna also recalls that, when Lenin was at last released from jail for a brief respite before Siberia Apollinarya Yakubova "ran and kissed him, laughing and crying at the same time." Perhaps Krupskaya had a rival until a relatively late date.[24] In any case Apollinarya found solace by marrying Lenin's successor as the leading spirit of the Petersburg Marxist underground, Takhtarev.

As for Krupskaya, her case with the police and with Lenin dragged on in uncertainty for some time after her release, under surveillance, in March 1897. It took the authorities until March 30 the following year to settle her fate, although tentative and incomplete information on their decision began to emerge as early as December 1897. As long as there was no firm reason to conclude that she would receive any sentence at all, Lenin did not try to get in touch with her. He presumably reasoned that it was best for her that the police have no additional reason to link the two. There is no reference to her in the surviving letters to his relatives from this period, although he made one inquiry about the fate of the "Bulochkins," the pseudonym of the Nevzorova sisters, whose sentence was very likely to prove similar to Nadezhda's.[25] Krupskaya, too, tried to avoid any new incriminating activity after her release. At first she was permitted to stay in Petersburg for her health, then to move for the summer to a cottage in Valdaika. She was not in close touch with the Ulyanov family and did not try to run errands for Lenin, such as buying books.[26]

Things began to move again only after the police gave signs of reaching a decision. Some time around the end of November 1897, they must have told Krupskaya's friend Zinaida Nevzorova that she would probably get three years' exile in some northern part of European Russia. Although Zinaida had formerly visited Sil'vin in jail, as

Krupskaya at age seven

A passport picture of Krupskaya in disguise (1917)

Lenin in 1897, shortly before he left for exile in Siberia

Inessa Armand (about 1910)

Lenin, Krupskaya, and Maria Ulyanova (Lenin's sister) at a military review on May Day, 1918

The room Krupskaya occupied in the Kremlin from 1918 to her death in 1939

*Krupskaya addressing a Red Army regiment in 1919,
during her trip on the Volga and Kama Rivers.*

Krupskaya and the convalescent Lenin, after his first round of strokes, at their country home near Moscow (1922)

Krupskaya and "Pioneers" in 1928. This activity was typical of her public role as the great maternal figure of her people

Krupskaya between Inessa Armand's daughter, whom she treated as her own daughter after Inessa's death, and her nephew Vladimir, Lenin's nearest male descendent (about 1932)

Krupskaya in 1936, three years before her death. She wears her "Order of Lenin," symbolic of her ceremonial status in the Stalin regime

Krupskaya's funeral on March 1, 1939. Stalin and others carry the urn to the Kremlin wall for burial.

his fiancée, she had plans to ask for a transfer to Siberia as the fiancée of Lenin's friend Gleb Krizhanovsky, who was settled not far from Lenin. So Lenin soon learned from Gleb about Zinaida's case, and he correctly deduced that Nadezhda would get about the same sentence. He also noted, in his letters home, that Nadezhda would probably ask for a transfer as his fiancée.[27] The context makes it clear that Lenin had not heard anything from Krupskaya, but felt that the signs pointed to the activation of a previous plan. Confirmation of his surmise reached him from Krupskaya in early January 1898. Knowing that she would receive a three-year sentence of rustication, she had nothing much to lose by letting the authorities know about her "engagement" to Lenin. She seems to have written him to this effect, informing him that they both should send the authorities petitions that she be permitted to join him. Lenin duly sent a telegram to the director of police, dated January 8, 1898: "I have the honor to request permission for my fiancée, Nadezhda Krupskaya, to move to the village of Shushenskoe."[28] Krupskaya wrote the Minister of Internal Affairs at somewhat greater length. She asked to be sent to Shushenskoe and implied that this exchange of a place of exile in European Russia for Siberia merited a year's reduction in the sentence, which would have had the effect of allowing her to leave Siberia with Lenin. She also asked permission for her mother to accompany her.[29]

Why should Elizaveta Vasilevna, who was not sentenced to anything, go to desolate Shushenskoe? Some of the Decembrists were joined by their wives, but certainly not their mothers-in-law. But was she really going to become Lenin's mother-in-law? Was her only daughter going to the ends of the earth as a fictitious financée, perhaps to live in sin with him? Elizaveta Vasilevna was an Orthodox Christian believer and no advocate of any sexual revolution. It is doubtful that her daughter had received any clear offer of marriage from this fellow, whom she had known for only a few short intervals in 1894-1895. Nor had Lenin promised the police, in his petition, that he would marry Nadezhda. At the time none of them were aware that the police would soon insist on immediate marriage. The whole uncertainty of Krupskaya's future with Lenin is probably chiefly responsible for her mother's decision to go along.

There followed three months of appeals and delays before the police gave final consent to Krupskaya's petition that she be allowed to join her fiancé. The official permission was dated March 30, 1898, and covered both Nadezhda and her friend Zinaida. Sometime during this period the police told Krupskaya that their consent to her petition would be approved only on condition that she marry her fiancé after she reached Shushenskoe.[30] Very likely the motivation for this ruling was annoyance with the abuse of fictitious engagements between radicals. Krupskaya must have sent word of this to Lenin, who responded (in a letter that is lost or hidden) by "calling her to him," that is, proposing that they accept the conditions laid down by the police.

Krupskaya is supposed to have replied to Lenin's offer of marriage: "Well, so what — if as a wife, then as a wife." The authority for this bit of lore is Vera Dridzo, Krupskaya's worshipful secretary between 1919 and 1939, who heard many of her reminiscences. While one may usually distrust reliance on word of mouth and memory, this peculiar choice of words was recollected very clearly by Lenin, who (in Dridzo's words) "often reminded her of this reply."[31] In Russian it sounds even terser, more careless and even contemptuous as an acceptance of a marriage proposal: *"Nu, chto zh, zhenoi tak zhenoi."* Odd as it is, the reply makes sense if considered as a reaction to the news that the police will insist that they marry, that Krupskaya may stay with Lenin not as a "fiancée" (*nevesta*) but only as a "wife" (*zhena*). The contempt in her reply is for the police and continues the attitude already adopted toward "engagement." This could be summed up: "We despise bourgeois 'engagement' and 'marriage' alike, and we accept these forms only to fool the police and aid our struggle for the revolution." But such an attitude obscured the question of their real emotions toward each other, and probably acted as an inhibition of any frank profession of love. How crushing it would be, and how unfortunate for correct socialist relations, if you were to tell your "betrothed" that you love him or her, only to receive a curt reminder that it is all just a tactical ruse — "And keep your emotions out of it, comrade."

However uncertain Krupskaya's status as a fiancée may have been in the winter of 1897-1898, it is clear that she had been chosen as Lenin's secretary. He needed one in Siberia even more than previously, precisely because enforced abstinence from political activism stimulated his interest in writing. The system of enforced settlement in remote areas, by which the Imperial government sought to isolate political troublemakers, was not bad for study or writing, particularly if you had family to send you the necessary materials. Typically the prisoner was simply ordered to live in a given locality, where he was registered with the police. He was paid a small stipend to live on and was left to find his own quarters and food. Lenin (and later Krupskaya, too) was paid eight rubles a month, not much, but a subsistence in a country town — over twice the wages of the more poorly-paid Petersburg workers and over three times the wages Lenin and Krupskaya were soon paying to their hired girl in Siberia.

Lenin had a strong scholarly bent and was deeply convinced that the cause of scientific socialism required learned theoreticians as well as popular agitators. In the last years of the nineties as he was chiefly engaged in economic studies of Russia that were intended to refute the current narodnik arguments. His major work in this line was a long book entitled *The Development of Capitalism in Russia,* which he started in Petersburg in jail and finished in Shushenskoe. It required a good copyist.

The prospective arrival of a helper, after he had been in exile for a year, was a valuable link with the metropolitan centers. Even with obliging relatives, it was hard for a vigorous worker like Lenin to have anything like the books and periodicals he wanted for his work. Things were mailed, but with continual delay and irritation. "As to what to send with N. K. — I think you should give her a real load of books," he wrote his mother. (Note that Lenin used the formal "Nadezhda Konstantinovna" or "N. K." rather than the familiar "Nadya" in his correspondence with his relatives until *after* she had settled in Shushenskoe.) In fact, Krupskaya had to find the books as well as pack them, for Anna forwarded the rather imposing list to her. She was also supposed to bring ready-to-wear clothing for him, moleskin clothing for hunting (at his mother's expense), and, of all things, his straw hat. "After all, it's a Paris hat, devil take it", wrote Lenin, without explaining whether he intended to impress the yokels or his fiancée. Anticipating heavier expenses after the arrival of the Krupskayas, whose financial affairs were probably not at all familiar to him, he added that his mother should give Nadezhda "as much money as possible" for transmission to him.[32] Lenin's mother, unlike Elizaveta Krupskaya, had both a substantial widow's pension from the civil service and an inheritance. She was able to afford vacations in Switzerland and the Caucasus in these years, while contributing to the upkeep of at least three of her four grown children.

The presence of Krupskaya in Petersburg for several months before her departure for Siberia could also be turned to good advantage by Lenin. She had better contacts with Marxist intellectuals than his relatives did, and was able to accomplish quite a lot as a literary agent. In January 1898, Lenin formed the idea of bringing out a volume containing several of his economic articles and had Krupskaya seek Peter Struve's help on this matter. He was the outstanding Marxist theoretician-scholar of the day in Russia, and, by keeping out of conspiratorial activities, kept out of jail. He edited a journal for a while and because of his good contacts among publishers was able to give Lenin invaluable help, which he did, generously. Krupskaya had a good introduction to Struve not only because of her impeccable credentials in the underground but also because she was a good friend of Nina Gerd, whom Struve was about to marry. Lenin made the job of dealing with Struve more difficult by taking an unjustly suspicious attitude toward him. At one point he told Krupskaya to withdraw the manuscript, because he was sure Struve would not really find a publisher for it. This must have been rather puzzling to Nadezhda, who had been taking a lot of trouble to cooperate with Struve, and who could not be expected to foresee that he would slip from Marxism to liberalism in a few years. Although she wrote disparagingly of Struve years later, when his apostasy was history, it is doubtful that she disliked him at the time, and she appears to have done her best to keep Lenin's contact with him. She even made the independent decision to accept, on behalf of Lenin, a commission from Struve to translate from the English (with the help of an existing German version) Sidney and Beatrice Webb's bulky *History of Trade Unionism*. In a letter to Lenin's mother Krupskaya admitted that she was not sure that Lenin wanted to take on translation, but she had decided to take up the offer because "it is a very interesting translation and the pay is good."[33] At this point Krupskaya was sufficiently naïve politically to be unconcerned about the unrevolutionary backsliding of Webbian socialism, but she seems to have been shrewd in guessing that Lenin could use the money.

In the middle of April 1898, the two Krupskayas started on the journey from Petersburg to Shushenskoe, approximately 4,000 miles east. Although Krupskaya's petition for a shortened sentence had been turned down, she had been granted permission not only to change her exile from Ufa to Shushenskoe but to travel at her own expense. This meant that, unlike some impecunious members of her group, she did not have to go with other prisoners, under guard. On the way they stopped for a short visit with Lenin's mother in Moscow. She already had met her

on several previous occasions, more because Maria Ulyanova took an active part in her son's travails than because
Krupskaya had been so close to him. Oddly enough, she
saw Maria almost as many times in the few years before
her marriage as in the many years afterwards. But this was
not because of any particular chilling of their relations.
Nadezhda was for years a model correspondent with her
mother-in-law, reporting cheerfully on Vladimir's welfare
and activities. It is hard to say what Lenin's mother thought
about her daughter-in-law. The surviving letters of Lenin's
mother, written well after her son's marriage, indicate that
she was solicitous of Nadezhda's welfare, but very reserved.
In her first letter from Shushenskoe to Maria Ulyanova,
Krupskaya complains that "Volodya [Lenin] is not satisfied
with what I had to tell him about all of you. He says it is
very little, but I told him all I know."[34] When they left
Maria gave the travelers a practical present: food for three
days so that they would not have to endure the meals available in railroad station buffets.

At last (on about April 15) Krupskaya was off to join
Lenin. Although neither her memoirs nor other writings
refer to it, the departure must have been an intense emotional experience for her, and not only because of her
forthcoming marriage to Lenin, with its uncertainties. She
was going not only as his bride but as a bride of the
revolution, fulfilling her childhood dream of devotion to
the cause of human betterment. If she found much that
was attractive in Lenin personally (as well as she could
recall what he had been like almost two and a half years
before) her devotion to him was surely based on the equa-
tion Vladimir Ulyanov = Revolution. But this is not to
deny that they were in love in their own ways, which were
inextricably intertwined with their ideas of revolutionary
mission: Lenin's self-image as a leader and Krupskaya's as
his devoted helper.

Considering that it was Nekrasov who had prepared
her emotions for this role, it is unthinkable that Krupskaya's mind did not turn to the favorite poem of her

childhood, "Russian Women," as she slowly crossed Siberia. In it Nekrasov hymns the spiritual nobility of the two princesses who left the comforts of Europe in order to join their husbands, whose devotion to the fight against tsardom had brought them to Siberia. Krupskaya could not have failed to see the parallels between the princesses' journey and her own. The husbands of the two princesses were "Decembrists," so called because of the month of their abortive revolution in 1825. Lenin and the members of the Group of Social Democrats who were arrested in the same sweep in December 1895 were known among their comrades as "Decembrists" — a conscious allusion to the earlier heroes. The great moral merit of the princesses was that they went to their husbands by free choice. Krupskaya had voluntarily requested to be transferred from enforced residence in one of the European provinces of Russia to Siberia to join her future husband. The parents of the princesses had tried to dissuade them from going. It is a safe guess that Krupskaya's mother did the same, and like the parents in Nekrasov's poem she probably argued that the harsh climate of Siberia is unhealthful. True, the princesses were going to join spouses who were condemned for life to Siberia, and they had to travel by wearisome sleigh, while Krupskaya faced only two years in Shushenskoe and could travel in the relative comfort of Count Witte's new railroad most of the way. On the other hand, her lot was harder than that of the Decembrists' wives because she was a political convict herself, not just a loyal spouse.

But the princesses had actually been married when they went to Siberia, and they knew pretty well where they stood with their husbands. Krupskaya could be reasonably certain that she would be married soon, thanks to the ultimatum of the police. But what kind of marriage would it be? The idea of an "engagement" had first been introduced as a ruse for the good of the cause. The Russian radical tradition in the later nineteenth century made quite a cult of marriages that also were intended as ruses —

to liberate radical women from their fathers' legal control so that they could serve the cause. It was a great point of honor, that the "husband" in such cases would not expect to have sexual relations with his "wife." Had Lenin, in the difficult circumstances since his arrest, ever made it clear that this engagement or marriage was not basically just a means to frustrate the attempt of the police to isolate him from a helpful comrade? Krupskaya had reason to feel more than the usual nervousness of a prospective bride.

As for Lenin, it seems likely that he had convinced himself by this time that he was in love with Krupskaya, and hoped that she returned his affection. But, he had not known her well before his arrest and had had only tenuous ties with her afterwards. As Lenin awaited the arrival of his fiancée and her straitlaced mother, he, too, had some cause for nervousness about the impending marriage, and it showed up in his letters home. "I am getting lodgings ready [for the two Krupskayas] — the next room in the same house", he wrote to his mother.[35] This is exemplary propriety for a radical who professed to scorn bourgeois hypocrisy and who liked a popular song called "We Were Married Out of Church." Why should a man of these convictions, who expects to marry soon anyway, plan for his bride to occupy her mother's room, not his? The most plausible explanation seems to be that he was not sure just what Krupskaya expected from their marriage, which she had agreed to with such diffidence. Did she think of herself as a comrade-assistant, with no intentions of really becoming his wife, with or without a "contemptible" marriage ceremony? If she did not love him, there would be little reason to expect her to offer herself to him simply for physical gratification. The Chernyshevskian model of the revolutionary male left little room for that sort of thing.

When his sister Anna innocently asked her brother, in a letter, when the wedding would be and who would be invited, Lenin irritably replied (to his mother) : "Isn't she hurrying! First of all Nadezhda Konstantinovna has to get here, and then we have to get permission from the authorities to marry — we are people without any rights at all. So how can I do any 'inviting'?"[36] And then he abruptly changed the subject. The crux of his annoyance seems to be that his family was not aware of the uncertainties in his forthcoming marriage. It is unlikely that Lenin would have discussed his intimate personal problems with his mother and sisters, and they would naturally assume that there would be an early wedding and a normal marriage. But Lenin was not at all sure that his bride intended to share his bed as well as his political convictions, and he found the whole question upsetting. After Nadezhda had arrived, and had suddenly become "Nadya" in his letters home, Lenin returned to Anna's question in quite a different spirit, jokingly inviting all his relatives, although he now expected that the haste imposed by the police would make their coming impossible.[37]

The journey through Siberia was uneventful. The railroad took the Krupskayas to Krasnoyarsk, where they were originally supposed to change to a horse-drawn vehicle to Shushenskoe. But they preferred to wait a week for the spring opening of steamer traffic on the Yenisei River. Although she was supposed to be under police surveillance, Krupskaya utilized her time in Krasnoyarsk to become acquainted with some of the older political exiles there. She also met two of her colleagues from Petersburg, who were on their way to other destinations under armed guard, since they were not traveling at their own expense. When the first northbound steamer of the season left Krasnoyarsk, the Krupskayas were on it, disembarking on May 6 at Sorokino, the most convenient river port that was functioning at that time. Continuing by road, they reached Shushenskoe at dusk on May 7.

Lenin presumably knew that they might arrive at any time, but he was out hunting when they reached the cottage where the two rooms had been rented, so they sat down to wait. When he did return, his peasant landlord added to the atmosphere of the meeting by telling Lenin, as a practical joke, that a drunken neighbor had been in

Lenin's room and had thrown all his books about. Frantically dashing to the disaster, Lenin met Krupskaya. What they said is not recorded, though Elizaveta is supposed to have remarked "Oh, how fat you're getting" (probably intended as a compliment, since he was peaked-looking in Petersburg before his arrest).

At this crucial point a curtain of privacy is drawn over the tangled affairs of the engaged couple. Krupskaya laconically records, "We had a good long talk that night." In all likelihood this was when they discovered, to their delight, that the uncertainties had been unnecessary, that both were in love and wanted a real marriage.

Krupskaya had affectionately brought Lenin, in addition to the many items he had requested, a green-shaded study lamp. She also brought the news that her final police orders required *"immediate"* marriage, or her departure for Ufa, the city in European Russia to which she had been assigned earlier. Although Lenin referred to this as "tragicomic," he was quite willing to comply with this condition, but found that he could not get the necessary papers from the bureaucracy. Even though he had been in Shushenskoe for over a year, it seems that the district offices in Minusinsk did not have him entered on their list of detainees. The situation became serious in June when no less an authority than the office of the Governor-General of Irkutsk, ruler of eastern Siberia, wrote to the office of the governor of Yenesei province to check with the police to find out if the marriage had taken place, and to deport Krupskaya if it had not. On June 30 Lenin wrote the governor of the province respectfully, but with a hint of malicious satisfaction, calling attention to this bureaucratic contradiction. His concluding argument was surprising, since it was based neither on sentimental grounds nor on the original order from Petersburg. He asserted that his bride was not receiving her monthly stipend because she was not yet married and that without this income she could not live. Considering the resources of the two families, this was not quite true, and it is certainly an unromantic pretext for marriage. But it seems to have worked, and on July 6 the provincial office wired the district police to issue a permit for the wedding.

This great event in Krupskaya's life, which perhaps ought to be the high point of this book, is plunged in obscurity. Krupskaya left no published memoir of the day, and neither she nor Lenin mentioned it *at all* in the letters to his relatives that have been published.[38]

The Orthodox ceremony, which was the only legal marriage in Imperial Russia (except for members of other recognized faiths), took place in the Shushenskoe parish church on July 10, 1898. The nuptial couple had hoped to have their friends over from the town of Tesinskoe, not too far away — Zinaida (Nevzorova) and Gleb Krizhanovsky. They had just been married under similar conditions and were to have been the legal witnesses for Lenin's marriage. Unfortunately the district police chief would not grant permission for this, arguing that one political convict who had been given a travel permit had disappeared. Elizaveta Krupskaya was doubtless present, as well as three peasant acquaintances of Lenin, who signed the church register as witnesses.[39] It is not recorded whether they also served as *shaferi,* the attendants who stand behind the bride and groom in an Orthodox wedding and hold crowns over the heads of the couple while the priest reads the service (the crowns symbolize the crown of martyrdom — a gloomy view of marriage). Although this ritual would have been galling to the likes of Lenin and Krupskaya, it is probable that the priest insisted on it (he had special reason to be unobliging to Lenin, because he had wanted to rent the room that Lenin had taken for the Krupskayas). He definitely insisted on another conventional ritual, wedding rings, a contingency that Lenin had not expected. Where to obtain a wedding ring in Shushenskoe, which had almost no shops? Fortunately one of the two other political exiles in town, a Finn named Oskar Engberg, was learning the jeweler's trade. At Lenin's request, Krupskaya had added a jeweler's kit to her luggage (it supposedly weighed over seventy pounds) to set up Oskar properly. This generosity now brought some return, for the neophyte jeweler fashioned two wedding rings of copper. According to the fashion of the radical intelligentsia, these were only to be worn at the ceremony, to satisfy the rotten capitalists — but Krupskaya kept hers, without wearing it.[40] Near the end of her life she donated it to the Central Lenin Museum in Moscow, which, however, was not sufficiently sentimental to include it in the Krupskaya room they set up after Stalin died. What Lenin did with his copper ring is anybody's guess.

Following the ceremony the bride and groom are reported to have returned to their cottage by separate routes, so as "not to attract attention."[41] They then gave a small reception, one of the few ever held in Siberia at which nothing stronger than tea was served.

CHAPTER III

Siberian Honeymoon

The Ulyanov's honeymoon in Siberia, which lasted about a year and a half, seems to have been as happy as could be expected of two austere personalities living in penal exile.[1] The sleepy, often frozen, pace in Shushenskoe (population 1,300) provided the couple with the most relaxed conditions of life that they were to know for any considerable period. Since exile limited the services that they could render to the cause, the pair had a good deal of time for themselves, despite their various literary projects. True, in her didactic memoirs Krupskaya stressed the well-disciplined work habits that they maintained: "First thing in the morning Vladimir Ilyich and I would sit down to the Webb translation . . . . After [mid-day] dinner we spent a couple of hours together copying out *The Development of Capitalism*."[2] This sort of recollection created an impression of self-denial that Krupskaya eventually came to regard as a misunderstanding of her early married life. Once, when reading a play about Lenin, she indignantly sputtered to her secretary, "Just think, we were young then, we had just been married, were deeply in love with one another. And he [the author of the play] says — 'They translated all of the Webbs' book.'" Or again, "We were newlyweds, you know — and brought beauty to this exile. If I did not write about this in my memoirs, that does not mean that there was neither poetry nor youthful passion in our life."[3]

From Krupskaya's perspective this romantic view of her early marriage is fair enough, even though she was responsible for the severe tone of her memoirs. Her letters to Lenin's mother and sisters from Siberia sound contented and affectionate. She seems totally devoted to "Volodya" (the diminutive of Vladimir and a more affectionate choice than the semi-official "Ilyich" that she later used in referring to her husband). Without belittling her admiration for him as a person or a revolutionary, Krupskaya brings a gentle touch of irony into her letters about Lenin in Siberia — a spirit that is missing after this honeymoon. She is amused by the zealousness with which he can undertake a fishing expedition, and then drop the subject completely after coming home "without so much as a tiddler." How he looked like "the giant from Hop-o'-My Thumb in his felt boots and quilted trousers" when he went visiting on one occasion. Or how he first "announced that he did not know how to gather mushrooms and did not like it," but now, after sampling this pleasure, "you cannot drag him out of the forest, he gets real 'mushroom fever.'"[4]

But even in her early affection for Lenin, Krupskaya did not expect too much in return. When he needed to have a tooth pulled and took a trip to Krasnoyarsk, she wrote that "the place seems empty without him," but she was happy that he could go because he had been "vegetating." She did not mind that he was "exultant" to have change of scene — just about two months after their wedding. Small services to him — mending his clothes, making him nightshirts, copying his manuscripts — were not tedious to her. She even displayed a tranquil temper when she was harassed by her sister-in-law Anna (as it seems from only one side of the correspondence). "It gave Volodya great satisfaction to read out to me all the reproaches that you have written about me," she wrote only a month after the wedding. "Well, I admit I am guilty [of what? not writing an adequate account of the wedding, perhaps?] but deserving of leniency."[5] Later Nadezhda suffered Anna's "indignant" reproaches because she had given Lenin her own letters to the Ulyanov family to "edit" before mailing them. Apparently it did not occur to the jealous Anna that if anyone deserved indignation it was her brother, who was certainly not having the role of censor forced upon him. The reason for this procedure, Krupskaya explained, was that she wrote in a bantering manner about Volodya (very, very mildly, one should add), and, "I would not write such letters if I did not give them to him to read before I send them off." This is a most revealing comment on the marriage, suggesting Krupskaya's sincere devotion to her husband and her perception in recognizing that he required a kind of reverence, even though he was not vain in the ordinary sense.

Her understanding of this side of her husband's character and her never-changing conviction that he deserved special devotion as a champion of the cause was the foundation for their successful marriage. Many years in advance of the rest of the country, Krupskaya had founded her private cult of Lenin, who was for her the embodiment of the revolution of her idealistic dreams. Her life could find its fulfilment in serving him, her love for him mingled with her firm devotion to the ideal of revolution. This bespoke modesty, the quality that Krupskaya's eulogists have emphasized above all others. In a way they are right. She scorned glamor and avoided public honor. Her modesty was probably not merely a pose but was a matter of sincere conviction. But conviction implies deliberate choice. Krupskaya, who was introspective, could not have been unaware of her modesty. Judging by her comments on what she found good in others, modesty was among her favorite virtues — and she was much concerned with virtue from childhood on. If she was sincerely modest it was because she was sincerely convinced that this was an essential part of being righteous. And can any person, if he knows that he is both righteous and modest, avoid inner pride? It is also easy to adduce a streak of the would-be martyr in such a personality. A little persecution may be quite welcome if it offers an opportunity for self-effacement and proof of total devotion.

So one need not be surprised to find the bride Nadezhda meekly accepting Lenin's "great satisfaction" in reading Anna's reproaches to her, or his censorship of her letters — or some more serious trials that Krupskaya later encountered in her marriage.

She did not seem to mind being taken for granted either, almost as soon as she had arrived in Shushenskoe. In general it is unremarkable that a young man should not be effusive in praising his bride to his mother and sisters, but Lenin's case deserves comment. He had spent almost eighteen months in this hamlet without the company of a single kindred spirit before Krupskaya arrived (the two fellow-exiles, ordinary workmen, were friendly but ignorant). Her coming surely transformed his existence there in almost every possible way, adding both love and political comradeship — even an unequal intellectual partnership — to his lot. But in the fifty surviving letters of Lenin to his relatives in this period he barely mentions "Nadya" at all and only in wholly uninterested allusions: "Nadya and I are making a fair copy of the Webbs' book." (This is all he has to say about her five days after the wedding — is it any wonder some Soviet writers formed a pretty ascetic view of the marriage?) "Nadya also wants to learn to skate, but I am not sure she will manage it." (His most long-winded reference to his bride during their eighteen months in Siberia.) ". . . Nadya copies it [his book] quite quickly as I write it." (The nearest to praise for her.) [6] Reading Lenin's letters, which deal at some length with family affairs, his own literary endeavors, visits to and from other exiles, and news of other exiles, one might suppose that he had been married for many years and that his wife was so familiar a part of the background of his life that no news concerning her could be expected. In reality this was hardly the case, and one is likely to conclude that Lenin's enormous confidence in his own powers and importance (really beyond vanity and modesty) led him to accept Krupskaya's devotion with the greatest of ease. Sharing her assumption that this was his due as a great man of the coming revolution, it was easy to take her for granted, once she had arrived and declared her feelings.

It was not that Lenin was careless of her well-being. When he left Shushenskoe to visit the dentist, he became quite solicitous for her safety, even asking Engberg, the exile-jeweler, to sleep in the cottage, and teaching Nadezhda how to use a revolver. This was her only personal contact with the tools of violence in her whole life as a revolutionary.

From her letters one gathers that he was relatively happy in her company and considerate of her happiness as well as he knew how. But for all that, Lenin's love for Krupskaya is a pretty pallid shadow of Andrei Kolosov's ideal love, which wholly possesses a man's being. The subject came up in the first year of their marriage, as an accidental result of Lenin's efforts to improve his German — not exactly a stirring pretext for a declaration of passion. As a device for self-teaching, Lenin had ordered a set of Turgenev in German, so that he could test himself by rendering it back into Russian. He particularly dwelled on certain passages that were dear to him, among them the key parts of "Andrei Kolosov."[7] But even though he supposedly took this opportunity to tell Krupskaya that he loved her in the ideal, total fashion, this could hardly convince anyone that Lenin was obsessed with her and not revolution. Since Turgenev's story suggests passion only as an abstraction, entirely lacking in emotional warmth, Lenin may be pardoned if he assumed that he understood ideal love, when in reality he wanted merely domestic tranquillity.

But passion is not the only possible distraction of marriage. What about the possibility of children? In later years Krupskaya said that she had wanted children very much and regretted that she never had any. ("But now all the young pioneers are little Leninists," she said, consciously donning the bridal robes of the revolution.) She also tried to depict Lenin as a kind of universal uncle, always playing with children and making a great hit. In Shushenskoe he is supposed to have been idolized by the five-year-old son of a poor, drunken neighbor, to whom he brought a toy horse from Krasnoyarsk. Minya, the boy, was supposed to have been a frequent caller, but it is fair to guess that he either learned to regulate his calls or was kept away from Lenin when he was working, by Nadezhda or her mother. The writing of *The Development of Capitalism in Russia* surely was not cheerfully put aside for any six-year-old. Quite possibly Lenin realized that his career as a professional revolutionary, and his nerves, would be better off without children about. But perhaps he did have a real fondness for children — from a safe distance.

Krupskaya, on the other hand, who really had known and loved children as a devoted teacher, was probably sincere in recalling that she had wanted a family. And she was evidently under some pressure from her mother-in-law to produce an heir — one more matter in which Lenin's female relatives presumably found her wanting. We find Krupskaya, after eight months of marriage, replying to Lenin's mother: "As far as my health is concerned, I am quite well but as far as concerns the arrival of a little bird — there the situation is, unfortunately, bad; somehow no little bird wants to come."[8]

While she lived in Shushenskoe she did enjoy good health. The region was far from being an arctic waste and was even known as "the Siberian Italy" because of its comparatively clement climate. True, the Rivers Shush and Yenesei, which met near the town, were frozen solid by early October and the ice broke up only in mid-April, leaving floating chunks as late as May. And there were periods in the winter, measured in days rather than months, when low temperatures or howling winds kept the whole family indoors. But the months of May through September were generally quite pleasant, if one wore netting against hordes of mosquitoes that arose from the large swampy areas.

There were natural charms. The Sayan Mountains, with peaks reaching about 7,000 feet, usually snow-capped, could be seen in the distance; the birch and fir woods nearby, though partly cut down, were pleasant; and the rivers provided recreation as well as transportation. In the summer Lenin and Krupskaya went swimming at a spot about twenty minutes' walk from their cottage; in the fall when the water was frozen but not yet snow-covered Krupskaya recalls it as "an enchanted kingdom" — "every little fish and pebble could be seen distinctly under the ice." And in the winter of 1899 Lenin and Engberg organized the local schoolmaster and some others to clear the snow off a part of the river to make a skating rink. Krupskaya, in her affectionately ironic mood, depicts Lenin as the slightly self-important figure-skating champion of the area, amazing "the Shushenskoe public with his 'giant steps' and 'Spanish leaps'," while she was only able to push a chair around the ice and, later, to "strut like a chicken." Her progress was not assisted by the attention of the rustic onlookers, who "keep relentlessly cracking nuts and showering the shells on our precious rink."

The chief outdoor recreations were hunting birds and rabbits and simply walking. Lenin had spasms of "hunting fever," as Krupskaya called it, and she sometimes accompanied him, along with their affectionate but inept bird dog, Zhenya. Together they did a lot of walking, just for exercise, gathering wild strawberries and mushrooms in season. With some fresh game, berries, mushrooms, and the produce from their kitchen garden in their second summer, the Ulyanovs were able to supply their own table to a fair extent, though there was no shortage of inexpensive local meat, milk or other staples. Neither of them had much taste for luxuries, although Krupskaya professed, in a thank-you note, greatly to enjoy the candy that Lenin's mother sent at Christmas.

At first Krupskaya and her mother did the cooking and housekeeping by themselves, and had some trouble learning to use the traditional Russian peasant stove — fundamentally a square brick oven — since they were city folk and accustomed to hired help as well. But in the fall of their first year in Siberia they partially solved their problems by hiring a scrawny girl in her early teens named Pasha Yashchenko, who was both illiterate and entirely untutored in city ways, though one suspects that she knew what to do with a peasant stove. Pasha must have been pretty poor, lacking even decent footwear at the beginning of winter, for her pay was set at "two and a half rubles a month plus boots." Interviewed in later years as a witness of historical greatness, she could recall only that on her first night with the family she slept on the floor, there being no spare bed, and Lenin stumbled over her in the dark. Also that they taught her to wait on their table, for even in this Siberian fastness Krupskaya had servant help, contrary to the teachings of Tolstoy. For her part Krupskaya recalls teaching Pasha to read, so that she soon was posting excerpts from the wisdom of Elizaveta Krupskaya, such as "Neva waste eny tee."

Krupskaya's mother, the matriarch of the household, was a bit worrisome about money, but not without some justice, since she was partly supporting the establishment. About two months after the wedding we find Lenin asking his own mother to send Elizaveta half the fee for the translation of the Webbs' book, which was expected to bring him a total of at least five hundred rubles. This was repayment of a debt to his mother-in-law.[9] A month later Krupskaya notes in a letter that her mother complained that "we grudged money [tips] for the postman but otherwise wasted it." But the debt was paid off, and life in Shushenskoe was simple enough to present none of the minor financial crises that faced Lenin and Krupskaya from time to time — until he took over the government of Russia. Elizaveta's main problem seems to have been boredom; she stayed indoors much of the time for fear of arctic weather. Krupskaya relates that one of her mother's rare walks in winter, to see the new rink, ended with her falling on the ice and cutting her head — "since that she is more afraid of the ice than ever."

Despite these dissatisfactions, the senior Krupskaya does not seem to have been a source of much discord in the family. Her religious views may have caused a few brushes with Lenin, who was so dogmatically anti-Christian that he even objected when Krupskaya proposed coloring some eggs and baking a cake in traditional Russian celebration of Easter. But on the whole it seems that Lenin and his mother-in-law managed to avoid such contentious topics.

The cottage (actually half of a cottage owned by a local family) was modest but comfortable. It was really a log-cabin in construction, with notched logs forming both the outer walls and interior partitions, but it was not wholly rude. The windows were good-sized, double-framed, swinging ones of the standard north-European type, with paneled wooden shutters outside and carved decorative panels above each window. To her mother-in-law, who kept thinking about coming for a visit in the summer but never did, Krupskaya wrote: "The apartment is a big one, and if you come, which we would very, very much like, there would be room for everybody . . . . It consists of three rooms, one with four windows, one with three, and another with one. It is true that the apartment has one disadvantage — the rooms are all adjoining."[10] It was warm enough even in mid-winter and had a pleasant garden, including flowers, in summer.

Nor were the newlyweds wholly isolated in their cabin. Although police permits were needed to travel to another town, these were usually available, and the Ulyanovs were either visitors or hosts quite frequently in their first year together in Shushenskoe, although not thereafter. Gleb and Zinaida Krizhanovskaya, their comrades in Petersburg and also Siberian newlyweds, were the mainstays, but not the only ones. The high point of gaiety in the Marxist community of the Minusinsk area was a week-long holiday held at the Krizhanovskys' new residence in the town of Minusinsk between Christmas and New Year at the end of 1899. There were chess games (Lenin was the champion, Krupskaya barely knew the rules), skating parties, songs with guitar accompaniment, and even some carousing. Krupskaya recalls that they mulled wine on New Year's Eve and that Lenin was "tossed" by his friends. She and Lenin never drank very much, and vodka or other spirits not at all, but they were not teetotalers on principle.

But fundamentally Lenin and Krupskaya remained hyper-earnest devotees of their cause. Lenin had long since disciplined himself to steady study and writing, and managed to utilize his exile to turn out an impressive volume of his own compositions and translation. He needed help, but mainly of a routine sort, and Krupskaya's role was primarily that of copyist, working first on the translation of volume one of the Webbs' book, then on Lenin's *The Development of Capitalism in Russia*. She also tried to make a modest critical contribution in completion of the latter work: "I play at being the 'un-understanding reader' and am supposed to judge whether the exposition of the 'markets' [Lenin's shorthand label for the whole book] is sufficiently clear; I try to be as 'un-understanding' as possible, but there is not much I can find fault with."[11] Surely it did not require much pretence on Krupskaya's part to play the non-expert in economics, and surely she did well not to find fault with her husband's labor of love, which was an important study that would probably still be read by economic historians of Russia if Lenin had, by chance, died in 1900. After this was sent off in February 1899, Lenin edited some other translator's botch of volume II of the Webbs' book. "He has to work alone because two of us take longer," Krupskaya wrote, although she did copy the final result and confessed that by the end both she and Lenin were sick of Sidney Webb.

In addition to writing and translating, the two devoted themselves to the study of foreign languages, principally English and German. Poor Krupskaya was trying to wrestle with spoken English without having had any practical instruction in its erratic rules of pronunciation. Even though she at one point promised herself to memorize twelve pages of "exceptions" in a Russian text on English, she admits that her pronunciation was all wrong — based on the way the French would pronounce the same letters. Her husband was better off in this, since his sister Olga had once had an English tutor in the language, but he does not seem to have offered much help. In German Krupskaya was relatively advanced, and even did some translation (for local, unpublished consumption) from the shorter writings of Marx and his disciple Karl Kautsky. German was the predominant language of Marxism at this time, and all of the Russian social democratic intelligentsia assumed that they should know it. Other major western languages were considered important partly because of the socialist writings in them, partly because people like Lenin and Krupskaya were very likely to go into emigration.

In addition to language study Lenin also tackled philosophy, an area in which Krupskaya showed no interest at any time in her life. "My joke is that it will soon be dangerous to talk to him [Lenin] because he has soaked up so much philosophy," she wrote to her mother-in-law.

Considering that Lenin's jobs for her came in fits and starts, and that he did not require a real collaborator, it is not surprising that Krupskaya at times felt that she was not as fully occupied as she should be. "I have no regular occupation, I just read. I have now been ten whole months in Shusha and have not managed to get anything done," she wrote to Lenin's sister Maria in March, 1899.

Sometime before mid-October 1898, she began to write her own political tract. Lenin encouraged her in this and, shortly after leaving Siberia, arranged for the publication of Krupskaya's first work. Much as he wanted her assistance as a copyist, he was far from wishing to confine her to this role alone. Realizing her limitations, he never urged her to take up the central problems of theory or current politics, but he evidently thought her well fitted to write about education and "the woman question" — areas that were traditionally "fitting" for women.

Her maiden venture was "The Woman Worker" (*Zhenshchina-Rabotnitsa*), a propaganda brochure, aimed at the ordinary working-class woman in simple, even childish, language.[12] Nevertheless, it takes a significant stand on several controversial issues, which are worth a moment's attention. Female Marxists who were concerned with "the woman question" were troubled by the problem of identifying the foe — were they engaged in a war of classes or of sexes? Klara Zetkin, the durable feminist of the German Left, in her pamphlet, "The Woman and Her Economic Position," almost seems to forget Marxism and the capitalist foe as she flails away at tyrannical males. Krupskaya, who cites this pamphlet in her own, shows a bit of the same spirit. She holds that factory labor is good for women because it helps liberate them from men, from the control of the tyrannical father or husband. And the only reference to socialist society in the brochure ignores its class content while noting that it will liberate women from the drudgery of child-rearing.

But the main drift of Krupskaya's preachment is more Marxist than feminist — perhaps because of Lenin's influence. The full independence of women can be brought about only through the victory of the proletariat, "only by fighting hand in hand [sic] with men in the workers' cause." And in Russia the absence of free expression or a parliament requires "political struggle" — the nearest Krupskaya comes to mentioning revolution, probably because she did not wish to frighten her feminine, not yet militant, audience.

This was clearly subversive propaganda, unlike Lenin's works in Siberia, which were mostly scholarly enough to be published legally. During the one police search of the Ulyanovs' rooms in Shushenskoe, the gendarmes evidently overlooked Krupskaya's manuscript as well as various secret letters to comrades. These had been "hidden" Krupskaya tells us, with some pride in her security know-how, on the bottom shelf of a bookcase. Fortunately the local police were fooled by this careless procedure. They quit after tiring of looking through Lenin's statistical reference works on the top shelves. The manuscript survived to be published, in Russian, in Germany in 1901 and again in Russia during the Revolution of 1905 — not to mention subsequent editions after Krupskaya became famous.

The argument of the brochure suggests Krupskaya's orthodoxy as a Marxist under Lenin's tutelage. Before her marriage it is doubtful that she thought much about ideological quarrels within Marxism and even maintained very friendly relations with narodnik socialists. She recounts that in the early days of her marriage she tried defending Lavrov's *Historical Letters,* which she had read in her first more or less Marxist circle in Petersburg. She dealt "very 'gently' " with Lavrov, but Lenin evidently made it clear that she should not entertain tolerant views of such non-Marxist books even if they contain some correct points.[13] To sharpen her conception of Marxism, he provided her, for the first time, with a copy in German of *The Communist Manifesto* and introduced her to the "orthodox" view, as represented by Karl Kautsky, of such heretics as Eduard Bernstein. It was just at this time that the latter, a leading German social democrat, published his "revision" of Marxism, emphasizing reform rather than revolution. This work and Kautsky's critique of it reached Lenin in Shushenskoe and Krupskaya naturally picked up his ultra-orthodox appraisal of the dispute.

By accepting entirely her husband's ideological dicta, Krupskaya was spared any agonizing doubts about the internecine quarrels of socialism and her own righteousness.

She was not a strong independent political thinker, but as long as he was able to set the line for her she rarely had problems in choosing the right side of any quarrel.

This came out in a rather minor episode in Siberia. A document called "Credo," which represented the views of one Kuskova, an emigrant Russian Marxist, was circulated in Russian social democratic circles and even reached Lenin in Siberia. "Credo" challenged several of the premises that Lenin and his friends held dear. It questioned the readiness of the Russian workers for a really revolutionary movement (as opposed to a movement for economic concessions) and the ability of the intelligentsia to lead them. Lenin was outraged and gathered with his wife and fifteen other exiled Marxists in Minusinsk in August 1899. There Krupskaya had the honor of signing a "Protest" against Kuskova, which has become enshrined in the annals of the party as an early example of Leninist rejection of deviation from the correct line.

In this Krupskaya's role was impersonal (although she did make a fair copy of the "Protest" for circulation elsewhere), but her change in attitude toward an old friend is something else again. Apollinariya Yakubova had been one of her closest friends among the teachers at the adult school, right up until the time of Krupskaya's arrest. Later "Lirochka," after escaping from a place of exile in Siberia, married K. M. Takhtarev, who had been the leading figure in the Petersburg Union of Struggle after Lenin's arrest. She was reported to be insufficiently outraged by Bernstein's ideas, and even to have contrasted their "practical" sense of "reality" to the "Protest," which she apparently thought of as "inventing" a path that reality ought to follow. Just a little earlier in her career Krupskaya surely would not have taken this kind of disagreement as a personal affront, but in early 1900 she clearly did. "Something has been happening to her in the past three years and I don't understand her any more," wrote Krupskaya. "She is not the Lirochka I knew . . . To tell the truth I cannot reconcile myself to her marriage. Her husband created the impression on me of a kind of narrow self-assurance . . . ." (Krupskaya knew Takhtarev in 1896.) [14] For Lenin's wife to think that someone else's husband was "narrowly self-assured" is perhaps the supreme achievement of uncritical loyalty, but Krupskaya was quite right in sensing that Takhtarev was about to become an "economist" heretic in Lenin's eyes.

Concern for the establishment of a correct line among Russian Marxists increasingly occupied Lenin's mind in his last months in Shushenskoe. He was eager to devote himself to the editing of a newspaper, published in the safety of emigration, which would help to unite Russian social democrats into a militant party. Although a so-called first congress of the Russian Social Democratic Workers' Party had met in Minsk in 1898, it had succeeded only in issuing a manifesto, written by Peter Struve, who did not attend and was suspect by Lenin. No real organization was established, and most of the handful of delegates were arrested just after the congress. Lenin was bent on holding a more substantial party congress, but believed that the way to it must be prepared by a newspaper. He entered into secret correspondence with several comrades in various other places of exile and soon worked himself into a state of tension that banished whatever remained of a honeymoon atmosphere. Always calmer than her husband, Krupskaya does not seem to have been greatly upset by this. In any case, she still had a year left in her term of exile, to be spent in northern European Russia, according to the original sentence.

The Ulyanovs' actual departure from Shushenskoe was full of emotion and excitement. Engberg, whom Krupskaya had tutored in Marxism, presented her with a book-shaped, hand-made brooch inscribed "Karl Marx." Pasha, the serving girl, "wept rivers of tears," and little Minya gathered up the paper and pencils that were being left behind. Elizaveta Krupskaya made quantities of small, supposedly frost-proof dumplings called *pelmeny* to eat on the first stages of the trip, in an open sledge. Zhenya the dog, who was being left with another exile, grew increasingly puzzled and concerned.

The party left Shushenskoe on January 30, 1900, and proceeded down the frozen Yenisei to Krasnoyarsk, where they could luxuriate in the warmth of the Transsiberian Railroad. They soon reached Ufa, where Lenin lodged his women in a hotel and left after two or three days. There was no question of his sitting out a year of Krupskaya's exile in a provincial backwater, but he certainly did not leave her flat. First, he attempted to get permission for her to reside in Pskov, some distance southwest of Petersburg, where he intended to set up temporary headquarters, employed in a government statistical office while secretly meeting comrades to discuss the forthcoming newspaper. His petition, dated March 10, was rejected. A fresh complication then appeared. Krupskaya was afflicted with some kind of gynecological ailment that put her in bed for some weeks. Lenin dutifully applied for permission to spend six weeks with her, but was turned down. Shortly thereafter, on May 4, he received permission to go abroad, as he had intended to do sooner or later. The police were remarkably permissive in granting passports for foreign travel to political suspects, partly because they seemed to think that this was one way of getting them out of action in Russia.

It is to Lenin's credit as a husband that he did not take this opportunity as soon as possible, but instead made a further effort to visit Krupskaya. On May 10 he applied for permission to go to Ufa. As a political suspect he was not allowed to travel freely in Russia, even though he had been given permission to go abroad. Only after his mother went to the police and offered to accompany her son (as if she were capable of keeping him out of trouble) was this permission granted. So in June, traveling with his mother and sister Anna, Lenin went all the way from Pskov to Ufa, partly by rail, partly by boat — a pleasant journey on the Volga, Kama, and Belaya rivers. There is little to be learned of this visit. Evidently Krupskaya still felt a mildly uncomfortable distance between herself and Lenin's mother and sister, who left Ufa before he did. In a letter to Lenin's sister Maria she wrote "There are so many things I wanted to talk about [with her in-laws]. When they arrived, however, I was so distracted that all my ideas flew away — and there were other visitors here besides the family. It turned out that I did not have a real talk at all and I do not know when I shall see them again."[15] Anna's memoirs give the same impression. She dwells on the lovely boat trip and studiously ignores Krupskaya.

By the time Lenin visited Ufa, Krupskaya had recovered, so he could leave in early July, proceeding quite directly to central Europe and his new life as a professional revolutionary in emigration. Krupskaya could not join him there until the following April — 1901. Her months in Ufa were a fairly dull interval although busy enough. She lived with her mother, first in an apartment on the corner of "Gendarme" and "Prison" streets, to Lenin's amusement, then in improved quarters with a less ominous address. Her husband could not contribute to her support, so Krupskaya went back to giving lessons. Here her status as a social democrat in good standing helped. A local radical, A. D. Tsuriupa, who eventually became a major Soviet administrator, found a place for her with a "local millionaire" who had five children. She liked the family in spite of their wealth. "They [the parents] are very strict, the way our merchants are, and I actually like the way the children are brought up. The parents do not dress them up, they have very few toys, no nursemaids, plenty of freedom, the youngsters are in the street all day, the children clean their own boots, tidy their own rooms (even wash clothes). In general, there is nothing aristocratic about them and they are not spoiled." The imprint of Tolstoy was still clear in Krupskaya's ideas about child-rearing. In particular she was "completely captivated" by the youngest, a pretty girl of seven — "Such wonderful children do exist. She is a happy-go-lucky kid, laughs a lot and has not been drilled (sometimes she wipes her nose on her frock)."[16]

This passage is perhaps trivial, but worth bearing in mind as a counter-weight to the volumes of stuffy, platitudinous homilies on pedagogy that Krupskaya later produced. In her younger days she did have real feeling for children, and it is not wholly her fault that this human warmth dissipated in later years when she tried to devise some "system" of education.

In addition to her teaching she continued her language study — German, French, and Polish (the latter not very well remembered from early childhood). There were also various revolutionary activities, even though getting caught might have meant that she would never be allowed to join Lenin abroad. Ufa was not a major intellectual or industrial center, but there were some political exiles living there, some others passing through on their journeys to or from Siberia, and some radical railroad workers. Within the limits of this situation Krupskaya played a fairly active role. She supposedly conducted a propaganda circle with some workers, and through her contacts with Lenin's friends arranged for the delivery of some revolutionary literature to Ufa. Judging by a note addressed to somebody at the time of her departure, she had been in effect the treasurer of a socialist group there.

Perhaps her most important service to the cause in Ufa was as a covert propagandist for Lenin's position in the internecine quarrels of Russian Marxism — a role she was to fill for many years to come. Unfortunately, only one of the letters that reflect this activity has survived, but this one has the honor of being the most substantial published letter from Lenin to Krupskaya. (They were together a great deal of the time after their marriage and did not correspond much when separated. After Lenin's death Krupskaya had only one, minor piece of correspondence — a telegram — from Lenin in her possession.)

There is a short, personal prologue to this letter, which is no more effusive than one would expect from Lenin, but nevertheless as affectionate in his peculiarly formal-hearty style as even his wife could expect:

"For a long time I have been trying to get around to writing you ["thee," *tebe* — the familiar form] about affairs [in emigration], but all sorts of circumstances have interfered. In the turmoil here I live rather fairly well, even too much so — and this in spite of special, extraordinary measures for defense against the turmoil! One might almost say that I live in loneliness — and in turmoil nevertheless! I dare say that in any novel situation turmoil is inevitable, unavoidable, and it would be a sin not to murmur thanks to God that I am far from being as nervous as our dear bookseller [meaning his comrade Potresov], falling into black melancholia and momentary prostration under the influence of this turmoil. There is much that is good along with the turmoil! Well, I shall now tell about the affairs of the emigrant 'Union of Russian Social Democrats,' I shall tell about them on the basis of facts and of the tales of the other side . . ."[17]

The remainder of the letter (about eight times the size of the above) is a purely political document, a polemical account of the split that had opened in 1900 between the supposedly orthodox Russian Marxists in emigration and the "young ones," who were allegedly guilty of the "economist" heresy. The hottest issue in the dispute at the time Lenin wrote was the published attack made by Plekhanov, the dean of Russian Marxists, on the "young" heretics, in which he used personal correspondence to show how conniving his ideological foes were. This led to a sharp quarrel over the ethics of Plekhanov's tactics, in which the "young ones" had a good chance of winning sympathy among their comrades back in Russia because they were operating a newspaper that was more widely received (illegally) than any organ of the orthodox. (Lenin's newspaper was not yet functioning.)

Lenin was solidly aligned with Plekhanov in this dispute, and the main point of his letter to Krupskaya plainly was to disseminate the attack on the alleged heretics. With characteristic belligerence he concluded with a call for "a decisive struggle against economism, . . . an irrevocable split with bourgeois 'criticism'." The point was not to harangue Krupskaya, whose loyalty he did not doubt, but to use her as a propagandist in the factional quarrels of the embryonic party. Just how she circulated Lenin's letter cannot be determined, but by way of example, it is fair to suppose that Krupskaya tried to send a copy to her friend Lidya Knipovich. During Krupskaya's stay in Ufa, Lidya secretly came to visit her, and they were in correspondence. Soon Lidya would serve as an underground agent for his newspaper.

On March 11, 1901, Krupskaya's exile was over, and in a few days, armed with a passport for foreign travel, she set off to join Lenin. Unfortunately, some of his encoded messages had not reached her. They had been sent in books (probably marked letters) to a presumably cooperative employee of the Ufa zemstvo office (local government). Unfortunately this man found the books interesting reading in their own right, and he simply kept them. At the same time Lenin's open letters in this period carried a return address in Prague, while he was actually living in Munich — a bit of conspiratorial hocus-pocus that accomplished little except to confuse Krupskaya. She expected to find him in Prague, living under the pseudonym of Modraczek, when he was really living in Munich as Herr Meyer. It should have been clear from Lenin's letters to his mother, as they are now preserved, that he was not masquerading as Modraczek, but merely pretending that this man was his landlord. Krupskaya briefly visited her mother-in-law in Moscow, but this evidently did not come out in conversation, which was quite possibly terse. So, after leaving her own mother in Petersburg, Krupskaya headed for Prague in early April. In all likelihood, it was planned that Elizaveta Krupskaya would follow her daughter after she settled down. In any case, she did this no later than mid-May.

Nadezhda expected to be met at the station, for she had wired her time of arrival. But nobody appeared, and at last she put her luggage in a cab and went to the Modraczek address. But Herr Modraczek turned out to be a Czech, who had some trouble grasping what was going on. Krupskaya's spoken German was apparently rather feeble in this crisis. At length he saw the problem and referred her to "Herr Rittmeyer" in Munich. Arriving there, Krupskaya, "wise by experience," checked her luggage at the station and took a tram to the address, which turned out to be a neighborhood beer-hall. "I approached the fat little German behind the bar," recalls Krupskaya, "and timidly asked for Herr Rittmeyer with a feeling that something was wrong again. 'That's me', said the publican. Absolutely crushed, I mumbled, 'No, it's my husband.' And there we stood, staring at each other like a couple of idiots. At last Rittmeyer's wife came in, and, glancing at me, said, 'Ah, it must be Herr Meyer's wife. He is expecting his wife from Siberia. I'll take you to him.'"

So it was that Krupskaya had her second dramatic reunion with Lenin, this one less sentimental than in Shushenskoe. "Pfui — Damn it, couldn't you write and tell me where you were?" she greeted her husband — the only display of annoyance toward Lenin that she ever recorded.[18]

CHAPTER IV

First Secretary of the Bolshevik Party

After three years in Shushenskoe and Ufa one might think Krupskaya would have found pleasure in her first stay in western Europe, from April 1901 until November 1905. The first two years of this sojourn were evenly divided between Munich and London, the remainder spent in Geneva — all places that have often charmed tourists and expatriates. Nor were the Ulyanovs living in squalor. As Krupskaya herself said: "We did not know the kind of need in which you don't know how you are going to buy bread. Did the emigrant comrades really live this way? There were some who were out of work for two years, who did not receive any money from Russia, and were literally starving. This never happened to us."[1] The explanation of this financial security lay partly in the assistance of their mothers and partly in Lenin's position as a party organizer, which usually permitted him to allot himself something to live on from funds in his control.

In Munich they moved after a few weeks from a single, impoverished room rented to them by a worker and his family to a new, pleasant apartment in the suburb of Schwabing. Krupskaya liked to boast of Lenin's love of mingling with poor workers. There might be something to this, for Lenin had chosen their first, proletarian dwelling in Munich, but it seems significant that when Krupskaya arrived they not only sought larger quarters but also moved out of the ordinary workers' district.

In London they had rooms at 30 Holford Square, a dreary but respectable lower middle-class neighborhood, which had the advantage of being fairly near the British Museum, where Lenin studied and wrote almost daily. Here the Ulyanovs' landlady found fault with her tenants: they had almost no furniture (each time they moved they sold what little they had acquired), did not put curtains in the windows, and Krupskaya did not wear a wedding ring (though she kept one). But they paid their rent, and no serious trouble came of this encounter with British propriety.

As for Geneva, they rented a detached house in the Sécheron section, which Krupskaya attempts to describe as a "working class suburb." But it was more petty-bourgeois than proletarian in atmosphere, and the house itself was nicely located near a park and the promenade along the beautiful lake of Geneva. Many people would find such capitalist oppression tolerable. The house, Krupskaya says, was crowded, with "three tiny rooms upstairs," and below a large, stone-floored kitchen, which had to serve as a living-room, an indignity that seems to have been gratifying to her yen for deprivation. There was also at least one other room on the floor, in which her mother slept. While Krupskaya says that the place was so crowded that they had to go for a walk if they wanted to talk to any visitors, V. V. Vol'sky (Valentinov), who called on them frequently there, recollects no trouble of this sort. He does, however, remember that he took long walks with Lenin because Krupskaya had taken a dislike to him and would not let him in. Lenin, not wishing to argue the matter, arranged to meet Vol'sky in the park.

After subletting their house while on summer vacation in 1904, they moved to a two-room apartment in a substantial-looking building at a good downtown Geneva address, soon changing to another two-room affair with kitchen after the return of Krupskaya's mother. It was a bit crowded. A comrade who visited them there recalls that Krupskaya and her *mother* occupied one room, Lenin the other.[2]

Apart from the question of housing, the Ulyanovs could partake of the attractions that Munich, London, and Geneva offer the public at large, as well as the charms of the nearby countryside. In Munich they liked a walk along the Isar River, and in London they took in the parks and the Museum of Natural History. Lenin was fascinated by a display of pickled embryos at different stages of development, she recalls. Geneva, of course, offered pleasant walks in the town or mountain hikes nearby. Lenin and Krupskaya were more attracted to mountain walks, especially in the Alps, than any other recreation, and in their fifteen years of emigration they had quite a lot of opportunity for this diversion. Although the idyllic quality of these hikes probably has been embellished a bit by Soviet writers, there is no reason to doubt that the Ulyanovs' alpine walks were very pleasant and a much-needed respite from their compulsive devotion to the cause. A Communist memoirist, M. M. Essen, recollects Lenin gathering wild flowers for Krupskaya, and the ex-Bolshevik Vol'sky recalls him reciting Nekrasov, to her applause, on reaching some magnificent view (and on another occasion getting scolded by her for forgetting the salt).

But even though she admitted to having had some pleasant walks in western Europe, Krupskaya always referred to emigration in the most depressing terms: "Akh, this emigration!," she wrote to a comrade at home in 1901. It was, in the words of her memoirs, a "dead sea." She believed that it had been torment to Plekhanov's generation, making a nervous wreck of Pavel Axelrod and driving Vera Zasulich to risk an illegal trip to Russia "just to see what kind of nose a *muzhik* (peasant) has." "To get the most out of a foreign country, you have to go there when you are young and are interested in every little thing," she wrote not long after she arrived in Germany.[3] Krupskaya was thirty-two at the time, and being away from her beloved Russia did not make her feel young.

In short, from her first days abroad and in all circumstances Krupskaya felt compelled to find living outside Russia an ordeal. This was partly a reaction to the distressing contrast between her comparatively secure life and the really grim existence of many of her comrades who stayed behind in Russia. To enjoy the charms of Munich, London, or Geneva while one's comrades were either in the hands of the police, or in danger of imminent arrest, was impossible for Krupskaya, who could not bear to appear self-indulgent in her own eyes. And the wish not to enjoy Europe was usually simple to fulfill, for Krupskaya was not a cosmopolitan at heart, despite her study of German, French, and English. Nor was her proficiency in these languages, especially English, great enough to provide easy contact with these foreign cultures. Her letters continually complain of linguistic difficulties, and report desultory attempts to take more lessons. Far from experiencing an initial thrill from her first encounter with life abroad she wrote her mother-in-law, "At first it was a bit miserable, very alien." She found even the German workers distressing because they celebrated May Day by going to a beer-garden, and English self-styled socialists worse, because they feared such things as being fired or going to jail. Krupskaya took pride in Lenin's supposedly superior knowledge of the countries they lived in, compared to most Russian emigrants, and seems to imply that she shared this understanding. But her few recollections about these places in which she spent so many of her best years hardly bear out the claim. In Munich they saw only a few Russian comrades, supposedly for security reasons. Of England she later wrote: "We know very little about English socialists in their home surroundings. They are a reserved people." Perhaps, but Krupskaya's description of the English enigma was partly her invention. Having been to a peculiar "Seven Sisters Church" in London, she knowingly informed her Russian readers years later that "in English churches the service is usually followed by a short lecture and debate."[4] In general her mind was quite closed to western Europe and its people. In fifteen years of residence there she never seems to have made a single friend, however casual, nor to have met anyone she respected, except Marx's daughter. Her world was the insular one of Russian emigrants who were in varying degrees obsessed by the vision of a *Russian* revolution.

Life within the Russian revolutionary emigration was for Krupskaya absorbing and at times really pleasurable. The diaspora of Russian Marxists in western Europe was an intimate and introspective community, even though it was scattered over some twenty cities. Everyone knew almost everyone else, even if only as enemies in the chronic feuds. There was a sense of mutual responsibility, and those members of the community who had some source of income contributed to various funds that were established to help their less fortunate comrades. A bewildering, continually changing variety of emigrant newspapers, representing every small splinter-group and sometimes even individuals, kept up communications within the community and provided inexhaustible fuel for the café conversation that was the main amusement — even the main occupation — of many emigrants. Above all the community had faith in the purpose of history and gave its members a sense of belonging to a great cause. At worst, they shared self-imposed misery with their fellow-exiles, at best a sense of close comradeship in the service of mankind.

Krupskaya's particular friend in the early years of her emigration was Vera Zasulich, the heroine of the 1870's, who had shot General Trepov at point-blank range. She had joined Plekhanov in emigration, and with a couple of friends they had formed the first circle of Russian Marxists. In Krupskaya's eyes Zasulich was the epitome of total devotion to the cause, even though she did not support Lenin after 1903 and had really contributed very little in words or deeds to the development of the movement. True, Zasulich had served as cook for a "commune" consisting of herself, Martov, and one Alexeyev in London (in all likelihood it was the most proper *ménage à trois* in history). Krupskaya's recollections of Vera's "unsuspected gifts for housewifery" leave one in doubt about the value of this contribution: "I remember her stewing some meat on an oil stove and snipping pieces off it with scissors and putting them into her mouth. 'When I arrived in England,' she told me, 'the English ladies tried to be sociable, and asked — How long do you stew your meat? All depends, I said. If you're hungry, ten minutes will do, if not — three hours or so. That stopped them.' "

Zasulich and Krupskaya saw each other almost daily during 1901–1903, when Vera was a member of the editorial board of *Iskra* and Krupskaya its secretary. Another editor, who moved with the Ulyanovs in these years, was Martov, a colleague in Petersburg and close friend of both Lenin and Krupskaya until 1903. He was given to non-stop talk, had no detectable life outside the socialist movement, and his relations with Krupskaya were described as "truly brotherly" by one witness.[5] In particular they are supposed to have enjoyed the daily ritual of sorting out *Iskra's* mail together.

During her year in London Krupskaya also saw a good deal of her Petersburg friend Apollinarya Takhtarev (née Yakubova), despite her deviation as an "economist." Krupskaya recalls that the Takhtarevs found the Ulyanovs their apartment in London and that "we saw Takhtarev very often," but she neglects to mention that much of the clandestine correspondence that Lenin's newspaper received in London from Russia came addressed to the Takhtarevs, which meant that Krupskaya probably saw her old friend almost daily to pick up the mail. It also meant that the Takhtarevs were generously increasing their own liability with the Russian police in order to protect the Ulyanovs, in spite of the ideological differences between the couples. "Our relations had a strained quality," recalls Krupskaya, and "once or twice there was an explosion and we had it out." Only a selfless sense of duty could have kept the Takhtarevs operating as a mail drop for Lenin after these outbursts.

Krupskaya also had the thrill of comradeship with G. V. Plekhanov, the dean of Russian Marxists and one of the half-dozen outstanding Marxist theoreticians of all times. In 1901–1903 Lenin and Plekhanov were political allies, and Krupskaya recalls with special pleasure the sojourn that she and Lenin had with Plekhanov in Zurich in September-October 1901, staying in the same hotel and taking meals together. The purpose of the gathering was to discuss relations of the Lenin-Plekhanov (*Iskra*) group with the so-called "economists" who were associated with *The Workers' Cause* (the same title that Lenin had wanted for his abortive underground newspaper in Petersburg in 1895). The *Iskra*-ites arrogantly broke off with their rivals, which seems to have given Krupskaya a gratifying sense of righteousness. Although she recalls that she was "still painfully shy" then, and no doubt too awed by the rather pompous Plekhanov to develop a friendship with him, she clearly savored her association with this founding father of the cause. One advantage of the association was that Plekhanov's wife Rosa was a physician, and on several occasions she gave Lenin and Krupskaya free medical attention.

For all the comradeship that Krupskaya found in the emigrant comunity she was rather withdrawn in her own household. This was less a matter of her shyness than of Lenin's determination not to waste hours talking over glasses of tea or mugs of beer. In place of these sociable addictions Krupskaya had her work for the organization and the companionship of her husband and mother.

Lenin and Krupskaya were very close to one another in the years of their first emigration, intimately sharing both work and recreation. In these years Lenin was rather rarely away from home for protracted periods, and Krupskaya accompanied him on several of the trips that he did take. True, Lenin secluded himself in their quarters or went off to a library for his study and writing much of the time. But he relied on Krupskaya as an audience — but not a critical one — for his emerging articles and booklets, such as *What Is to Be Done?* his most famous disquisition on the need for an elite of professional revolutionaries to direct the mass movement. It was started in their first, crowded apartment in Munich, Lenin pacing the floor as he thought out the booklet, Krupskaya discreetly keeping the pots and pans quiet. Over the following years she seems to have regarded herself as the guardian of his ideological muse, and severely fended off visitors when he was writing. Vol'sky recalls how Nadezhda or her mother blocked the door of their house in Geneva, telling visitors that Lenin was not at home, or "he is working and it is impossible to see him."

Elizaveta Krupskaya had rejoined the household very soon after her daughter had settled in Munich. (A letter written by Lenin on May 19, 1901, refers to Elizaveta as if she had been back with the family for some time.) Her presence was sometimes a trial, for she suffered frequently from the flu, or a cough, or rheumatism, and required a good deal of her daughter's attention. Toward the end of the family's stay in Munich Elizaveta decided that she had had enough of emigration, and returned to Petersburg. But she seems to have found life dull there and returned to her daughter in London, about May 1902, moving on to Geneva with the Ulyanovs the next year. Though she was not a self-proclaimed socialist, she felt at home in the emigrant Marxist community, more so than in Petersburg, her home town. According to Krupskaya she enjoyed the callers who were admitted to the house and was rather jolly, as well as being a useful housekeeper, when her health permitted. Vol'sky, who was not one to glorify the Ulyanov household, provides a rare glimpse of Elizaveta's good relations with her son-in-law. It seems that Vol'sky was explaining the correct technique of weight-lifting to Lenin, using a broom to demonstrate. Lenin had just taken the broom himself to imitate the correct form when "in the doorway leading into the kitchen-living room, where we were, I saw Elizaveta Vasilevna — Krupskaya's mother. Looking at our exercise with the broom and holding a handkerchief over her mouth, she was shaking with laughter. Lenin noticed her. 'Elizaveta Vasilevna, do not bother us, we are occupied with a very important matter.'" A few days later Vol'sky met her alone by chance and she volunteered her high opinion of Lenin. "'Truly, isn't Vladimir Ilyich clever? It's simply amazing how he caught on to all your tricks with the broom. Volodinka [a more intimate diminutive than "Volodya"] is clever in everything. If he loses a button somewhere, he doesn't come to anyone. He sews it on himself and better than Nadya.'"[6]

For a short time Lenin's sister Anna was also with them in Munich. She had left her husband, Mark Elizarov, to join Lenin in Munich in September 1900, while Krupskaya was still in Ufa. As already noted, Anna and Nadezhda did not get along well, and it seems quite likely that Anna was attempting to establish herself as Lenin's personal assistant before Krupskaya could appear on the scene. If so, she failed, and in May 1901, only a few weeks after Krupskaya arrived in Munich, Anna moved to Berlin, where she worked for Lenin's organization. Perhaps she gained some satisfaction in June-July 1902, when Lenin spent a month vacationing in Brittany with his mother and Anna. Krupskaya had declined to come "on various pretexts," according to Lenin's mother, who for her part had declined to go to London, where Lenin was then living. There seems to have been a bit of coolness in the family atmosphere.[7]

And what was Krupskaya's usual work in this first period in her emigrant career as a professional revolutionary? Formally she was the secretary of the newspaper *Iskra*. Lenin had arranged for this and the displacement of Inna Smidovich-Leman, who held the job until Krupskaya's arrival in Munich. It was a shrewd maneuver on his part, aimed at concentrating control over the newspaper, and through it the future party, in his own hands. The editorial board consisted of three members of the older emigrant group — Plekhanov, Axelrod, and Zasulich — and three of the young leaders — Lenin, Martov, and Potresov. In 1901 Lenin neither foresaw nor desired the approaching rift between himself and his colleagues, and he was not consciously trying to put them under his thumb, or expel them. But Lenin had a keen instinct for power, and, after some upsetting disagreements with Plekhanov in 1900, he probably wanted to be in the best possible position to influence the development of the newspaper and the whole movement. Unlike the others on the editorial board, he recognized that the seemingly routine job of secretary would be vital to the control of the emerging organization. In giving this post to the devoted Krupskaya, Lenin hoped that "all intercourse with Russia would be closely controlled" by his most trusted assistant. "Vladimir Ilyich told me that he had felt very awkward about doing this, but had thought it necessary in the interests of the cause," Krupskaya recollected.[8] Lenin's editorial colleagues did not understand what was involved in this maneuver. Plekhanov and Martov never shared Lenin's instinct for power, and apparently took it for granted that the really important work was in the realm of theory, that the mundane organizational tasks of the secretary could only serve the deep thinkers of the movement. In this they gravely underestimated the contribution that Krupskaya could make to the political survival of Lenin's faction, keeping up some semblance of regular organization even at Lenin's lowest moments in his quarrels within the party.

Iskra faced two main tasks: to win the allegiance of the active Marxists in Russia and to evade the efforts of the Russian government to suppress the revolutionary movement. In pursuing the first of these tasks the *Iskra* group faced suspicion and down-right hostility from many of the local, underground "committees" of Russian Marxists, who regarded the editors as high-handed in their ambition to control policy and to replace local publications with a single, authoritative organ. There was also considerable sympathy, especially in Petersburg, for the other main emigrant newspaper, *The Workers' Cause,* which Lenin and his allies were trying to brand as heretical. To overcome this resistance the Iskra organization relied on the distribution of their newspaper (fifty-one issues were published in 1900-1903, while Lenin was on the editorial board), along with other publications, including Lenin's *What Is to Be Done?,* Plekhanov's theoretical journal *Zarya (The Dawn)* and Krupskaya's brochure on "The Woman Worker." This in turn required a major effort to maintain a network of agents to smuggle the contraband publications into Russia, to store and distribute them, to solicit money to pay for them, and to politic on behalf of the editors. Considering that about eight thousand copies of each issue of *Iskra* were published abroad and that the police were watching for it at the border, this was a fairly substantial undercover operation. Its payoff was intended to be the convocation of a "congress" which would unite all the local Russian committees and most emigrant groups into a solid party. *Iskra* would be recognized as the official organ of the new party and, in effect, its editors would be the principal leaders.

Until this had been accomplished Lenin and his colleagues were content to conduct an essentially defensive operation against the tsar's government. Popular disturbances were welcome as a sign of dissidence, but a revolution was neither anticipated nor desired in the immediate future — before the new party could be prepared for it. But even defensive operations against the *okhrana,* or political police of the Empire, was a challenging task. The increasing number of active Marxists in Russia (albeit much less than one per cent of the total population) was partly matched by increased police vigilance. In Russia suspects were watched and often arrested and exiled. On the border a vigil was maintained. Since 1901 Krupskaya's name had been on a list of emigrants whose luggage was to be secretly searched and who were to be put under surveillance if they returned to Russia. Abroad, the *okhrana* maintained a secret headquarters in Paris and attempted to infiltrate emigrant revolutionary groups and to watch known subversives. In this they received assistance from the police of the major countries of Europe. The emigrants could not be arrested unless they violated some law of their host country, but a knowledge of their activities abroad could lead to the strangulation of the illegal work back in Russia.

Because of this, Lenin and Krupskaya, though they had left Russia on legitimate passports, attempted to disappear underground. In Munich Lenin had been living under the name Meyer without any passport until Krupskaya arrived. Then the two of them somehow obtained false Bulgarian passports as Dr. and Mrs. (Marcia) Yordanov, with which they entered England. Here they were free to forget identity papers, and they became Herr und Frau Richter, passing for Germans most of the time. But among her comrades in emigration in this period Krupskaya was "N. Sharko" or "Sablina," and to the comrades back in Russia she was usually "Katya" but sometimes "Minoga" or "Maria." Behind these masks the secretary of *Iskra* played "M" to a considerable network of agents — perhaps thirty or forty. Certainly her background offered little preparation for this role, and in her memoirs Krupskaya herself wrote that, in retrospect, "one marvels at the naïveté of our methods. All those letters about handkerchiefs (meaning passports), brewing beer, and warm fur (illegal literature), all those code-names for towns beginning with the same letter as the town itself (Osip for Odessa, Terenty for Tver, Peter for Poltava, Psaha for Pskov, and so on) all the substituting of women's names for men's [Gleb Krizhanovsky was "Clair" — that is "*K*ler" to give a hint of his real name — RHM] and vice versa — the whole thing was so thin, so transparent."[9]

And it was true, judging by the letters intercepted by the police and later published by the Soviets, that the *okhrana* rarely erred in identifying the code-names used in the underground. Nor were they unable to "develop" the "invisible" ink (no longer just milk) used in most of these conspiratorial letters, or in decoding them when that became necessary.[10] Some letters were written in invisible ink without a code, some in both invisible ink and code, and some mixed. The code was usually a simple one in which numbers were substituted for letters. It is even possible that the police were more adept than Krupskaya at developing invisible ink and decoding the letters. Her messages to the underground in Russia are full of complaints about illegible chemical ink writing, or invisible lines overlapping one another — or botched codes — all resulting in unintelligible correspondence. On the other hand, the police had to pluck these letters out of the mails in Russia, recognizing them by the address or place of mailing. The *Iskra* organization seems to have been reasonably successful in countering this by using more or less innocent addresses on both ends and by diversifying addresses or places of mailing. Krupskaya, on her end, used helpful, obscure sympathizers in various countries to post and receive letters. While she lived in Munich, for example, her letters were sent from Nuremberg, Liège, and Darmstadt as well as Munich itself. Or in London she received some letters not only at the Takhtarevs (probably not a very deceptive address) but sometimes from a bookstore manager named Mr. Raymond, who considered himself a socialist and exchanged Russian lessons for English with Lenin. On one occasion an incoming envelope, which he opened, contained an ostensibly blank sheet of paper, which Mrs. Raymond, who was not in on the conspiracy, confiscated to cover a marmalade jar. When Krupskaya realized that something was missing, she went to Mrs. Raymond and, with some difficulty, secured the missing letter, somewhat sticky by this time.

Thanks partly to the fact that the Russian police did not develop really large-scale foreign activities until after the Revolution of 1905, Krupskaya does seem to have succeeded in keeping them in the dark about her whereabouts. The archives of the Paris office of the *okhrana* suggest that only in February 1904 did they receive a memo from the director of police in Petersburg, identifying her as one who "occupies a central position in the organization of *Iskra* abroad. Beginning in the second half of 1901, under the name 'Katya', she conducted a lively conspiratorial correspondence with all the active committees of the Russian Social Democratic Workers' Party in Russia."[11] In fact, the police did not seem sure where she was at this date and were a bit behind the time, Krupskaya having quit *Iskra* in December 1903.

Still, this police report may stand as an impartial tribute to Krupskaya's remarkable one-woman operation as the center of a fairly complicated and effective network of agents in the period preceding the Second Party Congress. Even if her methods were in some ways amateurish, the fact remains that she succeeded in imparting to the *Iskra* underground organization a degree of coordination that no previous Russian revolutionary organization had known, and this with modest financial resources and not a single assistant in her one-room headquarters, which always smelled "of burnt paper from the secret letters she heated over the fire to read," as Trotsky recalled. He was one of the fairly numerous visitors from the Russian underground whom Krupskaya received (in the small hours of the morning in her dressing gown, in Trotsky's case). She tried to help such callers find lodgings in emigration and also was engaged in hearing their reports of affairs in Russia, or in giving them instructions if they were going back.

In all this Krupskaya obviously worked under Lenin's direct supervision, and there is no point in trying to inflate her independent role. She was not a policy-maker but a technician, battling relentlessly with trying tasks. Her contribution to the development of the organization that became Bolshevism required not genius but inexhaustible devotion, and on this basis it is no exaggeration to say that her role was essential. Lenin himself provided the conception of a party of a new type, consisting of professional revolutionaries who could put themselves at the head of the revolutionary movement, but he did not devote much of his own time to the essential practical work of keeping in touch with each agent, of sorting out incoming data and sending out letters to coordinate the underground work. Without suggesting that he was less than the leader behind the operation, it is clear that Krupskaya carried on her taxing work without a great deal of direct guidance from Lenin. She gave him many of the incoming and outgoing letters, and he answered a few letters himself, or added postscripts to her replies. A rare surviving letter from Lenin to Krupskaya, written in 1902 when he was on vacation in France with his mother and sister, shows how closely he was working with his wife at this time. In addition to routine details about money and printer's proofs, Lenin goes into considerable detail to give Krupskaya his latest information and opinion about a proposal to convene in Switzerland a "congress" of *Iskra* agents, which Lenin thought ill-advised. Indeed, this meeting never materialized, but the letter remains as a reminder that at this time Krupskaya, and not Martov, Plekhanov, nor any other, was Lenin's closest political confidant. "Who (first of all) thought up the 'congress'?" wrote Lenin.[12] "*Not we.*" The implication of the remark is a bit of tactical finesse. Lenin believed that if the congress convened (which it never did) he could load it in his favor. If his rivals objected, he could reply, "But it was *your* idea in the first place." He knew that Krupskaya would at once see the whole maneuver because of her close involvement in his daily scheming.

Lenin's own time was largely absorbed with his writing and the whole question of policy. He wrote numerous letters to his colleagues on the editorial board, which Krupskaya rarely did, even though she was secretary (only two of her surviving letters are to members of the board). But the correspondence with the underground was mainly Krupskaya's work, not Lenin's. A Soviet writer states that she received and answered about three hundred letters per month while she was secretary of *Iskra*. Although not nearly that many have been published, the figure is credible. The Communist Party archives today must hold many unpublished letters from Krupskaya, judging from footnote references in Soviet books.[13] Many other letters may have been lost, although Krupskaya kept the files of the organization as part of her job.

To understand her work as the director of the *Iskra* network, it is useful to read at least one more or less representative letter from beginning to end. The one that follows was divided by Krupskaya into eleven numbered points for clarity, and it is worth pausing after each point or two for a few words of explanation. The letter is to I. I. Radchenko, whom Krupskaya had known well in Petersburg and who still lived there as one of the main *Iskra* representatives in Russia. It was sent from London on August 20, 1902, probably in invisible ink but not in code, excepting individual words.

Dear Friend,
We received your letters of 10/VIII, without a number — with a password, and of 20/VII. We did not receive the swallows, the second letter with a password and about current matters. I don't know why they are late.

> [*Presumably the passwords were needed by agents whom* Iskra *was sending into Russia to deliver publications or make contacts. "Swallows" were journals, published legally in Russia, which the emigrant editors needed as sources for their writing.*]

1. A letter was received from Sonya at last. She writes that they have a great problem with passports, which they need badly. They also write that they intend to meet on 20/VII and lay down a further plan of action, and then send an agent to Fekla to reinforce the plan. All this is not bad, but thanks to the poor

organization of our correspondence, one feels somewhat cut off — Sonya doesn't know about Fekla's state
of affairs and Fekla doesn't know much about Sonya.
Sonya hasn't sent addresses, we wrote twice to the
old one, but what good will come of this, I don't know.

["*Sonya" is the Samara* Iskra *group, headed
by Krizhanovsky, and "Fekla" is the* Iskra *headquarters abroad. This point illustrates Krupskaya's unending struggle to try to keep up communications, which in this case are limping, even
though the agent is a good friend of hers. Without safe addresses for "Sonya" to use for incoming
mail, it is necessary to rely on personal couriers,
traveling all the way to London, crossing a
guarded border, to keep in touch. False passports
are needed for such trips.*]

2. Do you have connections with Petya? If so,
after having obtained the account, send even something there. They send letter after letter (in which
they write unfamiliar pseudonyms) and ask for fur.
Apparently Fekla's friends are being forced out by the
friends of Robert. Nobody knows exactly. The committee resents Fekla's letter in connection with the
May proclamation and is in revolt.

[*This concerns the feud between* Iskra *and*
The Workers' Cause *("Robert"), specifically in
ranks of the Kiev Social Democratic Committee
("Petya"). At this point* Iskra *was losing influence
in this committee, partly because their comments
on a May Day proclamation had been offensive
to local pride. To counteract this, Krupskaya
wants Radchenko to send some* Iskra *publications
("fur"), if Radchenko can arrange a safe method
of transport ("account").*]

3. Give your address to Semyon Semyonovich.
Dimochka will tell you about him in detail. We have
good, true friends among the friends of Semyon
Semyonovich, but up to the present they consider
only Semyon Semyonovich as *their own,* and regard

Fekla's activities from the side. Soon it will have its congress, at which the question of recognition of *Iskra* as the leading organ will be raised. It is necessary to be very diplomatic with Semyon Semyonovich. I have asked Semyon Semyonovich to see you without fail and talk things over with you.

[*In the "Northern Union" ("Semyon Semyonovich"), a cluster of committees centered on Yaroslavl,* Iskra *has better prospects than in Kiev, but Krupskaya is wary of offending local pride and losing the chance to be accepted as the leading organ. The problem of convincing local underground groups that an emigrant newspaper was really "their own", even if two thousand miles away, was a continual one for Krupskaya. "Dimochka" was a young woman, a mother at that, whom Krupskaya called "an enthusiastic, gushing girl", but who still had to be sent on this secret mission in the absence of any better agent.*]

4. About the beer, we have a person who can speak Swedish, but he is a great bungler, and we are afraid to let him go alone, the more so because it is not clear from your letter with whom he should speak, strictly speaking. We are thinking of assigning him a nursemaid — Laptya, in order to doubly equip the affair — true, this would be somewhat pointed, but thereby the affair will be more reliable. Write in detail about what needs to be arranged.

[*The problem of getting illegal publications, usually printed on onion-skin paper for compactness, across the border required continual ingenuity. In this case Krupskaya hopes to send Radchenko a consignment from the stockpile that Swedish socialists enabled* Iskra *to maintain in Stockholm ("beer" = printed matter stored there). But to cross the border she evidently hopes to use some unidentified person who will pose as a Swede, possibly carrying the contraband in a double-bottomed trunk — a favorite method. Unfortunately, the unreliability of this character may oblige Krupskaya to attach one of her most experienced men, Lepeshensky ("Laptya") to shepherd the Swedish-speaking smuggler. Even then, she doesn't know where they will be met in Petersburg.]*

5. It is necessary to see Uncle without fail. His address . . . I wrote him that he should meet with you, but he keeps silent for some reason.

[Another of Krupskaya's old Petersburg friends, Lidya Knipovich ("Uncle"), played an important role in the Iskra *network, as the chief agent in Odessa. For security, Krupskaya did not actually write secret addresses in the file copies of outgoing letters, so the present text does not include that information. Krupskaya kept elaborate address books as a separate, especially precious tool of her trade. Some of these, from a somewhat later period, have been found and published.]*

6. We are greatly worried about Arkady, let him be thrifty himself and not ask for money, better, let him not send it to Fekla.

*[*Iskra *cost quite a lot to publish: 1,500 German marks per month plus considerable transportation (smuggling) expenses, and the emigrant editorial board counted on supporters in Russia to pass the hat, especially among well-to-do sympathizers who were not actually in on the organization. One of Krupskaya's jobs was to keep after agents to send in money, but at the same time disbursements had to be made to keep some agents in the field, such as Babushkin ("Arkady"), a worker whom Krupskaya had known in the adult school years before. It appears that he was both sending in money and asking for a subsidy. Both Lenin and Krupskaya were worried about his security, and Lenin added a note to this letter, advising Radchenko to tell Babushkin to be very careful.]*

7. Address for money: Pinkau or Regnera.

[*Both considered safe places for collections to be sent. "Pinkau" was the name of a German photographer in Leipzig who received mail to be passed on to* Iskra. *Regnera was a member of the organization, living in emigration.*]

8. The musician arrived in Switzerland, we are summoning him here.

9. Vanya still has not arrived, when he comes I shall let you know at once.

[*P. A. Krasikov ("the musician") and V. P. Krasnukha ("Vanya") were both* Iskra *agents who slipped through the border for briefing and de-briefing abroad.*]

10. Rumors are circulating that "Freedom" is uniting with *The Workers' Cause,* in connection with which the latter has made a concession and has accepted terror. The Socialist Revolutionaries plan a weekly newspaper for the masses.

11. If Vanya sends the item relating to the Socialist Revolutionaries, it would be very good.

[*The last two points show Krupskaya's activity as a disseminator of intelligence on the rival revolutionary groups, and in order to perform this role she needs to gather intelligence, such as the Socialist Revolutionary materials.* Iskra *agents in Russia had to help in this job. "Vanya" in this instance stands for the organization of which Krupskaya was once a member: the "St. Petersburg Union for the Struggle for the Emancipation of Labor."*][14]

Such letters were the principal medium with which Krupskaya attempted to coordinate and direct efforts to bring the local Russian groups of Social Democrats to an acceptance of *Iskra's* leadership. And Lenin's. In her letters to agents Krupskaya took special pains to promote his writings, especially *What Is to Be Done?* This was not easy, as Krupskaya recognized in a report that she prepared in 1903: "In the majority of cases they [the local committees] regard the undertakings of *Iskra* as a matter that is wholly alien to them. One correspondent very accurately characterizes relations with *Iskra,* speaking for his committee: 'In general the committee is sympathetically inclined toward *Iskra,* but all the same they still think *this newspaper* and not *our newspaper.'* "[15] Some of the local groups never did fall into line, but in the course of 1902 and 1903 the prestige and argumentation of *Iskra's* writers, along with the persistent efforts of the underground agents, won many adherents. The competing newspaper, *The Workers' Cause,* was not mounting a comparable campaign, and there was at least fundamental agreement that an all-Russian party of some sort must be formed, for the 1898 party congress had done little more than provide a name for a party. As more and more local committees recognized *Iskra* as the leading organ of the movement, Lenin and his cohorts were encouraged to arrange the formation of an "Organizational Committee" in Russia, which met in November 1902, on the initiative of the *Iskra* agent Radchenko. The goal was the convocation of a party congress abroad. Since the majority of the members of this committee were *Iskra* agents, it was in a sense an extension of Krupskaya's little room in Geneva. In her report on the activities of *Iskra,* prepared for the Congress, she attempted to give the impression that after the appearance of the Organizational Committee her activities were made subordinate to it, as the most authoritative expression of the will of the movement. "*Iskra* transferred to the Organizational Committee all its links (transport, technical and other) ," she wrote, and went on to speak of *Iskra's* printed matter, funds, and agents being placed at the disposal of the Committee.[16] But in actuality it was Lenin who planned the basic strategy of the Committee and she who provided the coordination, while the Committee was in large measure a clutch of *Iskra* agents, aiming at the most favorable possible selection of delegates to the forthcoming party congress. Judging by the surviving, published correspondence, Krupskaya's role remained much the same, after the Organizational Committee had been established.

The success of this whole campaign was evident when the Second Congress of the Russian Social Democratic Workers' Party was opened in Brussels by Plekhanov on August 30 (N.S.), 1903. Thirty-one out of thirty-two delegates representing local committees at the congress supported *Iskra,* as did emigrant delegates with eight votes. They dominated such opposition as was present: five representatives of the Jewish Bund, which flourished in the western provinces of the Russian Empire, and three emigrant "economists."

The congress is renowned for almost simultaneously uniting and dividing Russian Marxists. Starting with an appearance of considerable *Iskra* solidarity, it ended with a rift between two factions of *Iskra* supporters, one that was never fully closed. Lenin's faction claimed that they represented the majority and took up the label "Bolsheviks" (men of the majority). The other faction, led by Martov, if anyone, foolishly accepted the label "Menshevik" (men of the minority), even though they commanded a majority against Lenin on the most volatile issue of the congress. This was the definition of party membership, which, both Lenin and Martov believed, would determine the whole character of the party and its historical role. Whether or not this was true, it does appear that Lenin's ideas about a narrow party of professional revolutionaries were running into resistance from among his former partners in the *Iskra* organization. Lenin felt betrayed by this unexpected opposition from his presumed allies and became so upset, Krupskaya recalls, that he could not eat the radishes and cheese that their Belgian landlady served for breakfast. He reacted vindictively, attempting to keep his opponents off the authoritative party bodies that the congress elected.

Krupskaya no doubt shared Lenin's shock and dismay at these developments. She had come to the Congress expecting to hear her friend Martov read a 7,500-word report that she had written on the work of the *Iskra* organization. It was her work, for only she had the knowledge to write in detail about the contacts of her secretariat and the underground agents. Lenin and Martov made only a few minor changes on her manuscript. Potentially it was one of the major reports of the Congress, which no doubt explains why one of the editors of *Iskra* was to read it in her stead. While it was not intended to be a dramatic document, the draft of the report shows Krupskaya's mastery of the tangled affairs of the underground apparatus. Perhaps it is most notable for its frank portrayal of the hostile or cool initial reception that *Iskra* had with many local committees in Russia, an implied reproach to many of the delegates present.[17]

But Martov never delivered it, and the draft remained unknown until it was published in a historical journal in 1928. The explanation of the elimination of Krupskaya's anticipated great moment at the Congress is surely the split between Lenin and Martov. It must have been a harsh experience for Krupskaya, the sort of thing that would harden her personality for the years of internecine strife that lay ahead. In fact the Congress produced such stress for Krupskaya that she fell ill, according to Dr. Rosa Plekhanova.

Beyond this abortive contribution, Krupskaya played little role in the Congress. She was one of fourteen delegates who had only a "consultative vote," meaning that she could speak and even vote in the assembly, though her vote would not count. But she did not exercise her right to speak during any of the twenty-seven sessions of the Congress, which started in Brussels and ended in London. The transfer, to avoid trouble with the Belgian police, was unpleasant for Krupskaya, who was miserable with seasickness.

In contrast with her reticent role at the Congress, Krupskaya played a fairly active part in the complex and acrimonious politics that followed after it, once the leading emigrant Marxists had returned to Switzerland. In the last months of 1903 Lenin's opponents were trying to crush his influence in various party bodies, and in all cases Krupskaya became involved.

One of these skirmishes occurred in the "Foreign League of Russian Revolutionary Social Democrats," a loose association of emigrants in twenty European cities (and also New York), which had been formed in 1901. It had not been very active in its own right, but had supported *Iskra* and had sent both Lenin and Martov to the party congress as its delegates. Since October 1902, Krupskaya had been one of five persons on the "administration" of the Foreign League, although it does not seem that this involved much of anything until Martov decided to try to use the Foreign League as a rallying point against Lenin. Through his ally, Lev Deich, Martov pushed for a congress of the Foreign League, so it could hear reports of the late Party Congress from its delegates, Lenin and Martov. The object of the exercise was to secure a condemnation of Lenin's policies. Krupskaya and another member of the administration of the Foreign League, M. Litvinov (Wallach), opposed the meeting but were outvoted on the administration. When the Foreign League met in Geneva in October 1903, Krupskaya, in recognition of her work as *Iskra* secretary, was asked to give a report on the relations of the Foreign League with Russia. Presumably, it was expected that she would present something like the draft she had written for Martov, which would by implication enhance the standing of the Foreign League, in the eyes of its members, at least. If so, the Mensheviks misjudged Krupskaya's character. Although modest and guileless in manner, she had been hardened by her recent experiences and was not about to lend herself to maneuvers against Lenin. Her report amounted to little more than a curt statement that "the League, as such, never conducted any relations with committees and other organizations in Russia — it did not have special personnel for relations with Russia, had neither addresses nor codes."[18] In other words, the Foreign League should not attempt to borrow the prestige of *Iskra* (or presume to judge Lenin).

But the name of *Iskra* was not as firmly in Lenin's hands as he thought it to be during the Congress. One of Lenin's apparent victories at the Second Party Congress had been to secure the election to the editorial board of *Iskra* (now called the "Central Organ" of the party) of Plekhanov, Martov, and himself. This eliminated three of the former editors (Axelrod, Potresov, and Zasulich), who had all turned out to be Mensheviks, and had placed Martov in a minority position, since both Lenin and Plekhanov had been Bolsheviks at the party congress. Martov in fact refused to serve at all on the board while his former colleagues were excluded, so *Iskra* for several months appeared to be definitely in Bolshevik hands. But just after the Foreign League congress Plekhanov weakened and told Lenin that he would insist on the return of the old board in order to reunite the party. Lenin was outraged and on October 19 it was he who left the board of *Iskra*.

This placed Krupskaya in a curious position. Formally she was secretary of *Iskra* in her own right, not because of her marriage. She did not in fact submit her resignation when Lenin did, evidently intending to continue to control the correspondence with Russia in Lenin's interest. But the Mensheviks were not so naïve as to permit this situation. On November 27 Martov wrote to her, asking if she intended to remain as secretary — implying that this would be rather anomalous. But she stubbornly replied, "I, from my side, have nothing against the secretariat." The editorial board could have simply voted her out of this job, but it is fair to guess that they feared her ability to sabotage their efforts by withholding the files of addresses, codes, and so on. They therefore attempted a more tactful approach, appointing a Mrs. Blyumenfeld as Krupskaya's deputy, charged with the job of conducting correspondence with Russia. At this, Krupskaya resigned, writing a rather huffy letter of December 5 to the effect that she had not been consulted about the need for an assistant and that it implied a lack of confidence in her work.

Having removed Krupskaya, could the Mensheviks obtain the vital files from her? In the following weeks they maintained that she obstructed this transfer, and she vigorously denied it. It is impossible today to be sure who was right, but it is fair to assume that Lenin would not have scrupled to use Krupskaya's position as far as possible against his opponents. We first find Mrs. Blyumenfeld asking for some address in Russia and being told by Krupskaya that she did not have it. The task of dealing with her was then passed on to Martov, who wrote a polite, formal letter concluding, "Without receiving this material, the editorial board cannot carry out its function correctly."

After this Krupskaya does seem to have handed some material over to Mrs. Blyumenfeld, but she did not satisfy the Mensheviks, especially with respect to current incoming letters. By December 28 they were sufficiently aroused to threaten that they would publish in *Iskra* a statement that Krupskaya was obstructing relations with the newspaper's correspondents, if she did not cooperate. Krupskaya answered angrily on the same day, saying that they could publish what they liked, but she would demand space for a reply. She denied withholding anything that the *Iskra* secretariat had coming to it, except several notebooks that she was supposedly still putting in order. As for current correspondence, she had already delivered it. "Nothing more, as far as I remember, has been received for the editorial board. Why the correspondence has ceased, I don't know. It isn't my fault." Showing a zest for combat that may have surprised her adversaries, she went on to accuse Martov of bad faith. She claimed that her notebooks contained a full set of incoming letters only, that only *some* copies of outgoing letters were retained, and "Martov could not fail to know this."[19]

In the same letter Krupskaya also called attention to the failure of *Iskra* to publish a notice advising correspondents to henceforth use different addresses for the

"Central Committee" and the "Central Organ." This distinction lay at the heart of Lenin's tactics of the hour, and Krupskaya's new secretarial role. The Second Party Congress had voted to establish a tripartite executive apparatus: a "Central Organ" (the *Iskra* board), a "Central Committee," and a "Party Council." Although this cumbersome plan never really worked, Lenin was attempting to manipulate it in his interest at the end of 1903. Having lost his control over *Iskra*, he believed that he could nevertheless direct the Central Committee, partly through the use of Krupskaya's special skills and experience. To further complicate the system, the Central Committee formed two branches: Russian and foreign (emigrant). By the end of August 1903 each of these had its own "Bureau", which presumably would serve to coordinate all the activities of the Committee. It is said that Krupskaya had become the secretary of the Russian Bureau, although it is not clear just who decided this or when.[20] Probably the appointment was slipped through unobtrusively on the pretext that only she had the experience to take over this kind of correspondence. In any case, when Krupskaya faced the hostile editors of *Iskra* in December 1903, she was already serving as secretary of the foreign bureau of the Central Committee and was in a position to decide as she pleased what records or incoming letters were rightfully the property of *Iskra* or the Central Committee. It is certainly true that she was writing letters in the name of this bureau, haranguing local committees in Russia about the iniquities of the Mensheviks, who were supposedly maneuvering to frustrate the wishes of the real party majority.[21]

Despite Krupskaya's strenuous efforts in this direction in the first half of 1904, Lenin's position declined. The basic trouble was that too many influential party members wanted to patch up the split with a compromise, not to end it by crushing the Mensheviks. By midsummer Lenin had lost all authority in the Central Committee and Krupskaya was no longer considered secretary of its foreign bureau. By September we find her writing to their remaining friends in Russia that they should mark his letters "Personally for L." or "Personally for N. K.", so that the letters would not "fall into alien hands" — meaning that correspondence intended for the foreign branch of the Central Committee was not being delivered to her.[22]

Lenin's fortunes were low indeed. He had no published organ of his own, no power in the executive bodies of the party. Lenin's only hope was to appeal directly to the rank and file of the party, which he did in a polemic of May 1904, entitled "One Step Forward, Two Steps Back." For her part, Krupskaya continued to write to local committees in Russia in support of Lenin's uncompromising line: "It is necessary," she wrote to Lidya Knipovich in Odessa, "to discuss the state of affairs with the comrades in Russia and to decide either on an open split [with the Mensheviks] or to yield the whole business into the hands of the Mensheviks."[23] This was no longer the gentle, adult school teacher, writing. The shock of "betrayal" by people whom she had taken to be as devoted as herself to the glorious mission of Marxism left an indelible mark on Krupskaya.

In the Bolshevik crisis of 1904 she was not only unwavering in her devotion to Lenin's extreme position, but was perhaps better able to stand the pressures of near-isolation than he. By the summer of 1904 he had pushed himself to the edge of a breakdown, and only a month's walking holiday in the mountains restored his nerves.

We have left our work and worries in Geneva", Krupskaya wrote to Lenin's mother, "and here [in Lausanne] we sleep ten hours a day and go swimming and walking — Volodya doesn't even read the newspapers properly; we took a minimum of books with us, and even those we are sending back to Geneva tomorrow, unread, while we ourselves at four in the morning will set out for a two-weeks' walking tour of the mountains. We shall go to Interlaken and from there to Lucerne. We are reading Baedeker and planning our journey carefully. In a week we have 'recovered' quite considerably and have even begun to look healthy again. It was a difficult winter and our nerves have been under such a strain that we cannot be blamed for taking a month's holiday . . . . Volodya and I have made an agreement not to talk about our work . . . as far as possible, not even to think about it."[24]

This was asking a bit too much. Maria Essen, a close comrade of both Ulyanovs at that time, who accompanied them on part of the hike, recalls that, after reaching a particularly breathtaking view, Lenin sat in meditation, then burst out, "Oh, the Mensheviks really foul things up!"

After their return to Geneva the fortunes of the Bolsheviks improved. Various local committees in Russia, with whom Krupskaya was in contact, supported them. A number of able new allies appeared in Geneva, including A. A. Bogdanov, a talented physician, philosopher, and propagandist. Heartened by these developments, Lenin established a newspaper of his own in December 1904, called *Vperëd* (*Forward*). Its editorial board, of which Lenin and Bogdanov were the leading lights, served as an organizational center for the Bolsheviks, and Krupskaya naturally became its secretary. Again she was immersed in grappling with a large correspondence, including the usual botched codes, missing addresses, and the need for funds. Lenin was deprived of the financial resources of the official party organization when he broke with it, and Krupskaya's letters throughout 1904 complain that they do not have "a groschen." It was no easy task proselytizing for Bolshevism, with the "legitimate" party organization in the hands of one's opponents, but Krupskaya, in her letters, steadily tried to undermine the enemy. To bolster her authority she signed a number of her letters to the underground with Lenin's name, though Soviet scholarship regards these letters as her compositions.[25]

Unlike her husband, she usually maintained a low-keyed approach to polemics, keeping clear of personal attacks on most of her opponents, probably hoping that they would once again be comrades together. The notable exception in this was Trotsky, the youthful firebrand whom Lenin had befriended in London and who repaid his patron with a rousing attack at the party congress of 1903. Although Lenin had been much taken with Trotsky in 1902, there is no evidence that Krupskaya shared this cordiality then, nor was she ever personally close to Trotsky during the political vicissitudes that pulled them apart or pushed them together during the next thirty years.

In 1904–1905 her letters reserved their sharpest barbs for Trotsky, treating him, rather than Martov or Plekhanov, as the main culprit among the Mensheviks. Speaking of one of Trotsky's contributions to the polemics of the day, she wrote to a comrade, "This brochure represents in itself the most scandalous perversion of the revolutionary movement in past years."[26]

Apart from Trotsky, her moderation helped put across the impression that it was the Mensheviks who were the conniving factionalists, while the Bolsheviks had a majority of the party behind their demand for a new party congress to put matters right. There was in fact considerable support in the underground committees for this, although not by any means because all the underground wanted to see Lenin prevail. By the opening of 1905 Krupskaya's correspondence was mainly devoted to the preparation of the congress — particularly the mustering of delegates favorable to Lenin. Ironically, one of the delegates whose mandate (document entitling him to represent some party body) was not arranged for in advance was Lenin. Only a week before the congress opened we find Krupskaya writing frantically to Lidya Knipovich, asking that Lenin be sent the official mandate for the Odessa committee, duly signed. It was in fact mailed, two days after the congress convened, but this formal point did not hinder Lenin.[27]

He was the undoubted leader when the so-called Third Party Congress opened in London on April 12, 1905, boycotted by the Mensheviks. Although not all the delegates, even those who were favorably inclined toward Lenin, would support him in everything, it was a comparative success. True, the Mensheviks were not regarded as complete heretics, cast out of the party, but Lenin now had staked a claim for his personal variety of Marxism, and he never wholly relinquished it. One of his achievements was to receive "official" recognition of his newspaper as the party organ (with the new name *Proletarii — The Proletarian*). Krupskaya again attended with only a consultative vote, but she did speak up briefly concerning several points on which her knowledge of incoming intelligence from Russia gave her special authority. The most important of these comments concerned the problem of whether to call for an armed uprising in Russia, where disturbances had been increasing since troops had fired on demonstrators in Petersburg in January 1905 ("Bloody Sunday"). She took a "left" position on the issue of an uprising, claiming that letters received by *Vperëd* showed that worker opinion in the southern cities was marked by "a militant mood."[28] Her other contribution to the congress was in editing the minutes that were published, a difficult job because the records had been kept by erratic amateurs.

Increasingly the question of revolution pushed aside the internecine squabbles of the emigrant Russian Social Democrats. As 1905 wore on, the Imperial government seemed to be losing its self-confidence and control over the situation. The advantages of an emigrant headquarters, beyond the reach of the *okhrana,* dwindled as police control in Russia declined and the need increased for on-the-spot leadership to deal with the opportunities that the crisis cast up. Lenin made some effort to play the revolutionary leader in exile. He met Father George Gapon, the priest who had led the demonstrators of "Bloody Sunday," and a sailor from the *Potemkin,* the battleship whose crew had mutinied. He even took up the study of street fighting, in the quiet of a Swiss library. But none of this could replace actual participation in the revolution, nor could Krupskaya's correspondence keep up with events. Faced with the possibility of becoming isolated from both Bolshevik and Menshevik factions, which were drawing together on the local level, Lenin returned to Russia on November 8, 1905. Krupskaya remained in Geneva a few days longer to put their affairs in order and then followed her husband, traveling through Germany, Sweden, and Finland.

The Petersburg to which Krupskaya returned in November 1905 was a strange place indeed. The tsar still lived in his palace outside the capital and his soldiers and police still maintained their garrisons and headquarters in the city. But a railroad strike and general strike in Petersburg and other important cities in October had badly shaken the poise of the regime. On October 17 the tsar had issued a manifesto proclaiming various civil liberties. It also stated that the forthcoming parliamentary body, the Duma, which had been promised in August, would be broadly representative and that no new law could be adopted without its approval. The revolutionaries certainly were not satisfied with these concessions, but readily sought to utilize the new freedoms to intensify the revolutionary situation in the country. In Petersburg a Soviet (Council) of Workers' Deputies was established as something less than a revolutionary government but more than an opposition party. It did not call for the overthrow of the government, but it did attempt to direct a general strike to protest the prosecution of naval mutineers and the establishment of martial law in Poland — almost a call to insurrection. Such provocative anti-governmental acts, which scarcely would have been permitted in the parliamentary democracies, were initially tolerated by the "autocracy" which once had been accustomed to arrest any person whom the police considered guilty of any kind of political activity.

Such an unexpectedly easy reversal of fortunes for the Russian Social Democrats was too good to be real. They were not yet sufficiently well organized to take full advantage of the weakness of the regime, which was not as great as it seemed, for the armed forces were, in the main, still usable as the final arbiter of the situation. Still, the tsar's government moved cautiously. Even after it had succeeded in arresting the Executive Committee of the Petersburg Soviet, and in crushing an armed insurrection in a working-class section of Moscow (both by the end of 1905), the government did not attempt to locate and arrest all revolutionaries right away. Even after it had restored its former authority in most of the Russian Empire, the police scrupled to offend public opinion in Finland by openly violating such autonomy as this "Grand Duchy" of the tsar enjoyed.

Thus it was that Krupskaya, like many other active socialists, was able to remain on the territory of the Russian Empire, including Finland, through 1906 and 1907, even though the high tide of the revolution had passed by the end of 1905. Her status in this period was legally ambiguous. She was not wanted by the police as a criminal and she re-entered Russia as she had left it, on her own legal passport, joining Lenin as guests of a friend in Petersburg, then moving to a furnished apartment on the Nevsky Prospekt. Both Lenin and Krupskaya at first kept their legal passports, as if trusting the new freedom, but, rather inconsistently, they risked prosecution for a relatively minor offense by failing to register with the police. Still, in early December, they moved again (why is not clear), becoming guests of a friend of Lenin's younger sister Maria, and this time they did register with the police. "The moment we registered our house was surrounded by a swarm of police spies," recalls Krupskaya, though one wonders if two or three might seem a swarm. The watching police did not arrest Lenin when they easily could have done so, but he was uneasy about his security, and evidently decided that there was less risk in living underground than in relying on the self-restraint of the authorities. So around mid-December the couple obtained false passports from some comrade who handled this kind of service. This forger was either very tired or a bit impudent in Krupskaya's case, for he transformed her into "Praskovaya Evgenevna Onegina" — that is, the unmarried daughter of Pushkin's tragic hero, Eugene Onegin. No such woman exists in Pushkin's verse novel. If this conspicuous absurdity were not enough to attract attention, Krupskaya continued to see her mother, and could not persuade that aging lady to go along with the conspiracy. Having been addressed as "Nadya," Krupskaya would protest, "But Mama, you know I am Praskovaya," to which her uncomprehending mother would answer, "That now I should suddenly call my own daughter Nadya 'Praskovaya'! What nonsense."[29] Equally risky, if there really were a danger of arrest, were Krupskaya's visits to Lenin's mother, either at her Petersburg flat or at a country cottage that she owned at the nearby hamlet of Sablino.[30] Nor did they make any thoroughgoing effort to avoid one another's company. Although they lived apart for intervals at the end of 1905 and approximately February 1906, Lenin and Krupskaya otherwise occupied modest furnished rooms at several addresses. Since their false passports indicated at one point that they were Mr. Chkheidze (the name of one of Lenin's prime adversaries in 1917) and Miss Onegina, their landlords and neighbors may have formed the impression that they were living in sin — if so, it should have given the couple, who had been forced into Orthodox wedlock, some ironic satisfaction. When not occupying the same rooms, Lenin and Krupskaya even managed to stage a kind of parody of an illicit love affair (though their motivation for intrigue was political), Krupskaya sneaking in the rear entrance of the building where he lived and talking to him in a whisper; or fixing a rendezvous on the street and going by cab to dinner in a private dining room in a stylish hotel on the Nevsky.

After about nine months of residence in Petersburg, Lenin decided that the risks there were too great, so in August 1906 he moved with Krupskaya (soon joined by her mother) to a comfortable country house called the Villa Vaasa, just over the Finnish border and not far from Petersburg. While her mother and a hired maid looked after domestic cares, Krupskaya could commute to the capital by rail, leaving early and getting home late, seeing to Lenin's affairs in town. The risk of arrest was considerable for Krupskaya, for the police definitely kept an eye on travel in and out of Finland at this point in particular. Also, according to her memoirs, one of her close associates in party work in Finland was a woman who turned out to be a police agent and who did arrange the arrest of a fair number of comrades. It is not clear why they failed to nab Krupskaya during one of her visits to the capital, or why the only police report on Krupskaya in this period (dated March 1, 1907) emanated from the Paris office and merely alluded to her as a resident at the Villa Vaasa.[31] Perhaps the explanation is Krupskaya's comment in her memoirs (in one of the moments when she was not seeing spies everywhere) that "the police force was still pretty disorganized," or perhaps they thought it necessary to leave her alone in order to protect the cover of their agent, Katya Komissarova, who was working as Krupskaya's assistant.

Krupskaya's Finnish sojourn does not seem to have left unhappy memories with her, probably because of the excitement of her frequent trips to Petersburg. But, she remembers that she often found her husband in a downcast mood when she returned at night. He was able to travel from Kuokkala to various Social Democratic conferences in Finland and the West, and to receive news from Petersburg by a special daily courier (in addition to Krupskaya), but Lenin nevertheless suffered from bouts of depression and nervous tension. By June 1907 he was so exhausted by the strains of his running feud with the Mensheviks that he took an extended holiday with Krupskaya, her mother, and Lidya Knipovich. Lidya's family owned the cottage where they stayed at a seaside hamlet called Stjernsund on the Finnish coast. Judging from Krupskaya's letter to her sister-in-law Maria, it was a highly successful restorative:

. . . we are, at the moment, 'outside public interests' and are leading a holiday life — bathing in the
sea, cycling (the roads are bad, by the way, so you
can't go far). Volodya plays chess, fetches water, at
one time we had a craze for the English [card] game
of 'donkey', and so on. . . . Everybody here is putting
on weight splendidly. We could read a lot but none of
the books here are very suitable and anyway we don't
feel like reading.[32]

By this time, about a year after she had become a
commuter between Kuokkala and Petersburg, Krupskaya
was no doubt needing a rest, too. And what was the sub-
stance of her feverish activity during this, the first of the
two Russian revolutions that she was to experience? The
answer is not altogether clear, although it is fair to say
that she was not active in central dramas of the revolution,
such as the Petersburg Soviet or the Moscow uprising. Nor
was Lenin, for that matter. Her official biographers maintain that she was "the secretary of the Central Committee"
throughout the revolution, and no doubt she was serving
in this capacity with respect to the Bolshevik wing of the
party until the end of 1905. In her memoirs she relates that
the pressure of work shortly after her return to Russia kept
her busy, along with a newly-appointed co-secretary, Mikhail Sergeyevich Weinstein, and an assistant, Vera Menzhinskaya. Weinstein, Krupskaya recalls, was mainly concerned with the "fighting organization" (which did not
amount to much), while she operated a reception service
for comrades arriving from the provinces — to make ap-
pointments with Lenin or others, to find them false passports, to provide them with printed propaganda, or some
other form of assistance. To evade the police, Krupskaya
and her colleagues kept moving their "office," using at
various times the rooms of two Social Democratic dentists
(a good cover because callers were routine there), the
premises of a Social Democratic bookstore (a poor loca-
tion, where Krupskaya was once apprehended but allowed

to go away after merely giving a false name to the officer), the canteen of the Technological Institute (a hotbed of radicalism for fifteen years, the scene of meetings of Soviet, and therefore not a very clever choice), and various flats occupied by comrades. This shifting about for the sake of security produced its own risks. When she first went to one of the dentist's flats to receive callers, she was given the wrong address and blundered into the apartment of the very colonel who was in command of the regiment that crushed the Moscow uprising. But he was not in, and Krupskaya left, pretending that she had a toothache and was searching for a dentist. The colonel's servants, apparently fearing an assassination attempt, were only too happy to see her go.

There were also, no doubt, many odd jobs to perform, for example, sitting for three days in a print-shop, reading the proofs of one of Lenin's minor writings as quickly as they came off the press, in order to speed up publication. Or the curious task of seeing that local Social Democratic committees were instructed to send two copies of all their *illegal* publications to the manuscript division of the library of the Academy of Sciences, the highest learned agency of the tsar's government. This library had undertaken to make a collection of such publications, and Lenin, with a lifelong respect for libraries — and perhaps with the quiet conviction that one day it would be *his* library — asked Krupskaya to make arrangements for this cooperation.

But perhaps the most important, and most sensitive, of Krupskaya's tasks during the revolution lay elsewhere — as the chief accountant and paymaster of the Bolshevik organization. It is impossible to provide a full picture of this side of Bolshevik operations, because Lenin had good reason to keep it well concealed. Both the sources of revenue and its expenditure were highly sensitive points. Fund-raising often involved shoddy or even criminal tactics, and disbursements provided vital intelligence on the size and thrust of his organization, and especially the extent to which Lenin kept his own funds strictly for his own faction, even after Bolsheviks and Mensheviks supposedly closed ranks in 1906.

Krupskaya was the only one who had full access to the party's accounts. Her correspondence amply demonstrates that she was the authority to whom party workers applied for funds, and we are told that she was a member of the "economic commission" of the Bolshevik center, a shadowy body which may have existed principally in her desk drawer.[33] This responsibility probably was fairly simple before the revolutionary upsurge of 1905, when Lenin disposed of only modest funds which would support only narrow operations — mainly a single party newspaper. But the enthusiasm of 1905 brought very extensive new donations, and an accounting of May 1907 showed that a small fortune — over sixty thousand rubles — had been spent by the party in the period since Lenin's return to Russia. This accounting was signed by "Zimin" and "Maksimov" (Bogdanov), but it seems likely that they merely gave it formal approval, while Krupskaya actually prepared it. For one thing, it was sent as an attachment to a letter she sent Lenin in May 1907, while he was in London for a party congress (see below, p. 127). Furthermore, the financial statement utilizes Russian accounting terminology that was probably familiar to Krupskaya as a result of her year with the accounts department of the tsar's railroads, but was not the sort of thing that just any comrade would know. (But this experience did not guarantee accurate addition; her total figure for expenditures is fifty rubles more than it should have been.)

Finally, it is hard to imagine who but Krupskaya could have provided the figures, including 51 rubles for "petty disbursements," 1,285 rubles for the party's "passport bureau," 2,270 for bail bond put up on behalf of arrested comrades who proceeded to forfeit their bail, 4,994 for the publication and transportation of the newspapers *The Proletarian* and *Forward,* for which Krupskaya was secretary, and 20,924 rubles and fifty kopeks for "local committees." Granting that some of the funds were disbursed in good-sized lumps, and that Krupskaya had some assistance, it remains that there is a lot of work involved in disbursing sixty thousand rubles, and keeping the books for it.[34]

Although reliable statistics simply can not be collected, it is clear that the Social Democratic Party multiplied in membership by at least several-fold in late 1905 and early 1906, and this no doubt helped to keep Krupskaya's secretariat busy. At the same time, however, this complete change in the size of the party — and in its opportunities to organize openly — almost nullified any ideas of running a tightly-knit, centrally-controlled organization. The drastic change in the size and the pace of the movement made it impossible to direct it through a small network of professional agents or to keep up communications by mail between the center and the local branches. Krupskaya's old skills as a corresponding, coordinating secretary were temporarily less important, and there is no evidence that she, or the secretariat of the Central Committee as a whole, busied themselves much with incoming and outgoing mail.

The practical executive authority in the party in this exciting but chaotic time lay mainly in the various city committees, which maintained only loose communications with one another. They did this more by special emissary than by communications through some center, such as Krupskaya's secretariat. Moreover, the tendency within the local committees was strongly toward a reunification of Bolsheviks and Mensheviks, with little regard for the sectarian reservations that the leaders, recently returned from emigration, felt about this. As early as late December 1905, the formation of a reunified Central Committee, which apparently did not recognize anyone as its secretary, further undermined Krupskaya's authority. Her position declined still more sharply in April 1906, when the party held a "Unification Congress" in Stockholm, with the Mensheviks holding the upper hand. She had arranged to come to this congress as the delegate of the Social Democrats of Kazan, but the mandate commission decided that she did not qualify because fewer than one hundred party members had voted for her. Krupskaya protested this ruling in writing to the congress, maintaining that nobody had established that she lacked the hundred votes — not an implausible argument in view of the impossibility of actually running these elections on regular lines. However, nobody, not even her husband, came to her assistance, and it is questionable that she was offered a "consultative vote," though this is claimed in Krupskaya's memoirs.[35] This humiliation no doubt reflected a general Menshevik desire to minimize Bolshevik strength at the congress, but there may also have been some special rancor for Krupskaya, as Lenin's wife. She had been a particularly unpleasant adversary around the time of her resignation from the *Iskra* secretaryship.

More important than the injury to her pride was the removal of any basis on which Krupskaya could claim to be secretary of the Central Committee (now reunited with a Menshevik plurality) or Central Organ of the party. The main basis for a separate Bolshevik organization had received a severe setback, and the leaders of the precariously united Russian Social Democratic Labor Party did not want to appoint Krupskaya to any office whatsoever. Nevertheless, she could continue as Lenin's personal assistant, playing a particularly important role as his observer in the capital. It is difficult to illustrate this activity with documents, for most of the communication between husband and wife was in conversation, but when Lenin went off to London for the fifth party congress Krupskaya wrote at least one letter to him, summarizing current party affairs in Russia. The *okhrana* helpfully intercepted this letter and copied it for posterity. Dated May 8, 1907, it is highly impersonal in tone and even uses the formal *"vy"* in place of the familiar *"ty"* in reference to Lenin, a faint effort at concealment of identity rather than a sign of marital estrangement. What is most impressive is the range of topics on which Krupskaya had late intelligence and her willingness to make her own political judgments. Because this letter is both a rare example of Krupskaya's political collaboration with Lenin and an interesting insight on the state of Bolshevism in 1907, it is worth quoting in full, interpolating some explanations of Krupskaya's cryptic style, which was intended only for a single, expert pair of eyes:

> Things are bad with us. These days 47 persons (Miron, Nikol'sky, Evgenii, Ryazanov, Iordansky, Volna, and others) have been appearing in the fraction [the Social Democratic bloc in the Duma, which contained 65 members in all], predominantly Mensheviks, but there are Bolsheviks, too, for example the delegate from Samarra, somebody from among the workers. Neither in Piter [Petersburg] nor in Finland are any sort of meetings organized. A passport and and admission permit (*propusk*) are required for everyone in Finland. [That is, border crossing between Petersburg and places such as Kuokkala had been tightened up.] The *pitertsy* [comrades in Petersburg] are sitting without money, without literature [propaganda], which is a complete fiasco, without people.
>
> In Moscow the last member of the Regional Bureau, Danilo, has vanished, and the Regional Bureau has ceased to function. In general there is a complete collapse in Moscow. Vladimir [a city] is also a mess. Yesterday I received a letter from our man there (the one who was arrested in Androkyanua). They probably released him, or found nothing and did not press any charges. N. [Nikitin, Menshevik] is released, we must think [about what relations we should have with him?] one of these days. Correct relations are established with them [the Mensheviks]. They designated an executive commission during his [Nikitin's] absence and in general have taken care of everything. For the present there is no money. If Tstsa and B-' had helped, perhaps there would be something to do.
>
> Tomorrow Herman is leaving directly for you. The other day we obtained a pair of thousands [of

rubles] (yesterday 3,000 rubles were already received) . And for the moment I ask you not to print that account which I sent you yesterday; this is necessary in conspiratorial relations.[36]

And even though party "unity" prevented Lenin from controlling an official "central organ", he would not remain without his personal newspaper, started in August 1906, again using *The Proletarian* as its name. It was edited in Kuokkala, printed in nearby Vyborg (Finland) , and smuggled into Russia — the kind of operation with which Krupskaya was familiar. As usual, she served as secretary for her husband's enterprise, this time assisted by Vera Menzhinskaya and the police spy Katya Komissarova. It may have been through Katya's efforts that Krupskaya was shadowed when she went to the capital in April 1907, to sit on the mandate commission of the fifth party congress. This body met in London at the end of the month, without Krupskaya. But even though arrests were being made among the socialists who were on their way to the congress, she made it back to Kuokkala safely — and found seventeen delegates waiting for her to fix them a meal.

But the risk of arrest was definitely increasing during the fall of 1907. By that time the new premier, Petr Stolypin, had restored the authority of the regime throughout the Russian Empire, and the *okhrana* was acting more boldly in Finland. Lenin, never one to take unnecessary risks, left his wife (with Mrs. Bogdanov) in Kuokkala to burn the more sensitive part of the files, while he moved to a hideout near Helsinki. After spending some weeks there he made his way to Stockholm, at some date before December 13, 1907, catching a steamer from a small island near Åbo, and almost drowning as he crossed the thin ice to make this melodramatic connection. Krupskaya seemed more confident that the police were not looking for her in earnest. She risked another trip to Petersburg to install her ailing mother in quarters of some sort, then proceeded to Stockholm without any histrionics.

CHAPTER V

Comrade Inessa

Krupskaya had liked emigration in the West little enough the first time, when she had left Russia to await the Revolution. It was still more bitter the second time, leaving the homeland because the Revolution, having happened, was gradually, dismally fading into the past. As if this were not gloomy enough, both Lenin and Krupskaya, while stopping off in Berlin, had a bad attack of food poisoning. The onset of this misery came at the end of an evening with Rosa Luxemburg, which may explain why Krupskaya could not recall anything very favorable to say about the outstanding female Marxist of all time. Reaching Geneva, both Lenin and Krupskaya felt that they had reached rock bottom. "I feel as if I have come here to be buried," Lenin remarked soon after their arrival, still half-sick, in the middle of January 1908.

They remained in "this damned Geneva," this "awful hole" (as Lenin put it in a letter to his sister Maria), for less than a year, living at first in one room in a boarding house, but moving to an apartment after Krupskaya's mother joined them once more in the spring, taking over the kitchen chores. There was the usual work for Krupskaya — the secretaryship of Lenin's revived factional organ *The Proletarian* — but the difficulties were even more discouraging than usual. The *okhrana* in Russia, and also in western Europe, operating under the direction of its Paris headquarters, had grown more active and efficient. The pages of *The Proletarian* and Krupskaya's letters maintained a brave front. "I think", she wrote in a letter that the police intercepted, "that relations with Russia [the underground] will develop strongly."[1] But in retrospect Krupskaya recalled, "as for letters, we expected them more than we received them," and a letter to her from a comrade in the underground, accused *The Proletarian* of being excessively optimistic, when in fact "a downright liquidation of the party is going on; the Moscow committee is in the full sense of the word *introuvable* (seriously) ; in Piter [the capital] there is nothing . . . and you say that 'a renewal of the personal membership of the party is going on.' "[2]

With revolutionary parties in general and Lenin's personal following in particular in a state of disarray, the distribution of *The Proletarian* (and a newspaper in which Mensheviks also participated, *The Social Democrat*) was an especially hard problem for Krupskaya. This time she had neither the money nor the contacts at her disposal to ship printed matter to Russia by the *pud* (36 pounds) . Her surviving correspondence shows that she relied heavily on a single collaborator named M. V. Kobetsky, who settled in Copenhagen in 1908, after fleeing Russia.[3] The method was to send him relatively small stocks of the two newspapers (a few hundred at a time, judging by the records) , and he would then mail smaller quantities to specified addresses, wrapping the thin newspapers in a heavier paper to conceal their nature when placing them in envelopes. In her instructions to Kobetsky, Krupskaya tells him not to send all the envelopes in a consignment off on the same day, and to use assorted envelopes, so as not to attract attention. Clearly she was counting on the casualness of police checks on the mail, especially coming from Copenhagen, which had not been known as an emigrant revolutionary center. And she was correct in this, for she was still keeping up her orders to Kobetsky after almost two years, which indicates that letters received by Krupskaya from Russia reported the safe arrival of much of the material. But the delivery cost per copy of a newspaper was very high, and the total number that could be shipped through Kobetsky was small. The geographical variety of the addresses that Krupskaya sent to Kobetsky suggests that he was responsible for most of Russia; it is doubtful that Krupskaya had several such mailing agents working at once.

If pressure from the police on the Social Democratic Party was not bad enough, Lenin and his closest colleague of 1904-1907, Bogdanov, were falling out over issues of philosophy and practical tactics, creating acrimonious divisions among the emigrant Bolsheviks. To put it as briefly as possible, Bogdanov, with some moral support from Lenin's erstwhile benefactor Maxim Gorky, was interested in various abstract conceptions that Lenin regarded as totally anti-Marxist, and at the same time Bogdanov led a vigorous group of Bolsheviks who were convinced that Lenin was wrong to have dropped his tactic of boycotting the elections to the Duma, following the first election in 1906. A good deal of Lenin's time in 1908 was occupied in writing a polemic on the philosophical issue, and also in reluctantly accepting an invitation to visit Gorky at his villa on Capri. Krupskaya had at first considered going too, but in fact stayed in Geneva. The philosophical battlefields were never her milieu.

In the summer of 1908 Krupskaya "had a lot of free time on my hands," and so she turned again to the study of French, and to pedagogy, which she had not touched for over ten years. Initially this involved merely some visits to Swiss schools, which she found opresively regimented, and some reading. But from this time to the end of her life Krupskaya never again set aside her active interest in education. Another distraction in Geneva was the arrival of other emigrant Bolsheviks, including Kamenev, Zinoviev, and their wives. Lilina Zinoviev became one of Krupskaya's close friends, and the two men were later to play an important role in Krupskaya's political life. Still, she was relieved in December 1908, when Lenin decided to move his headquarters to Paris — partly because Lenin was convinced by two comrades that in a big city he would be less likely to be spied on. One of these advisors was in fact a spy, who most likely realized that it would be more convenient for the Paris headquarters of the *okhrana* to keep an eye on Lenin if he were close at hand.[4]

The three and a half years (1909 through mid-1912) that Krupskaya spent in Paris were fairly settled, physically. They first rented "a large, airy flat that even had mirrors over the fireplaces" on the prosperous Rue Bonier. At this time Lenin's sister Maria was living with them, so they could use four rooms plus kitchen and storerooms. She had joined the family in Geneva to pursue a higher education, which she continued in Paris, staying until the fall of 1909. Krupskaya got on well with Maria, who was nine years her junior and did not seem to take the same possessive attitude toward her brother as did elder sister Anna. Still, Maria's presence must have been something of a strain, because she had to have an operation for an ear ailment in Switzerland and for appendicitis in France. With her mother intermittently ill, too, Krupskaya must have had a lot of nursing on her hands for about a year.

After Maria was well enough to return to Russia in the fall of 1909, the family moved to smaller quarters (two bedrooms and kitchen) at number 4 on the Rue Marie Rose, a very short street of stolidly bourgeois Parisian apartment buildings, which must have been fairly new at the time. Krupskaya preferred this to the larger apartment because it had central heating. Here the Ulyanovs remained until July 1912, when Lenin transferred his headquarters to Austrian Poland.

In the early years of his second emigration Lenin traveled a good deal, usually to give lectures to Russian emigrant groups or to attend conferences, including meetings of the Second International, in which he became active in 1907. He visited Geneva, Berne, Brussels, Nice, Capri, Copenhagen, Stockholm, Berlin, Stuttgart, Zurich, Antwerp, Liége, London, Lucerne, Prague, and Leipzig once or more while Krupskaya stayed home in Paris. Her party functions presumably required that she keep close to the incoming mail, and her mother (or Maria) probably needed her care. In three and a half years she got out of Paris only on summer holidays, and on two of these three trips not very far away at that. In 1909 Lenin, Maria, and Krupskaya spent about a month in an inexpensive pension in a town called Bombon (Saône-et-Loire). In Krupskaya's opinion the place was depressing, but Lenin apparently liked it fairly well. She found the other guests at the pension were intolerably petit-bourgeois, combining pretentious airs and vulgarity. The worst culprit was a saleslady who "liked to tell risqué stories, of which she had a large store, yet at the same time she dreamt of how she would lead her daughter Martha to her first communion."[5]

The following year, 1910, Krupskaya and her mother set off for a French socialist summer colony on the Vendée coast of Brittany where Elizaveta Krupskaya had spent the previous summer. But Krupskaya, as usual, did not feel at home with foreigners, who struck her as unfriendly to Russians. Soon some more Russians arrived — one couple and an unattached man. Even though they were adherents of the heretical Bogdanov faction of Bolshevism, they were Russians, and Krupskaya evidently found them exceedingly congenial. With them, she spurned French socialism — "There were hardly any workers there" (as if the leaders of Russian socialism were mainly proletarians) — and moved to the nearby town of Pornic, where Lenin joined the colony.

In the summer of 1911, they hardly left Paris, spending over two months in the town of Longjumeau, near Orly airport, where Lenin ran a school for Bolshevik underground workers. This was a poor sort of vacation, mostly work or boredom in the unattractive little town, with only a few breaks for bicycle trips to the palace at Fontainebleau or various woods. Krupskaya liked the food — "the cuisine is Russian, filling, home-cooked food" — but complained that they had to walk a "verst" (over half a mile) from their lodgings at one end of the town to the school's "commune" at the other end of the village. And it was beastly hot, there was no grass or garden around the tanner's house where they had rented rooms, and her mother was in poor health.

To add to the discouraging picture, her husband was showing a good deal of interest in another woman. This was Inessa Armand, Krupskaya's only known rival for the affections of Lenin after their marriage.[6] The Inessa-Lenin-Krupskaya triangle poses a number of riddles that can neither be fully solved nor simply ignored in a life of Krupskaya. For one thing, it *was* a triangle, not just a "V" formed by one person's relationship with two others, as in so many alleged triangles. In time, at least, there was a close personal bond between Inessa and Krupskaya, as well as between Inessa and Lenin.

It is highly probable that Inessa was Lenin's mistress for about a year in 1911-1912 and quite possible that they renewed their love affair for a bit more than a year in 1914-1915. In any case, Krupskaya's marriage was subject to considerable stress because of Inessa, although Nadezhda did in time accommodate her life to Inessa's presence. To be sure, all the parties to this episode treated it with considerable discretion, and Soviet archivists and writers have been careful not to publish anything that would establish a Lenin-Inessa love affair. It is possible that Lenin and Inessa were not lovers, physically. Such aberrations as total monogamy or impotence do occur, but in this case they seem pretty unlikely. The French Communist biographer of Inessa, who had access to unpublished papers in Russia, seems to accept that there was an affair. "As for Lenin," he writes, "how could he not be seduced by this exceptional being who combined beauty with intelligence, femininity with energy, practical sense with revolutionary ardor?"[7]

Inessa's background was exotic. She was born in Paris on May 8, 1874, or June 16, 1875, depending on which of her principal biographers one prefers.[8] Her parents were theatrical people, father French (d'Herbenville) and mother English, which presumably accounts for Inessa's being officially recorded as a member of the Church of England when she married — a rare affiliation for a future Leninist. Because her father died when she was a child, Inessa-Elizabeth (as she was named in the church register when married; some writers say she was born simply Elizabeth) was sent to live with her grandmother, a governess employed by the Armand family near Moscow. The Armands were Russified French émigrés who had become wealthy industrialists and, at the same time, liberal-radical intellectuals. They treated the child Inessa as one of the family, and enabled her to obtain the educational qualifications to become a domestic tutor (like Krupskaya). But before she could begin this career, Alexander Armand, the eldest son of her benefactor, married the eighteen- or nineteen-year old Inessa. She lived with him for about ten years (1893-1903), the attractive young wife of a wealthy young businessman and the mother of his four children, two boys and two girls who were born between 1894 and 1901. By 1903, if not earlier, Inessa fell for her husband's younger brother, Vladimir, who had become a youthful radical (while her husband remained vaguely liberal). At some time not specified by her Soviet biographer, Inessa moved in with Vladimir, with the indulgent consent of her husband, who remained her friend and financial support. Although the dates are not certain, it seems quite likely that her fifth child, a son born in 1903, while Inessa was in Switzerland, was fathered by Vladimir. A letter to him in August of that year suggests that they were close then (of course, they had lived in the same house since childhood, so this is inconclusive), and the trip, supposedly for Inessa's health, might well have been an unsuccessful attempt to cope with the domestic crisis.

According to Krupskaya's recollection of what Inessa told her, it was prostitution that first aroused Inessa's concern for social problems. Upset by this institution, she joined a Moscow "Society for Improving the Lot of Women" sometime around 1900, specifically its branch which attempted to rehabilitate prostitutes. At this time she was deeply religious and an admirer of Tolstoy (again like Krupskaya at one stage). However, a member of her group wrote to the sage to ask him what could be done about prostitution. He could qualify as an expert, both as an outstanding customer in his younger days and a moral uplifter later. He replied: "Nothing will come of your work. It was thus before Moses. It was thus after Moses. Thus it was, thus it will be." Which finished Tolstoyism for Inessa and turned her to socialism, the only creed that really looked on women as the equals of men, she believed. According to an unpublished memoir, available to Inessa's Soviet biographer, she became a "revolutionary" in 1901, yet she told Krupskaya that she had retained her religious convictions until the birth of her fifth child (whatever that had to do with it) in 1903. But such eclecticism is not impossible by any means. Police records show that she was under surveillance in 1905 and her rooms were searched. She was arrested in 1907, and the police considered her a Socialist Revolutionary (a narodnik, non-Marxist), although Krupskaya says this was just because a relative had given her some of their publications.

Whether or not Inessa's political affiliations were clear at the time, the police sent her into exile in Archangel province. She was accompanied there by her Vladimir (Armand, that is), who was still so smitten with her that he would not stay behind, even though he had been given no sentence. This was real women's liberation: a Russian man reversing the pattern of Nekrasov's poem "Russian Women." He contracted tuberculosis in a year there, and went off to Switzerland. Inessa arranged to escape through Finland and joined him, but he died soon after her arrival in 1909. Heartbroken, Inessa Armand moved to Brussels where she made some effort to study pedagogy (again, an interest dear to Krupskaya). It has been asserted, that she met Lenin sometime in 1909, but there is no reason to think that they were well acquainted when she moved to Paris in October 1910. She arrived with three of her children, who recently had come from Russia, and took a flat at 241 Rue St. Jacques. It was her husband who enabled her to follow her emigrant revolutionary career in comfort.[9]

At about 35 Inessa was still youthful-looking, a reddish-haired, passionate woman, who certainly did not believe in "bourgeois hypocrisy" about sexual relations. From her photographs (including one police "mug" shot in which Inessa sought to annoy the cops by keeping her eyes shut), we gather that she was not a conventional beauty, but one of those people who combine a purely personal kind of good looks with an intense vitality. And, speaking of physical attraction, it is worth noting that Krupskaya had not reached middle age gracefully. An objective police description, written just a year before Inessa moved to Paris, said of Krupskaya: "tall, about forty years old [correct], medium brown hair, thin, stoops, grey eyes, small nose, thin lips. Dressed always slovenly."[10] Two Bolshevik witnesses testify that in this period Krupskaya slept in her mother's bedroom, not Lenin's.[11] Inessa, who had her husband's largesse, always seems to have been neatly, though not daringly dressed. In 1915, Inessa wanted to publish a book advocating "free love," praising the superiority of "a temporary passion and a love affair" to "kisses without love" of "vulgar and worse than vulgar spouses."[12] And by 1910, or 1911 at the latest, Inessa had become a politically ardent Leninist. Certainly the ingredients for an amorous affair were present on her side.

The early meetings of Lenin and Inessa in the winter of 1910-1911 are a blank, but they must have become quite well acquainted then, because Lenin selected her to join the "faculty" of his summer school for Bolsheviks in Longjumeau in 1911. This was a signal honor for a woman who had no particular experience either as a theoretician or as a practical organizer. Most of the lectures were by Lenin and his two chief colleagues of the time, Zinoviev and Kamenev. According to one account Krupskaya gave some classes on how to establish an illegal newspaper, which she was certainly qualified to do. At Longjumeau Inessa and her children lived in the building that was used for the classes and meals, and it is quite clear that she was in close association with Lenin (politically, at least) all through the summer. When Lenin and Krupskaya moved back to their apartment at 4, Rue Marie Rose in September 1911, he, or Inessa, or both, arranged for her to take a flat at No. 2, the building next door.

Until the following July there is no doubt that Inessa and Lenin saw each other constantly and were closely associated in their work. Both of them, and Krupskaya, were leading members of the Paris group of the "Emigrant Organization" of the party, a cell of about thirty-five members at this time. In fact, Inessa became the secretary of the "Committee of Emigrant Organizations," which was the executive body of all the groups of emigrant Russian Social Democrats that existed in about fourteen different western European cities. Before the Revolution of 1905 Krupskaya had held just this post in the same body, then called the "Foreign League of Russian Revolutionary Social Democrats," and during the First World War she again carried this responsibility. But in the period when Inessa was living next door, it was she whom Lenin chose to handle the correspondence and other administrative work connected with the emigrant branch of the party.[13] Krupskaya continued to serve as secretary of Lenin's factional newspaper, now called *The Working-Class News* (*Rabochaia Gazeta*), writing her accustomed letters in defense of the Bolshevik cause (with special digs at Trotsky, who was more than usually at odds with Lenin in 1911-1912).[14] But the more important task was the one entrusted to Inessa, for Lenin's chief tactical objectives at this point were closely involved with the politics of the emigrant community, while the Russian underground was still in the doldrums.[15]

The initial shock of Inessa's affair with Lenin must have been very hard on Krupskaya, leaving emotional scars that were still tender years afterwards. In her memoirs of this period, written for mass consumption in 1928, she tries to leave the impression that Inessa established close relations with the family only *after* 1912, when all of them turned up in Austrian Poland. "That autumn," (1913) writes Krupskaya, "all of us — our entire Cracow group — were drawn very close to Inessa. . . . We knew her, of course, in Paris, but the colony there had been a large one, whereas in Cracow we lived together in a small, close and friendly circle."[16] No mention of Rue Marie Rose, complete contradiction of Krupskaya's own writing for a much more select, well-informed public a few years earlier: "We saw each other every day [in Paris]. Inessa became a person close to us. She loved my old mother very much."[17]

There may be a kind of truth in this self-contradiction. It is possible that the two women saw each other constantly in Paris, but without cordiality. Only in 1913 did a real friendship between Inessa and Nedezhda grow up. By that time Inessa had left Lenin, returned to Russia, suffered imprisonment and was released. In her memoirs Krupskaya implies that her rival took the initiative in bridging the gap between them: "during this visit [near Cracow] she [Inessa] told me a great deal about her life and her children [three of whom had lived next door to Krupskaya for a year, previously!], and showed me their letters. There was a delightful warmth in her stories. Ilyich and I went for long walks with Inessa."[18]

But in the first year of Lenin's attachment to Inessa Krupskaya was not ready for long walks with her rival. According to the recollections of Alexandra Kollontai, as reported by her one-time colleague, Marcel Body, Krupskaya offered to leave, but Lenin asked her to stay.[19] This is certainly plausible. Kollontai was not in a position to know much at first hand, never having lived in close proximity to Lenin in emigration, but after the Revolution she became friendly with Inessa Armand. For her part, Krupskaya no doubt thought that she opposed the "bourgeois" concept of marriage, and was obliged to free her husband when he wished. But it could not have been easy for her. Surely Krupskaya, who secretly kept the wedding ring that she could not wear (because of the inverted prudery of her set), regarded marriage — and especially her own marriage — with a lot more reverence than many non-radical women. She never expressed approval of any alternative to monogamy, and most certainly never followed Inessa Armand and Alexandra Kollontai in advocating "free love." Quite apart from her ideology, Nadezhda Krupskaya was a child of the Victorian middle class when it came to sexual conduct. Like many women of this background, she was pretty innocent in sexual matters — she once wrote that the Russian Old Believers (dissidents from the official Orthodox Church) did not, as a group, suffer from syphilis because they did not eat out of common bowls, which, she obviously believed, accounted for the spread of syphilis among other Russians. For such a naïve person, the sexual conduct of an Inessa or a Kollontai (who had a series of lovers) would be both frightening and shocking, no matter what Chernyshevsky had said.

Kollontai left a fictionalized version of the Lenin-Inessa-Krupskaya triangle in a novella published in Russia in 1927.[20] Entitled *A Great Love*, the resemblances between the three real persons and "Senya" (diminutive of Semen or Simon), Natasha (for Inessa), and Annyuta (for Krupskaya) are unmistakable. He is an emigrant Russian revolutionary leader who has a beard and wears an old cap. His wife has a heart disease and cannot be excited. (Something approximating this soon developed with Krupskaya.) The other woman, Natasha, has known other lovers, and is more exciting than his wife. Natasha also has ample independent financial means (unlike her lover), works as a party secretary, and is an excellent linguist. At the end of the story Natasha leaves Senya to return to underground work in Russia (as Inessa did in 1912).

This exit ends Kollontai's story, but it does not exclude the possibility of a sequel, which the lives of the real people did in fact provide. The conclusion of this act in the fictionalized account also concurs with Kollontai's statements to Body about Lenin's decision to remain with Krupskaya. The novella has it that the initiative in breaking off the affair came from the mistress, who was disappointed that her lover did not esteem her revolutionary activities more highly. At the same time, both felt that their passion was spent and that they should part. This is precisely the kind of conduct that Lenin had found so admirable in Turgenev's Andrei Kolosov.

There is some fairly persuasive, if complicated, evidence that Lenin and Inessa reached such a decision in the middle of May 1912, while taking a holiday in the resort town of Arcachon, near Bordeaux. This setting, incidentally, resembles one of the places that Kollontai's fictitious lovers enjoyed together — "a southern landscape." The point of departure of the real-life evidence is a police report, dated April 30, 1912, which states that Inessa, though normally a resident of Rue Marie Rose, is now taking a vacation at Arcachon.[21] Lenin confirms this in a curious way in a letter to his mother dated March 8 or 9: "E. V. [Krupskaya's mother] thinks of going to Russia, but I do not expect she will. We are thinking of sending her to friends of ours in Arcachon in the south of France."[22] Of course, it is possible, but exceedingly improbable, that Lenin had several friends in this small town. But it seems that he was thinking of sending his mother-in-law to stay with his mistress for a holiday. This may seem to be a unique idea in the annals of philandering, but it is not quite as improbable as it sounds. As noted above, Krupskaya specifically said that her mother and Inessa were chummy in Paris. So it is not out of the question that Elizaveta Vasilevna was invited to Arcachon by her son-in-law's mistress. The old lady's mind was failing in these years, and it seems likely that she was innocent of the nature of the Lenin-Inessa relationship.

But she did not go. Instead, the chronological list of events in Lenin's life (as published in the fifth, most recent and most exhaustive edition of his collected works) states: "Before May 10 — Lenin leaves Paris for several days.''[23] Among the thousands of entries in this reverent list of his every known activity, this one is unique. Where did he go? And why, in this one case, do his latter-day Soviet Boswells not tell us? In other cases, they are happy to explain where he went and why. Possibly they don't know (and it is true that they do not have the archives of the Paris office of the *okhrana* at their disposal to provide a clue). One can't be sure, but it seems pretty fair to surmise that Lenin joined Inessa Armand at Arcachon.

If this were so, the outcome of the visit appears to have been more in Krupskaya's favor than Inessa's. Lenin came back to Krupskaya from wherever he had been and within a few weeks moved, without Inessa but with his wife, from Paris to Cracow. This transfer of his operational headquarters is usually presented as a change in tactics, a response to the need to be closer to the Russian border because the workers' movement at home was heating up. This is true, but it also seems quite likely that intimate personal considerations were involved in planning the move. Who was to go where, and with whom? Why just at this time? In actuality Krupskaya (and her mother) accompanied Lenin to Cracow, while Inessa, after stopping over with them for two days, proceeded on to Russia as an underground agent. She was still wanted there as an escapee from her term of exile, and everyone involved surely knew that the chances of her arrest were high, considering how good police intelligence on their organization was at this time. But Inessa went, possibly with deliberate recklessness, soon to be arrested and put in prison, where she began to develop symptoms of tuberculosis. This martyrdom may have altered her position in Krupskaya's eyes, especially if she had voluntarily relinquished her husband at the same time.

Krupskaya left Paris forever, without regrets. The high point of her years there had been a brief meeting with Laura Lafargue, the aged daughter of Karl Marx and wife of a French socialist. Although their short conversation evidently lapsed into awkward silence after Krupskaya had tried out a few remarks on Russian women in the revolutionary movement, she had been "quite excited — I was actually walking with the daughter of Karl Marx." Otherwise the French had been a trial. On a fairly rare occasion, when Krupskaya and Lenin had gone to the theater in Paris, she found that "the play was idiotic, but these French fairly yelled their heads off. Still there was some wonderful music during the entr'actes — Tschaikowsky, Rimsky-Korsakov, Borodin."

Things were better in Cracow. Being good Russian patriots, both Lenin and Krupskaya noticed the difference: "Almost in Russia! Even the Jews are like Russians," wrote Lenin. "It was only half emigration . . . . Ilyich liked Cracow very much. It reminded him of Russia . . . . I liked Cracow, too," echoed Krupskaya. And there were more Russian comrades to see in Poland — almost all devoted Leninists, not the exasperating diversity of emigrant factionalists that one met in a city like Paris. Kamenev and Zinoviev, with their wives and children, followed Lenin to Poland and lived close at hand, so Krupskaya had the pleasure of their company almost daily, and especially the comradeship of Lilina Zinoviev, with whom she happily shared her secretarial functions. As in the past she also acted as the party accountant.[24] Other Bolsheviks visited them, Bukharin coming from Vienna and notables from the Russian underground, including almost all of the Central Committee on two occasions. A new, Bolshevik, Central Commitee, had been formed by Lenin at his Prague Conference of January 1912, giving him additional leverage in his attempt to run his own party. Although there was no formal post of secretary of the new Central Committee, Krupskaya, as in earlier years, filled this role, not only taking care of correspondence but also carrying the main burden of organizational details, including false passports and housing, when the committee met secretly in Austrian Poland. Although not a member of the committee, she participated in its meetings at this time, and once gave a major report on the activities of the local underground committees. According to the memoirs of G. I. Petrovsky, who was present, she even disagreed with Lenin on one occasion. At one point, he was advocating emphasis on small groups of conspirators, around which larger party units would form. But Krupskaya said that things would not work that way in life and that he was too much attracted by the idea of little groups.[25] Did she really grasp the full implications of this criticism, which went right to the heart of Leninism, echoing the charges of his most acute critics?

Perhaps her comments were inspired by the poor state of affairs in the Bolshevik underground in Russia at this time. The government was comparatively permissive, and Bolshevik deputies openly participated in the Duma (Krupskaya wrote a speech for one of them, attacking government policy on education, but it was never delivered).[26] Several party publications were permitted, including *Pravda* (*The Truth*), which had been founded in 1912. At the same time, the police had greatly improved their techniques for penetrating and smashing conspiratorial organizations. As Krupskaya wrote to Elena Stasova on February 21, 1914, "The illegal organization is cut to ribbons. There are no solid regional centers. The local organizations are cut off from one another and in the majority of cases everywhere there are only workers in the organizations, the professionals [professional revolutionaries] have vanished long since. There are no secret addresses anywhere, nor any such conspiratorial practices.'[27]

As a result of this curtailed activity concerning the underground, much of Krupskaya's secretarial attention was connected with the legal Bolshevik newspaper *Pravda*. Unlike Lenin's previous journalistic ventures, it was published in Petersburg, but with editorial supervision from Lenin's emigrant headquarters. True, there were frustrations in attempting to carry out this operation by remote control. Krupskaya notes in a letter of February 1, 1913, to an emigrant comrade, Shklovsky:

"Of course, *Pravda* is very badly run. Mainly because the people in the editorial staff [in Petersburg] were chosen at random ['like pines from a forest,' a colloquialism] the majority are not literary people, there are even undesirable elements, like Salin, who is completely reconciled with his Bundist center, is serving on *Pravda* only to earn a living, and frequently does us dirt [literally, 'passes us a pig,' a colloquial expression for a really mean betrayal]"[28]

"Salin" is none other than Iosif Vissarionovich Dzhugashvili, who used "Salin," "Solin," and other pseudonyms but was just settling on one of them — "Stalin" — about this time. He had not played a prominent role in the Bolshevik organization until 1912, when Lenin coopted him onto the Central Committee and appointed him to the *Pravda* editorial board, with sorry results. Krupskaya had met him for the first time in Cracow in the weeks immediately preceding the quoted letter, and it is obvious that seeing him in person only reinforced the antagonism that she already felt toward him. No comment on any comrade, including the Mensheviks, in the hundreds of Krupskaya's letters that have come down to us conveys such contempt. In fact, her outraged feelings seem to have misled her about Stalin's political deviations. True, he had shown "conciliationist" leanings in his work with *Pravda,* meaning that he was not sufficiently militant in his attitude toward non-Bolshevik socialists. But it is uncertain why Krupskaya tied him in with the Bund, the Jewish socialist party of the Russian Empire. Stalin not only disliked Jews (which Krupskaya probably did not know), but had never in his career been close to the Bund and had just written rather extensively against its policy on the "national question" (how to cope with the multi-national make-up of the Empire). It seems likely that the real basis of Krupskaya's loathing of Stalin was his personality, that crude, sly manner which offended most of the intelligentsia socialists who met Stalin in his younger days. And led them to underrate him. It has been suggested that in the years before 1913 Stalin had been an agent of the *okhrana,* and this is possible, although it seems equally possible that Stalin was tricking the *okhrana* to gain their protection and to betray his numerous enemies.[29] Whatever the facts of the matter, it is quite definite that Krupskaya did not mean to imply that kind of betrayal when she spoke of Stalin "passing us a pig." Krupskaya took a good deal of pride in relating in her memoirs how she had forced an agent named Brendinsky to quit the party (and his police vocation) by questioning him and reporting the case to Burtsev, a Socialist Revolutionary, who acted as a kind of volunteer security officer for any Russian socialist party. But Krupskaya took no such course with Stalin, who was arrested on February 23, 1913, not to be released until 1917.

Despite some signs of improvement in the prospects of the workers' movement in Russia, 1913 proved to be a year of trial for Krupskaya. Living in cramped quarters (a two-bedroom apartment, though in a new building), she had to take over most of the domestic work because her aging mother was becoming "pretty helpless," in the words of the Polish socialist Bagocki, who had helped the family get settled in Cracow. Cooking was never Krupskaya's strong point, though it is not clear that she realized this. Years later she boasted to her secretary that she could prepare eggs twelve ways — but when questioned it turned out that they were all the same, except for the addition of onions, or bread, or tomatoes, and so on. Bagocki comments on her cooking as only a reverent Leninist could:

"Her culinary abilities, in the presence of other, more important functions, did not yield especially good results. But Vladimir Ilyich was not particular and limited himself to jokes, such as saying that he had 'roast' too often, meaning somewhat over-cooked boiled meat."[30]

A more serious problem was her health. During 1913 Krupskaya was increasingly bothered by the symptoms of the thyroid disorder known as exophthalmic goiter, or Graves' or Basedow's disease — general weakness, headaches, bulging eyes, heart palpitations, shaky hands, swelling on the neck. This made it increasingly difficult for her to keep up her work, and worried her husband greatly. Many moral accusations have been laid against Lenin, but nobody can fault him concerning the close personal attention he gave to Krupskaya's health at this time. It appears that the symptoms were becoming troublesome no later than April 1913, and for three weeks Krupskaya spent a good deal of her time at a free clinic in Cracow, taking electric treatments and bromides on the theory that she had a nervous disorder. But her condition only worsened, so on April 23 or 24 they took the advice of a physician and moved to the mountain town of Poronin, at the edge of the Tatra mountains, six or eight hours' trip by rail from Cracow. Here they rented a big country villa ("a huge one, far too big," wrote Lenin to his sister Maria), planning to spend five months there.

Still her condition declined. While Krupskaya believed that the summer's rest would restore her, Lenin anxiously pursued his own researches into the problem. He wrote to his brother Dmitri, a physician, who consulted some texts and advised against surgery, much to Krupskaya's relief.[31] But Lenin had little confidence in Russian doctors, especially socialists. One explanation of this distrust is that a radical Russian medical student had tried to cure Lenin of baldness in 1903, with no success.

Disregarding Dmitri's advice and his wife's preference, he followed the suggestion of his Polish friend Bagocki, a student-neurologist himself, and sought the services of Professor Theodor Kocher in Berne. Kocher was a 1909 Nobel laureate in medicine, having pioneered surgical treatment of thyroid disease. In early May Lenin wrote to a Russian friend in Berne to find out how one approached the eminent specialist. By mid-May he had determined to take Nadezhda to Kocher, and she was now willing to go, having been alarmed by renewed heart palpitations.[32]

As one whose life belonged to the party, Krupskaya could not have a surgical operation without its peculiarly Bolshevik aspect. Lenin's personal finances were stretched, and he implored the editors of *Pravda* to send him money to pay for Nadezhda's operation. "I beg you not to be late," he wrote on June 16, but they must have let him down, for the request was repeated soon afterwards (". . . my wife is going to have an operation. The money is badly needed.") [33]

Arriving in Berne on June 10, they found that Kocher was a busy man and not inclined to rush his cases, which upset Lenin. "There was a great row with Kocher — a capricious character," he wrote to Kamenev after it turned out that they would have to wait their turn.[34] But Lenin, who would hardly have tolerated such annoyance in other circumstances, was willing to put up with it for his wife's sake. Finally, after two weeks of preparatory treatment, Krupskaya had the operation on June 23, removing part of the thyroid gland. It was considered inadvisable to use anesthetics, so it must have been a great ordeal. The next day, Lenin wrote to his mother, Nadya ran a high fever and was delirious — "I was pretty scared." But she improved quite rapidly after that — "Kocher is, of course, a wonderful surgeon, and everyone with thyroid trouble should go to him," Lenin wrote to his mother on July 26.[34] While Krupskaya recuperated in the hospital Lenin spent half his days with her, the other half in a library, but as soon as she was pronounced fit to leave his impatience finally got the better of his solicitude, and they returned directly to Poronin on July 24, rather than spending two weeks recuperating in the Alps, as recommended.

Krupskaya lived for twenty-five years after the operation, working at an exhausting pace much of the time, so Kocher's surgery must be considered at least a qualified success. On the other hand, she had renewed heart palpitations in 1914, and Kocher, having been consulted by mail, wanted to see her again, perhaps for another operation. She evidently resisted the idea, and tried to spend the summer of 1914 resting at Poronin. In April 1915 Krupskaya consulted a second distinguished Bernese specialist, Professor Hermann Sahli, who believed in treating Basedow's disease as a psycho-neurological problem, not to be dealt with surgically. At his advice she spent a long summer holiday in the Alps, and by September claimed that she was wholly recovered, having twice climbed to the summit of the Rothorn (7,500 feet) without getting tired. Sahli's opinion of her condition, which was fairly optimistic, seemed justified. He still maintained that she was not seriously ill, with no heart disease, in April 1917, when she paid her last visit to him. Judging by his cryptic clinical notes, and his prescriptions of rest and sedatives, it seems that Professor Sahli considered that Krupskaya suffered mainly from nervous tension, though not mental illness.[35]

While Krupskaya was recuperating from the operation at the villa in Poronin in September 1913, Inessa Armand reappeared on the scene. After she had developed signs of tuberculosis in prison, her loyal husband, with whom she had not lived since about 1902, persuaded the authorities to release her on bail — the very substantial sum of 5,000 rubles. Inessa immediately fled the country, which may or may not have been what her husband had in mind, and went directly to Poronin. Here she stayed until December. As already noted, this was the time when Inessa rather abruptly became friendly with Krupskaya. Perhaps Inessa had given up Lenin, and the grateful Krupskaya found that she had much in common with this martyr from the tsar's jails. Or perhaps Inessa did renew an amorous relation with Lenin, but Krupskaya now accepted this. In any case, Krupskaya recalls in her memoirs how the three of them constantly went for walks in and around Cracow, to which they had returned from Poronin on October 7, about a week after Inessa had appeared.

In the "ism"-ridden humor of the Bolshevik community in Cracow, two "parties" were identified at this time: the "walkists" and the "cinemists," a schism reflecting the two available forms of diversion. Lenin, Krupskaya and Inessa headed the former faction, and therefore called themselves "anti-cinemists", which they punned into "anti-Semitic."[36] This heavy-handed wit foretold a cruel irony, which none of the Cracow group could guess. A generation later, Zinoviev and Kamenev, who "led" the "cinemist" ("Semitic") group in Cracow, and who were of Jewish origin, were shot by Stalin's police as part of a purge with truly anti-Semitic overtones. In addition to walking, Inessa talked the Ulyanovs into subscribing to a series of Beethoven concerts, but this seems to have turned out rather sourly: "For some reason the music made us terribly miserable, although an acquaintance of ours, an excellent musician [Inessa], was in ecstasies over it," Krupskaya wrote to her mother-in-law shortly afterwards. And even though it does appear that Krupskaya and Inessa had become very friendly in this period, something happened to Inessa's feelings about life with the Ulyanovs. At one point in the fall, Inessa had planned to move from her rented room in the house where the Kamenevs lived to better quarters, and to bring over some of her children. Krupskaya, whose Polish was weak, but better than Inessa's, even helped her look for a place.[37] But in early December 1913 Inessa decided that Cracow was too dull, and she abruptly moved to Paris, staying there, or in a resort on the Dalmatian coast, until the war broke out in August 1914.

Both Lenin and Krupskaya remained in close touch with Inessa by letter during this period. Twenty of Lenin's letters to Inessa, from the time she left Cracow until they all reached Switzerland in 1914, have been published, though none of Inessa's to Lenin have been released (some are known to exist; Krupskaya quoted one in her memorial essay, and Fréville was allowed to see them much later). Bertram Wolfe, in scrutinizing the Lenin-Inessa affair, has pointed out that it was only shortly after Krupskaya died that Lenin's letters to Inessa were published, that parts of some letters are alleged to have been lost, and that Lenin addressed Inessa with the familiar *ty* in these letters, a verbal intimacy that he reserved for only his relatives, and, in his early days, just two of his comrades, Martov and Krizhanovsky. They are mainly concerned with the important role that Inessa played in Bolshevik politics at this time, especially as Lenin's representative in certain fruitless conciliation talks concerning the Mensheviks. The tone of the letters at some points suggest the mood of a man who thinks he has parted on friendly, even paternal, terms, with his love: "I am *very* pleased that you [and here Lenin uses the formal form, *vy*] are entirely well, not sick, and that you [*vy*] are busy. . . . I wish you [*ty*] all the best and the very best."[38]

Or had they parted? On January 5–12, 1914, Lenin visited Paris, without his wife, and while he was there received an invitation from Inessa to give a speech to a meeting commemorating Bloody Sunday, 1905. According to the chronological list of events in Lenin's life, he sent Inessa a letter accepting the invitation, but this letter is for some reason excluded from the "full" collected works, probably to preserve Lenin's privacy.[39] Short as this visit was, it cheered Lenin as few things ever did. "I have been to Paris and not to London and have had quite a good trip," he wrote to his mother (to whom he never mentioned Inessa in any way). "Paris is a very unsuitable town for a man of modest means to live in, and very tiring. But there is no better and more lively town to stay in for a short time, just for a visit, for an outing. It made a good change!"[40]

At this very time, Krupskaya and Inessa were collaborating by mail on a project that Krupskaya had initiated while Inessa had been in Cracow. This was the legal publication, in Russia, of a socialist newspaper for women, to be called *The Working Woman* (*Rabotnitsa*). In a letter to an unidentified underground comrade, asking for help in founding this publication, Krupskaya says that Zinoviev had given special encouragement to the Bolshevik women who were discussing the project: Krupskaya, Zinoviev's wife Lilina, and Inessa.[41] In another letter, to her sister-in-law Anna, who also helped make the arrangements, Krupskaya was glowing in praise of Inessa in particular, whom she called "a still more steadfast person [than Ludmilla Stal', another editor living abroad, a loyal Bolshevik herself] in matters of principle, and who does well everything that she undertakes."

Such admiration is particularly interesting in view of the critical opinions that Inessa expressed on Krupskaya's outline of the first issue and a draft of an appeal for support of the newspaper. Speaking of the latter, Inessa wrote, "We don't like your appeal — I must tell you this," while she completely rewrote the outline. (Inessa mixed *ty* and *vy* in addressing herself to Krupskaya.) Soon, however, both women were in full agreement in their annoyance toward the editors in Russia, Rozmirovich and Samoilova. They omitted Krupskaya's article, which led her to complain (to Samoilova) : "The first number of *The Working Woman* upsets me terribly." Inessa shared the reaction: ". . . it [issue number 2] is altogether empty and in my opinion, in this sense, useless . . . evidently, some conciliators, or even worse, occupy the editorial board [in Russia]." The same letter is particularly interesting because Inessa goes on to demonstrate her close personal feelings for Krupskaya: "how long it is since you [*ty* throughout this letter] have written me, dear one! How shameful for you to have forgotten me and not to have written! Write soon. I recently received a letter from Inessa [her daughter, whose letter is not published] — I am sending it to you; it seems to me that it will interest you, yes, and I want to share my joy with you. The letter is quite bold, it is quite refreshing. Sixteen is a wonderful age — this is indisputable . . . I firmly, firmly embrace you, Inessa." The problems that Inessa and Krupskaya were encountering with their newspaper were soon solved by the police, who arrested the editors in Petersburg. Krupskaya had some desultory correspondence with sister-in-law Anna about the future of the project, but new editors could not be found and the journal languished. It would not be surprising if the whole affair reinforced the ill-feelings between the sisters-in-law, for Anna had been partly responsible for the arrangements in Russia and apparently liked the published results.[42]

In May 1914 the Ulyanovs returned to the rented villa at Poronin, which was considered good for Krupskaya's ailment and was in any case an attractive place to spend a summer. Here it was that the First World War caught the Ulyanovs unprepared, for Lenin had not taken the Serbian crisis seriously enough. He should have, because his presence in Austrian Poland was doubly dangerous. The Russian armies intended to invade this border region, and the *okhrana,* which knew where Lenin was, instructed General Alekseev, the commander of the offensive, to arrest Lenin if possible and send him to Petersburg. To the local Austrian authorities, however, he was a highly suspicious Russian, who had been lurking on their border for several years. On August 8 (N.S.) he was arrested in Poronin and sent to prison in the nearby town of Novy Targ. Lenin was in danger of being shot as a spy of Nicholas II, which would have been a supremely ironic end to his career. There was panic in the area. A local priest told his flock that Russian agents were poisoning wells, Krupskaya learned from a neighbor's six-year-old boy. When Lenin was arrested, a police search showed that he had considerable material on the agrarian question in Austria — obviously strategic intelligence. And to make matters worse the case was transferred to a court martial, which could easily have been more interested in shooting a few "spies" for the good of morale than in making inquiries.

To make matters worse, they had a hired maid who, as Krupskaya remembers it, "had been telling the neighbors all kinds of stories about us and our connections with Russia." Krupskaya got rid of her by sending her to Cracow with wages paid in advance, and then set about trying to get Lenin out of jail. Fortunately, she had the assistance of Jacob Fürstenburg (Hanecki), one of Lenin's most trusted agents at this time and a very shrewd fellow. He threatened the local officials with dire results if anything happened to their distinguished prisoner, a member of the International Socialist Bureau. He arranged for Krupskaya to have visiting privileges at the jail, and began an attempt to mobilize the Austrian Social Democrats to intercede with the government. Among other maneuvers, Fürstenburg and Krupskaya wrote a letter, over her signature, to Viktor Adler, the leading Austrian socialist, who knew Lenin through the International. Adler was the sort of moderate socialist whom Lenin was constantly excoriating. If Adler had been a good "militant" socialist, he probably would have been in jail himself in 1914, but as it was he was a respected member of the parliamentary opposition and Lenin needed his help. He did in fact heed the appeal of Krupskaya (signed "With party greetings, Nadezhda Ulyanova") and persuaded the minister of internal affairs to free Lenin and let him proceed to Switzerland, where it was hoped he could continue to work for the downfall of the Russian government.[43]

After twelve days in jail, during which Krupskaya worked hard packing their things and commuting by rail from Poronin to Novy Targ to visit Lenin, he was released. After a week's journey they arrived in Switzerland, greatly relieved. Throughout the excitement, Krupskaya's aging mother had been unable to grasp what was going on. Part of the time she was convinced that Lenin had been drafted by the Russian army.

The Ulyanovs' third and final sojourn in Switzerland (August 1914–April 1917) was the hardest of all. The war isolated them from other European countries, and Lenin's appeal to turn the war into a civil war alienated most other socialists. Krupskaya's health was intermittently poor, and both their mothers died, Elizaveta Krupskaya in 1915, and Maria Ulyanova in 1916. With the death of these widows, their government pensions ended, removing a source of financial support at a time when Lenin faced the poorest fortunes of his career. He received some hundreds of rubles from his sisters in Russia after his mother's death, presumably an inheritance, but he had three living siblings, and the estate could not have been large. Fortunately, Elizaveta Krupskaya had inherited the substantial sum of 4,000 rubles from one of her sisters, who died in 1913. It represented the life-savings of the deceased, a school-teacher in Novocherkassk, the capital of the Region of the Don Cossack Army. Even though it required an agent's commission of fifty per cent to transfer this money from Cracow to Switzerland in wartime, the remainder was the mainstay of the Ulyanovs' existence until 1917.

With this modest capital, supplemented by some small earnings, they rented a succession of dreary rooms in Berne and (after January 1916) Zurich. The gloom was relieved by summer trips to a hotel in Sörenburg or a simple pension-nursing home at Tschudiwiese, both in the Alps. Without a healthy cook, or a kitchen, most of the time, they generally had frugal meals at boarding houses when not in the Alps. For a while, one of their regular tablemates was a prostitute, which seems to have given Krupskaya a gratifying sense of mingling with the victims of capitalism.

Judging from her memoirs, one of the most cheering features of this difficult period was the comradeship of Inessa Armand. She arrived in Berne in September 1914, and lived just across the street from them in the suburb of Distelweg. The three of them were together much of the time. "Sometimes we would sit for hours on a sunny wooded hillside, Ilyich putting down notes for his articles and speeches, and polishing his formulations, I studying Italian with the aid of a Toussaint textbook, Inessa sewing a skirt in the autumn sunshine."[44] In the evenings they would often gather at the Zinovievs' tiny room in the same neighborhood.

There is little detailed information on the character of the triangle at this time. We do know that when Lenin and Krupskaya moved to the Hotel Marienthal in Sörenburg, around the end of May 1915, they were soon joined by Inessa, and that they stayed there together until the fall, when they all returned to Berne. If Lenin and Inessa had an amorous relationship in this period, Krupskaya left no sign that it bothered her, unless there was an implied dig in the passage in her memoirs that described the idyllic mornings at Sörenburg, Lenin and Krupskaya working diligently, while Inessa (a dilettante?) played the piano.[45] Certainly it was widely taken for granted among socialists who knew Lenin that Inessa was his mistress in 1915. In the opening months of the following year Inessa went to Paris as his agent to contact French members of the anti-war Left, traveling on a passport in the name of "Sophie Popoff," supposedly born in Baku in 1881. The French *sûreté* kept an eye on her and sent reports to the Russian *okhrana,* which show that the detectives did not realize that "Popoff" was really Armand, although they did understand that she went by the pseudonym "Inessa" and that she was *"la maîtresse de Lénine."*[46] The impartiality of this police report cannot be doubted. At the time it never occurred to the French detectives that there was anything sensational involved. The *"maîtresse de Lénine"* reference was simply a matter of identification, and no thought of puncturing future Soviet deification of Lenin could have crossed their minds. Why shouldn't this obscure Russian emigrant have a mistress?

Very likely they were correct, except for timing. When Inessa left Lenin in January 1916, to go to France, she left him forever. When she returned from her trip to France, Inessa did not settle in Berne, but instead moved restlessly among several other Swiss towns, seeing Lenin only once more in Switzerland — at a political conference — before joining him on the famous sealed train across Germany in April 1917. Whatever the reason for this renewed separation, Lenin missed Inessa's companionship and wrote a stream of letters to her in Switzerland, fairly often complaining that he had not heard from her. Clearly he wished that she had stayed. "After the flu," he wrote to her in Paris, in January 1916, "my wife [not 'Nadya'] and I went for a walk on that road to Frau-Kappelle for the first time — do you remember? — we three had wonderful walks there once. I remembered it all and was sorry that you weren't there."[47]

During the war there was no friction between Inessa and Nadezhda in their party work. Inessa, with her fluent French, Russian, German, and English, was especially useful as Lenin's agent on the trip to Paris, which has been mentioned, and as a delegate to various international conferences. One of these was a conference of socialist women in Berne in March 1915. Both Inessa and Nadezhda wrote letters trying to prepare the conference so as to maximize the Left (more or less Leninist) position, Inessa propagandizing Klara Zetkin of Germany and Krupskaya tackling Alexandra Kollontai, a Russian emigrant in Norway, who had close ties with the Left there. And both Nadezhda and Inessa attended the conference as Bolshevik delegates, meeting with some disappointment because a "compromisers'" resolution against the war was adopted over their votes. In a perceptive post-mortem of the conference, addressed to Kollontai, who could not come after all, Krupskaya put a good deal of the blame on Zetkin, who as chairman wavered and then threw her support to the non-Leninist resolution. Later Krupskaya and Klara Zetkin became good friends in the faith, but their relations began on a sour note.[48]

Inessa, but not Krupskaya, also attended a conference of socialist "youth" in 1915, which perhaps suggested an unflattering comparison. But Inessa, at forty, was a pretty implausible young Bolshevik herself, chosen as much because of the absence of any real Bolshevik young people in Switzerland as for her girlish complexion.

Krupskaya alone carried on the regular secretarial functions of the party abroad, and had the satisfaction of being right in the middle of Lenin's web at all times, while Inessa remained on the edge. In particular, Krupskaya reoccupied the post that Inessa had held in her stead a few years before — the secretaryship of the Committee of Emigrant Organizations.[49] As at other times when revolutionary activity in Russia seemed to be at a low ebb, as it did from the outbreak of the war until 1917, the main focus of Lenin's politics lay in the emigrant realm. In this case he was trying to line up as much support as possible for his anti-war, pro-revolution position, and surviving letters show Krupskaya busily concerned with the details of this task. For example, she circularized the Bolshevik emigrant organizations, urging that they support the formation of "Internationalist Clubs" — essentially front organizations to attract the largest possible numbers of anti-war people.[50]

There was also important political work among a special class of "emigrants" — Russian prisoners of war who were interned in Germany or Austria-Hungary. In the short run, these men were incapable of helping the cause of revolution, but they included disillusioned and disaffected victims of the war who were prime candidates for recruitment to the party after their release. Posing as a philanthropic body, the "Commission for the Aid of Russian Prisoners of War" was largely a Bolshevik propaganda organization, of which Krupskaya was secretary and main executive. To keep the prisoners from boredom, books and periodicals were sent to the camps, with German permission. The Germans were ready to cultivate the tsar's domestic foes.

Krupskaya had twenty different prison camps on her mailing list and more than fifty individual prisoners as contacts — mostly Social Democrats, preferably Bolsheviks, who could serve as agitators among their fellows. One of these was Roman Malinovsky, a one-time member of the Bolshevik Central Committee and Duma deputy, who had quit amid charges that he was an *okhrana* agent, and later had become a prisoner of war. Still later, he returned voluntarily to Soviet Russia, despite the knowledge that the Soviet government would by then have the police records. He was tried and shot, despite an appeal to Lenin. Was he an agent, double agent, or triple agent? It is not generally known that Lenin, through Krupskaya, was in touch with Malinovsky during the war (there were five letters from her, presumably eliciting replies), and it could be that a knowledge of this correspondence might help unravel the mystery of Malinovsky.[51]

Another political philanthropy with which Krupskaya worked was the central secretariat of the six funds (*kassy*) for the welfare of the Russian political émigrés in Switzerland. Many were impoverished and tuberculosis was more than ever epidemic among them, so much so that a major enterprise of the funds was an attempt to establish a special Russian sanatorium in Switzerland. Krupskaya took the job as secretary (meaning the main day-to-day administrator) of the central office of the funds with the hope that it would pay a modest salary. It seems to have been disappointing in this respect, for cash was extremely scarce among the Russian refugees, but it did keep her fairly busy.

In October 1916 she traveled to Geneva (without Lenin) for a two-day conference of the funds. There she delivered the main report on the work of the secretariat, noting that this body had started the program for tuberculosis care, that it had attempted to survey the émigré community by means of a questionnaire, and that the establishment of an employment bureau was under consideration. In the version of her report that was copied down by the dutiful *okhrana* agent who was present, she concluded by noting that an employment bureau would be particularly important "because of the possibility, *after the end of the war, of a new, re-enforced emigration.*"[52] Krupskaya was far from expecting the events of the coming year. Still less did she imagine that her prediction would come true "after the war," but that the re-enforced emigration would consist of socialists (among others) who had fled the persecution of a *Bolshevik* government.

As for correspondence with the Russian underground, Krupskaya tried to carry on, but most of the comrades had been arrested early in the war, if not before. We find her complaining to Alexander Shlyapnikov, one of Lenin's chief agents in Scandinavia at this time, that she was getting almost nothing in the way of incoming mail from Russia, even though her letters to and from relatives proved that it was possible for mail to get through.

Throughout the personal and political travail of her second emigration, Krupskaya found some relief in the study of education, her original mission in life. Despite her party work, she often had a good deal of time available, and, being a compulsive worker, she did a lot of reading and some writing on pedagogy. There was plenty to learn. Krupskaya's secondary education and her experience in the school for factory workers had only limited relevance to the mainstream of educational theory and practice. Her task of making up what she had missed was complicated by the vigorous cross-currents of criticism and new theories of education. Although she attended some lectures on education in Paris, Krupskaya coped with this body of knowledge mainly on her own, in libraries and by subscribing to various periodicals. Perhaps the chief monument to her diligence in the decade before the revolution is the twenty-six notebooks on education that she compiled for her own use. They still exist, it is said, in their original blue bindings, but mercifully, they have not been published.[53] From what she wrote for publication, however, it is clear that she read quite widely and with critical intelligence. While Krupskaya does not have a place in the annals of education (outside the Soviet pantheon), either for her creative thinking or for erudition, the fruits of her decade of self-instruction are not negligible.

She learned a good deal about the various ideas that are vaguely described as "progressive education," and she developed her own point of view about them. As one who had been an admirer of Tolstoy's ideas on education, Krupskaya had already rejected "formalism," "routine," "schools separated from life," well before the new German and American schools had reached maturity. Not that she underrated these foreign developments. On the contrary, she clearly had read quite widely in foreign writings (especially German) and was generous in her praise of American public education. She professed great admiration for local, popular control of schools in America and the "brilliant results" of this system, in the "land of highly-developed self-government."[54] Like most progressivists, she favored co-education. She rejected the opinion of one writer, who believed that mixing boys and girls in school would lead to the dying out of interest in sex — one of the few prophecies of doom that can be safely forgotten. Her own theory seems to have been at once "progressive" and conservative (the reverse of "free love") : if boys and girls are not to sleep together, she said, they should work and study together. This, she reasoned, will bring "spiritual nearness" without endangering traditional morality, which she implicitly approved.

Most of Krupskaya's early writings on education were pedagogically radical but not noticeably Marxist. This no doubt reflected her desire to find legal publishers in Russia for her work. Most frequently she sent her short articles to the educational progressive I. I. Gorbunov-Posadov, editor of a magazine called *Free Education* (*Svobodnoe Vospitanie*) — meaning "liberated" education. He had been an active Tolstoyan and one-time director of the publishing organization for which Krupskaya had checked the text of *The Count of Monte Cristo*. His wife, Elena, had been acquainted with Krupskaya in the Petersburg "Union for Struggle" — the Petersburg intelligentsia was a small world. Eleven of Krupskaya's articles, all fairly short, appeared in *Free Education* between 1909 and 1915, and she engaged in an extended correspondence with Gorbunov and his wife. In her letters Krupskaya was the meek novice — "I want to write a lot but I lack self-confidence," she confessed to Gorbunov after he had accepted her first article. A year later she most humbly asked that some kind of cash honorarium could be paid — "our financial affairs are getting worse, and even a small sum would be very timely." She tried, without success, to venture into fiction, submitting a short story called "Lelya and I", based on a childhood friendship with a cousin. She also sounded out Elena Gorbunova on the idea of a longer story on "The History of One Teacher," evidently based on her girlhood acquaintance with "Timofeika," the narodnik rural teacher.[55]

But *Free Education*, or the few other non-socialist journals that accepted bits of her work, were not very satisfactory outlets. By 1912 Krupskaya had turned to the legal Bolshevik press for most of her writings on education, and a more class-conscious note appeared in them.

No specifically Marxist theory of education had yet been worked out, but in 1915 Krupskaya attempted to cope with at least a part of this problem. Whiling away the wartime months in Switzerland, she did some earnest reading in Rousseau, Pestalozzi, and Marx, as well as current pedagogical works on "labor schools" — general education based on the idea that everyone should have practical instruction in manual skills. From this emerged a booklet of 30,000 words, Krupskaya's longest single publication, entitled "Public Education and Democracy" (*Narodnoe obrazovanie i demokratiya*).[56] It is an uninspired essay, heavily laden with quotations and not very cohesive. But it did set forth the basic idea about proper socialist education that Krupskaya held, and fought for, in the last twenty years of her life. The main point was that all schools should include a large dose of physical labor, not to teach any particular trade (only bourgeois trade schools wanted that), but to instil a proper moral attitude toward labor, on which the socialist order must be based. Although Karl Marx, no educationist himself, said very little on the whole topic, Krupskaya could rejoice in his resolution for the first Congress of his International, in which he urged that all people have practical experience of labor from age nine. Relying on some general books by other people, Krupskaya acknowledged that a good deal had been done in this direction in Germany and, especially, America. John Dewey is mentioned in passing as a good influence. But, she concluded, "As long as the direction of schools remains in the hands of the bourgeoisie, the labor school will be a weapon directed against the interests of the working class."

There was not much of a market for her booklet, written in Russian, in 1915. Both she and her husband wrote to Maxim Gorky about it, somewhat diffidently attempting to enlist his help in finding a publisher.[57] At the same time Krupskaya wrote to Gorbunov-Posadov and to both her sisters-in-law about this — all in vain, until the Revolution of 1917 radically changed the atmosphere in Russia. Eventually Soviet educationists decided that the work was a classic, and it was translated into several languages and widely reprinted.

While this booklet was in search of a publisher, Lenin and Krupskaya were also trying to develop a bigger project for her: the editorship of a "Pedagogical Dictionary." The motivation for this was financial rather than ideological. As Krupskaya wrote to Maria Ulyanova on December 14, 1915, "We shall soon be coming to the end of our former means of subsistence and the question of earning money will become a serious one. It is difficult to find anything here. I have been promised a pupil, but that seems to be slow in materializing. I have also been promised some copying [of business correspondence, by hand] but nothing has come of it. I shall try something else, but it is all very problematic. I have to think about a literary income. I don't want that side of our affairs to be Volodya's worry alone. He works a lot as it is. The question troubles him greatly."

"Volodya" was equally enthusiastic about increasing his wife's earnings. He wrote on February 18–19, 1917, to his brother-in-law, Mark Elizarov, overstating Nadezhda's competence to prepare the "Pedagogical Dictionary" and urging that they publish it themselves, "borrowing the necessary capital or finding a capitalist who would come in as a partner in the enterprise." Otherwise, Lenin feared, the publisher would "grab *all* the profit for himself and enslave the editor."[58] This is pretty conventional Marxist economics, and it offered an attractive alternative to revolution: if you can't overthrow the capitalists, become one yourself.

Krupskaya gently chided her husband for this letter when she wrote her memoirs, after his death. She called the plan "fantastic," although at the time she had prepared a draft letter to be sent to some publisher, attempting to sell the idea. And it was an intrinsically sound plan.

Such reference books existed in other languages, and the remarkably rapid growth of Russian public education since about 1906 guaranteed a solid market there for a good pedagogical guide. What seems fantastic today is the notion that Lenin, only *three weeks* before the onset of the Russian Revolution of 1917, had so little idea of what was imminent that he was excited about a purely bourgeois publishing project which would have required years to complete.

Krupskaya was equally unprepared for an early downfall of the Russian autocracy. On March 12, the day that Nicholas II abdicated, we find her writing to a tubercular comrade, who was in a sanatorium for Russian socialists at Davos:

"It is hard to make sense today because of the telegrams that have excited all the Russians here: about the victory of the Revolution in Russia, the seizure of power by the Kadet-Octobrist [liberal] bloc, the three-day battle, and so on. Perhaps it is another hoax, but perhaps the truth. . . ."[59]

A Quiet Revolution

The downfall of the tsar opened the way for Lenin and Krupskaya to return to their beloved homeland, but not without difficulty. The emigrant Bolsheviks in Switzerland were surrounded by two states (France and Italy) that regarded them as traitors to the allied war effort and two other states (Germany and Austria) that considered the Ulyanovs to be enemy aliens. Clandestine travel was not a promising alternative. Since about 1914 Krupskaya seems to have been the main emigrant Bolshevik expert on doctored passports. We find her writing from Poland to Comrade Shklovsky in Switzerland in July 1914, soliciting all possible passports belonging to friends who were residing in Switzerland and therefore not in need of them.[1] During the war she arranged Inessa Armand's phony passport that took her to Paris as Sophie Popoff and later tried to find her one that would get her to Norway or Sweden and perhaps from there to Russia. Inessa even suggested that she borrow Nadezhda's passport, presumably with a new photograph, but Krupskaya vetoed this and nothing came of the whole effort.[2] Lenin thought of trying to obtain a Swedish passport, but Krupskaya persuaded him that this was too risky without a knowledge of Swedish. "Imagine yourself falling asleep and dreaming of Mensheviks, which will start you off swearing juicily in Russian!" she protested.[3] She had reason to think so. A visitor to the Ulyanov hearth at just this time recalls that he arrived to find Lenin reading a speech by the Menshevik Chkheidze, then chairman of the Petrograd Soviet and later Lenin's official greeter at the Finland Station.

"It's simply shit!" Lenin burst out.

"Vladimir! What language!" Krupskaya's phlegmatic voice was heard from the next room.

"I repeat: shit!"

"Vladimir! Don't get excited!"

"Shit!" insisted the furious Lenin.[4]

It remained for the German General Staff, negotiating through Swiss socialists, to arrange their passage back to Russia through Germany and neutral Sweden. When the news that this arrangement had been settled reached the Ulyanovs in Zurich, Lenin insisted on catching the first train to Berne, the collection-point for the car-load of Russian socialists who were to go home. This gave Krupskaya only two hours to wind up housekeeping. Along with the routine chores she wanted to fetch her mother's ashes from the crematorium in order to fulfill a promise that they would be interred in Russia. They never were, although later Krupskaya asked a comrade who was going abroad to place some flowers on her mother's grave.[5] She suggested that she stay behind a day and try to catch up with the expedition in Berne, but Lenin would not hear of this. On March 26 they joined thirty Russian socialists, not all Bolsheviks, who were to make the trip across Germany in the sealed railroad car (that is, they were to be immune from normal border control, and were unable to have any subversive links with German leftists while on German soil). Their friends the Zinovievs were with them, as was Inessa Armand, but her relations with both Lenin and Krupskaya during the historic trip seem to have been rather distant. When they reached Petrograd she left them at once and went on to Moscow.

Judging by Krupskaya's memoirs, the dominant personality during the five-day journey across Germany was the four-year-old son of a Jewish Bundist woman who was in the group. Conversation was trivial, the German meals good. The stopover of one day in Stockholm was a blur in her memory. When at last they crossed from Finland into Russia, Ludmilla Stal was among the greeters who boarded at Beloostrov, near Petrograd, and she urged Krupskaya to say something to the "working women" who were at the station, "but words utterly failed me."[6] Late at night on April 3 she arrived with Lenin at the Finland station of Petrograd, where Lenin was ceremoniously greeted by Chkheidze, representing the Petrograd Soviet of Workers' and Soldiers' Deputies. Krupskaya was greeted by Alexandra Kollontai, who presented her with a bouquet of red roses.

Making speeches to the workers was not the kind of contribution to the revolution that one would have expected from Krupskaya, quite apart from nervousness. For about twenty years her main service to the cause had been in the secretarial field — organization, communications, accounting, records. No Bolshevik could equal her experience in this area, and the party never had greater need of these services. The removal of the autocracy had made Russia the "freest country in the world" (Lenin), or at least the belligerent country with the fewest constraints in its internal politics. All parties, including the Bolsheviks, were free to recruit, organize, and propagandize, and all of the socialist parties could participate in the Soviets that had been elected in all the main cities of Russia. Although Lenin's party was not by any means the largest in the spring of 1917, it was one of the big four (the Constitutional Democrats, Socialist Revolutionaries, and the Menshevik Social Democrats being the others), and it was rapidly attracting new adherents, especially those who opposed continuation of even a "defensive" war. To take advantage of this unprecedented opportunity the leading Bolsheviks who were not in Siberia or in emigration when the tsar abdicated had set up an open headquarters in the large house of the ballerina Mathilde Kshesinskaya in Petrograd, before Lenin returned to Russia. Although the Provisional Government, then headed by Prince George Lvov, was far from wishing to abolish the rights of private property, it ignored legality when it came to the confiscation of buildings belonging to people closely associated with the former court of Nicholas II — and Kshesinskaya had once been mistress to the tsar, who had given her the house. It was not ideally suited as an administrative headquarters, and for a time the secretariat of the party was relegated to a bathroom, but the house commanded a splendid view of the heart of the capital, across the River Neva, and its transfer from the hedonistic Kshesinskaya to the austere Bolsheviks was excellent stagecraft for the opening of a revolution.

Shortly after her return to Russia, Krupskaya did go to work at the secretariat, but in conditions that displeased her and pose a problem for her biographer. Her well-founded claim to seniority in the secretariat was ignored and she was subordinated to Elena Stasova, who was *the* secretary of the party. Stasova was a long-time member of the party, who had been acquainted with Krupskaya even before her marriage (see above, p. 33) , but Stasova had no special accomplishments in her career as schoolteacher, Bolshevik, and political prisoner. When the revolution released her from a term of residence in Siberia and she went to Petrograd, it was not surprising that young Vyacheslav Molotov should invite her to act as secretary. At this stage, in early March 1917, there were few established party members on the scene, and fairly junior people, like Molotov himself (who was not a member of the Central Committee) , had to improvise with whatever personnel could be found. What is surprising is that Lenin failed to place his wife-secretary in her accustomed position in the organization. After all, he was bent on confirming his personal leadership among the Bolsheviks, and he had no qualms about asserting *himself* over Stalin and Kamenev, who had played a leading role for a time after they had been released from Siberia and had bumped Molotov from the top of the party organization in the capital. In fact, in the weeks before Lenin's return, the party leadership of Stalin-Kamenev had taken a definitely un-Leninist line in accepting the Provisional Government and the idea of a defensive war. Lenin might well have felt that he should replace Stasova, the secretary who was working under this leadership, with his wife, claiming seniority on her behalf.

But he did nothing in this direction, and left Krupskaya to receive what seems to have been a deliberate snubbing at the hands of Stasova. In her memoirs, despite their general effort to convey an image of modesty and harmony, Krupskaya could not wholly conceal the rancor that she felt about her treatment in 1917. "I went to work at the Secretariat of the Central Committee in the Kshesinskaya Mansion," she recalled, "but it was nothing like the secretarial job that I had done abroad or that of 1905–1907 when I had done rather important work on my own under Ilyich's direction. Stasova [who, unlike many female comrades, is *never* favorably recalled by Krupskaya] was the secretary, and she had a staff of assistants to do the clerical work. My job involved talking to the party workers who visited us, but I knew little about local activities at that time. Central Committee members often came in, especially Sverdlov. I was a bit out of touch though, and the absence of any definite duties was irksome."[7] The excuse of being "out of touch" is unconvincing. Nobody was fully prepared for the turmoil of 1917, including Stasova, who did not have anything like Krupskaya's accumulation of personal knowledge of party members in all localities in which there had ever been a Bolshevik committee. The real point is that she was shoved aside. Stasova, in her own memoirs, does not even mention that Krupskaya appeared at the secretariat, though she names her four assistants (Menzhinskaya, Slovatinskaya, Pavlova and Itkina) .[8]

Why did Lenin ignore Krupskaya's humiliating position in the secretariat? Conceivably he was too preoccupied by his struggle to convince his comrades of the rightness of his "April Theses," which outlined his open hostility to the new government and the continuation of the war. Conceivably he was not fully aware of the situation, for Nadezhda saw little of her husband from the time they arrived in Petrograd until he became the head of the Soviet state. Their daytime activities kept them apart, and Lenin was rarely at home in their single room in the apartment of his sister Anna and her husband, in which sister Maria was also living at the time.

It seems much more likely, however, that Lenin knew of the situation but was for the moment not inclined to press Krupskaya's claims to seniority over Stasova. A Russian named George Denicke, born in 1887, who joined the Bolsheviks in 1904 and left them in 1917, has an interesting recollection in this connection. In his generally sober and credible memoirs, he recalls that a close friend and party comrade named Pinkevich had chanced to stand beside Krupskaya when Lenin first presented his militant April Theses. "Pinkevich told me that even Lenin's wife, Krupskaya, was scared by the violence of her husband's position. . . . He [Pinkevich] stood beside Krupskaya [during Lenin's speech] who after some time turned to him, obviously scared, and said: 'It seems that Ilyich is out of his mind.' "[9] This is plausible. The April Theses probably came as a shock to her, because Lenin's expressed opinions shortly before they left Switzerland, while predictably hostile to the liberal Provisional Government, did not include the slogan "All power to the Soviets!" If Lenin came round to this stance during the trip to Russia, he told nobody; Krupskaya recollects of the trip that Lenin "withdrew completely into himself."[10]

There is also evidence that, as late as June 6, 1917, Krupskaya was still willing to disagree with Lenin, in public, on the tactics of proletarian revolution. In a party meeting of that date, which considered the desirability of a militant demonstration involving pro-Bolshevik army and navy units, Lenin was enthusiastically affirmative. The possibility of a violent outcome positively attracted him. Krupskaya, however, took the opposite position. Referring to the proposed demonstration, she said "It won't be peaceful, so perhaps it should not take place."[11]

The April Theses advanced an extreme position concerning the continuation of the war, defensive or not. Most Russian socialists and many Bolsheviks were so elated by the replacement of autocracy by a democratic regime that the overthrow of the new government was not regarded as an immediate question. While strongly disapproving of a war of annexation, most Russian socialists initially accepted the premise that the new revolutionary state should defend itself against the Kaiser's army. Kamenev, a friend of Krupskaya, was only the most influential and outspoken Bolshevik to hold this opinion just before Lenin returned. The second article that Krupskaya wrote for *Pravda* upon arriving home suggests that she shared Kamenev's tendency. Her subject was child labor, and reflected her continuing fascination with "labor education." Basically she wanted to forbid hired child labor and *require* socially productive labor of all children aged twelve to sixteen. What is interesting with respect to Lenin's political position is Krupskaya's attitude toward the war. After opening with a good Leninist declamation against the capitalists of all countries, in whose interest the war is being fought, she goes on to say, "We clearly see the task that lies before us — to organize the productive forces of the country. The war sets us this task, it makes it a question of life or death."[12] In other words, despite her conventional Bolshevik antipathy for the "capitalists," Krupskaya was willing to take for granted that the revolutionary country would strive to strengthen its war effort, and this provided her with a pretext for arguing the case for her educational hobby-horse: compulsory "labor education."

If Krupskaya could take this approach to the situation in the country well *after* Lenin had presented his theses, then it is quite possible that she was speaking of herself, among others, a decade later when she wrote in her memoirs: "The comrades [who first heard the April Theses] were somewhat taken aback for the moment. Many of them thought that Ilyich was presenting the case in much too blunt a manner, and that it was too early to speak of a socialist revolution."[13] In short, there is considerable reason to think that Krupskaya wavered in her support of Lenin's ultra-militant position in April 1917, and this could easily have affected his interest in promoting her career in the secretariat. There is even reason to think that Lenin himself snubbed her while she was in the secretariat. According to an unspecified document in the archives of the party, quoted in a Soviet article: "In the secretariat she 'continued in essence to be called Ilyich's private secretary.' "[14] This contradicts Krupskaya's recollection that she was no longer working directly under Lenin as she once had, or that she lacked specific duties. On the contrary, it suggests that she *was* to have been Lenin's personal representative in the party secretariat, a job in keeping with her experience, but that he did not wish to rely on her after their political differences developed.

By late April Krupskaya simply abandoned any attempt to continue her career in the secretariat, and turned to the problems of youth organization and education. In so doing she did not reject the party or Lenin. Her devotion to both was too deep-rooted and she was incapable of imagining any alternative political commitment. But she did not act or write as if she thought that the preparation of a second revolution in 1917 was her main concern.

Quite possibly Krupskaya was asked by Lenin or some party body (one Soviet essay says that it was the party conference that met in late April 1917) to specialize in youth affairs as a way of smoothing her exit from the secretariat.[15] There was as yet no Communist youth organization, and Krupskaya held no formal office, but a good deal of her time in mid-1917 was devoted to youth. With the complete establishment of the right of association, a variety of more or less left-wing youth leagues appeared in Petrograd. At first Krupskaya interested herself especially in one called "Light and Knowledge," which included Bolsheviks, Mensheviks, anarchists, and others. Apparently its homemade program was not revolutionary in a political sense, one of its points being that all members, boys and girls alike, be required to learn to sew. Krupskaya recalls that a Bolshevik boy who objected to this on the grounds that wives would do the sewing anyway was overwhelmed with criticism of his ideas about relations between the sexes.

Krupskaya's writings in 1917 on the question of youth organization were staunchly socialist, inveighing against the "boiskaut" movement and other "chauvinist" youth organizations, but she did not propose a specifically Bolshevik youth auxiliary. Instead, in a draft of by-laws for a hypothetical "Union of the Working Youth of Russia," published in *Pravda* on June 7, 1917, she proposed what might be called a "front" organization. All youth "who live by the sale of their labor" could join the "Union," and no special ties to the Bolshevik Party and its discipline were specified. Apparently she assumed that such a youth organization would have a protracted existence in a "bourgeois" society, for the draft by-laws called for the union to carry on a campaign for a six-hour working day for minors and increased pay.[16] Such goals are reformist, not revolutionary, and they imply that capitalist society would be around for some time: under socialism no such campaign would be necessary, or permitted.

Krupskaya submitted this rather incomplete proposal to a Petrograd city conference of the Party in July, and received the approval of the gathering, which meant very little in practice. The leaders were preoccupied with questions other than youth organization in mid-1917, and Krupskaya was forced to look elsewhere to find an active career of public service at this time.

She found it in the new city district dumas (councils) which were being elected under the Provisional Government to increase popular participation in government. In the elections of June 3-5 Krupskaya ran and won as a Bolshevik candidate for the duma of the Vyborg district, a body of sixty-two representatives in a district of about 170,000. This in itself was no great achievement and not a full-time career, but when the duma met on June 16, she was elected to its seven-person executive committee (*uprava*) as the head of the public education section (soon renamed "culture and education section"). This distinction is easily explained. The Bolsheviks held a majority in the duma in this working-class district and chose only their own for the executive committee — and Bolsheviks with a background in education were rare. Thus it was that Krupskaya from mid-June until the October Revolution was immersed in the problems of developing a new, more democratic network of schools for young and old, reading rooms, nurseries, and parks in the Vyborg district. There already existed a system of public schools, and some other cultural institutions, but Krupskaya was bent on greatly improving the quantity and quality of these amenities, a goal which appeared quite possible without any socialist revolution. True, Krupskaya for years had been making various general statements about the need for a proletarian revolution to build a truly democratic system of education. But when she was faced with opportunities for democratically-based reform, she seemed quite content to apply her devotion and energy to this work, which could be undertaken legally and without delay. When Krupskaya asked a fifteen-year-old Bolshevik named Liza Drabkina to start a playground, the zealous Liza (according to her own recollections) said that she wanted "to complete the revolution, not wipe kids' noses." Supposedly Krupskaya replied with a preachment to the effect that the revolution needed this kind of work, too, in order to show the proletarians of the Vyborg district how the Bolsheviks care for the working people. This is humane and all very well, but it is safe to say that Lenin's ideas about the Bolsheviks' role in 1917 were closer to Liza's (before she succumbed to Krupskaya's sermon) than to his wife's.

Some of the Soviet stories of Krupskaya's work in the cause of public welfare in this period depict her as a kind of weepy sentimentalist who can only be considered the psychological opposite of Lenin, especially during his climactic ordeal of political determination. In another tale, young Liza Drabkina tells Krupskaya how a lad at the playground loved to draw flowers, always with a dirty-blue square above them. Drabkina visited his poverty-stricken home and found that the view from his window was just such a square of blue—the nearest he had come to actually seeing nature. When Drabkina reported this to Krupskaya, "she listened to me, laying her trembling, fine hands on the table, and large, silent tears ran down her cheeks." Another memoirist recalls finishing a soap-box speech at a factory, "And there, trembling, forgetting all words, I saw in the crowd encouraging, pleasant eyes, full of tears. . . . I heard a soft voice saying something, but I was so excited that I don't remember what, but I do remember that because of my inept but sincerely delivered speech N. K. Krupskaya kissed me."[17]

Such stories probably contain a pinch of hokum, but they tend to confirm that Krupskaya was absorbed in her educational work in the Vyborg district. One of her pet projects was the establishment of classes, on company time, for illiterate or semi-literate factory workers in the district — there were said to be eight thousand in the textile plants alone. Another project was the establishment of playgrounds, for which unused land had to be obtained and cleaned up. Still another was the establishment of public reading-rooms (mostly current newspapers and the like), of which there were forty by the October Revolution, and improved libraries. To handle this growing program subsections dealing with extra-school, in-school, and pre-school education, and with libraries and art were established. The cooperation of the industrialists was sought, with some success. Reporting on the work of her organization in a nonpolitical journal, Krupskaya noted that the "Russian bourgeoisie is quickly learning anew in the European mold," which implied some approval for reformist socialism. In one factory the management had donated one hundred thousand rubles for cultural work, though there was a difference of opinion about worker and management representation on the cultural affairs committee that they were forming.[18]

Krupskaya was justifiably pleased with the progress that she was making, and boasted of her district's achievement at a city conference on educational work. Countess S. V. Panina, the most noted philanthropist of public cultural activities in the Empire and a deputy minister of education in the provisional government, reported on the government's work in this field, but admitted that its plans were not being fulfilled. Krupskaya then reported on the fruitful work of her Vyborg district group and concluded "There is what the ministry and the city duma have done, and here is what the public and the Bolsheviks have done."[19]

Another of her activities, quite apart from her post in the district duma committee, was as chairman of the Vyborg district branch of the "Committee for Relief of Soldiers' Wives," which almost smacks of helping the war effort, and is certainly not very Leninist. She took over this job from her old school-friend, Nina (Gerd) Struve, the wife of the now-liberal Peter Struve. Supposedly this work, which was essentially a non-party, welfare activity, helped to introduce Krupskaya to public speaking, as did her educational work, and in her memoirs she pays tribute to the experience.[20]

Yet none of this had much to do with the real business of the Bolshevik Party in 1917: the seizure of power. Krupskaya's involvement with this struggle came mainly as a result of the personal attacks on her husband by his political opponents. Shortly after the time of his arrival, there had been some criticism of his return with German help, especially when he revealed his sharply anti-war (hence "pro-German") theses. Krupskaya did not share his political line in early 1917, but she could not abide attacks on the integrity of her husband. As early as May 13, she had published in the party organ *Soldatskaya Pravda* a biographical sketch of Lenin, entitled "A Page from the History of the Party." While not mentioning Lenin's position in 1917, the little essay was not a bad synopsis of the history of Bolshevism-Leninism before the war, and sought to dismiss the accusations of collaboration with the enemy as simply a disreputable product of class conflict. Her argument faltered when it came to rebutting the accusation that the Germans let Lenin return from emigration because it would be harmful for Russia. In reading the draft of his wife's article Lenin, therefore, made some interpolations, attempting to divert the reader's attention from his own case by noting that other socialists, including non-Bolsheviks, had also come home through Germany and that socialists of neutral countries had made the arrangements.[21]

Soon a much more serious campaign against Lenin, involving formal criminal charges of treasonous relations with the enemy, reinforced her defensive devotion to her husband. In early July, there was a violent demonstration of armed military units in Petrograd. The demonstrators now supported Lenin's slogan, "All Power to the Soviets!" The Provisional Government succeeded in defending its existence, but only with the aid of reports that the upheaval was inspired by the Germans, who were working through Lenin. The state prosecutor tried to bolster this charge with purported documentary evidence. At the beginning of this crisis Lenin and his sister Maria were taking a short holiday not far from Petrograd in the Finnish town of Neivola. Krupskaya recalls in her memoirs, which never intend to emphasize any differences between herself and Lenin, that "I saw still less of Ilyich when I started work in the Vyborg District" (by mid-June). She had been invited on this holiday by Lenin's friend and holiday host, V. A. Bonch-Bruevich, but she chose to stay home.

The July crisis helped to rally Krupskaya to Lenin in spirit, even if events soon separated them. When it became known that there were criminal charges against Lenin, he and his colleagues had to decide whether he should surrender himself and take a chance on his trial, or to go into hiding, which could be seen as an implication of acknowledged guilt. Krupskaya saw Lenin only twice, and briefly, during this crisis, but both meetings emphasized the danger to him and drew them closer. On July 5 she evidently acted as a guide to escort him into the Vyborg district, a working-class quarter that he probably did not know well, where he stayed in an obscure worker's apartment to avoid the police. Then, on July 7, she went with Maria to another apartment, belonging to Sergei Alliluev, Stalin's future father-in-law. Lenin had moved over there, and Stalin was a steady boarder at this time. He was present, along with the Bolsheviks Nogin, Stasova, and Ordzhonikidze when Krupskaya and Maria called. In her memoirs Krupskaya makes this sound like a rather intimate personal meeting. Lenin said that he and Zinoviev would stand trial. "I got up hastily. 'Let's say goodbye,' Ilyich checked me. 'We may not see each other again.' We embraced."[22] With that she went off to convey the news to Kamenev, who was hiding in a nearby apartment. But Lenin thought better of courting martyrdom and reversed his decision later that day. Departing from Petrograd secretly, he went into hiding in the country, just over the nearby border of Finland. From this refuge he supposedly wrote several letters to Krupskaya, but these were not preserved. Soon he moved on to Helsinki, which was practically the capital of a sovereign state by this time.

Meanwhile, Krupskaya was caught up in the government's search for Lenin. On the night of July 7 two military officers came to their room at the Elizarovs and asked if she knew where Lenin was, a question that she could not have answered even if she had wished to, for she did not know of his decision to flee. "They took some notes and documents of mine off the table" — very likely something fascinating on the playgrounds in the Vyborg district. Two days later "a gang of cadets came charging in and ransacked the whole apartment." This time they took Krupskaya, her brother-in-law Mark Elizarov (Anna's husband), and an illiterate servant girl who "had no idea who Lenin was" down to military headquarters for questioning. When it was determined that Lenin was not in the haul, they were released late at night.[23]

Since Helsinki was secure from the Russian police, Krupskaya felt that she could risk visiting her husband there, with elaborate security precautions. Her procedure was to go to the border town of Razliv, and meet the family that had sheltered Lenin before he went to Helsinki. They provided her with the passport of a relative, Avgafya Atamanova, to which Krupskaya glued her own photograph, wearing working-class clothes, a babushka on her head. Thus disguised, she crossed the border into the Finnish forest. A road took her about four miles to a small railroad station where she could catch a train for Helsinki. The first of the two arduous trips that she made had a frustrating conclusion because to find Lenin's room she had to rely on a sketch-map sent to her by him in invisible ink. The paper had been burned while being heated to develop the ink, so Krupskaya had to blunder about the streets of Helsinki, not wishing to ask directions, for some time before she arrived. The second time she almost got lost in the woods at night finding her way to the railroad.[24]

When Lenin returned secretly to Petrograd he put up at the apartment of a young Bolshevik woman named Fofanova. It seems quite possible that he did not at first get in touch with Krupskaya, presumably for reasons of political, not amorous, conspiracy. His wife recorded in her memoirs the impression that he returned to Petrograd on October 7, which is very likely the earliest that she learned of his presence in the city. Others who assisted in the conspiracy, including Fofanova, place the arrival about two weeks earlier.[25] In any case, the absence of stringent police measures against the Bolsheviks on the part of the waning Kerensky government soon convinced whoever was in charge that it was all right for Krupskaya to start visiting her husband at Fofanova's, serving him once again as a courier. Beyond that her contributions to the "Great October Socialist Revolution" were modest. In August Krupskaya was a delegate to the Sixth Party congress, which met in Petrograd while Lenin was away in hiding. However, her only recorded act at this gathering was to sign a petition in which thirty-two delegates protested the late arrival of their comrades at morning meetings. On October 5, she was in a seven-person delegation from the Vyborg district party committee to a meeting with the Central Committee to consider the question of armed uprising. This delegation was solidly for the rising, and one memoirist has her saying a few words in this sense.[26] She was not present at any of the crucial meetings, however, and was certainly not one of the main advocates of Lenin's current tactics, although it is safe to say that she no longer opposed them. When the great event came, and pro-Bolshevik forces seized the key centers of Petrograd, Krupskaya had little to do. It was a hectic time, and her memory of it is rather confused. Apparently she sat around the party headquarters of the Vyborg district during the evening of October 24, while units of Trotsky's Military Revolutionary Committee mobilized for the seizure of the key points in Petrograd. Having nothing to do in the Vyborg district, she went to Fofanova's apartment in the early hours of October 25, only to learn that Lenin had left for the headquarters of the operation at the Smolny Institute. She then returned to the Vyborg district and shortly before or after dawn went off to Smolny in a truck, along with Egorova, who was the district party secretary, Fofanova, and others. There was nothing for them to do at Smolny either, and Krupskaya confesses that she cannot recall whether she saw Lenin there. In her memory the scene is the one usually depicted in dramatic Soviet versions: the

Institute illuminated by spotlights. Actually Fofanova thinks that they arrived well after dawn, which seems much more probable. Krupskaya must have been excited and exhausted at the time, and it would not be surprising if latter-day paintings and films eventually replaced her own confused recollections in her mind's eye.[27] Krupskaya had been a spectator of the Bolshevik revolution, and not one with a very choice seat at that.

Her one specific service to Lenin during the critical days of the seizure of power was domestic. On October 27, she took Fofanova and Maria Ulyanova on a shopping expedition. They returned with a fine overcoat with karakul collar and a winter hat with earflaps, both of which we see on Lenin in many photographs.[28] It appears that Lenin, a bourgeois in his own life-style, wanted to stock up on a few of the amenities of capitalism before he dismantled it.

CHAPTER VII

First Lady

At nine in the evening on Oct. 26/Nov. 8 Lenin addressed the Second All-Russian Congress of Soviets and, along with his decrees on peace and land, announced the composition of the executive organ of the Soviet government.[1] This was the Council of People's Commissars, and its chairman (in essence the prime minister) was "Vladimir Ulyanov (Lenin)." His long and often discouraging struggle to take power in the name of the workers had succeeded. He was the head of the world's first self-proclaimed socialist state and his wife Krupskaya was transformed from an obscure female Social Democrat to "first lady" of the Soviet Republic. But how was this role to be played? Nobody had given any advance thought to this minor question, but it was immediately assumed that the old aristocratic and bourgeois customs were finished. Women were comrades, not decorative possessions now, and an experienced party member like Krupskaya could better serve the cause as a responsible official in her own right than by shaking hands in reception lines. In mid-1919 when a British newspaper reporter interviewed Krupskaya and then wrote an article in which he called her Soviet Russia's "first lady," Lenin professed to be highly amused that his wife should be given this bourgeois dignity. According to Krupskaya's secretary, he took to calling her "first lady" (in English) when they were at home, as if to emphasize how ludicrous it was to think of his workaday spouse in so frivolous a role.[2]

He was right. Krupskaya rarely appeared as "first lady" in any conventional sense. She witnessed her husband's self-proclamation as head of state from an obscure seat in the Congress of Soviets, ignored by the multitude, and in the early weeks of Soviet rule she did not even live with Lenin, who had taken up a modest room next to his office in the Smolny Institute, the Soviet command post. A month after the Bolsheviks came to power she still gave her residence address as "Petrograd, Petrograd Side, Malyi Pereulok (Little Lane) number 256, Apartment 5."[3] When Krupskaya moved into these humble quarters is uncertain, but it must have been after Lenin had fled to Finland in July, offering her a welcome opportunity to cease being the guest of her sister-in-law Anna. Only by the close of 1917 is it clear that she was back with Lenin as his wife. The two took a brief vacation in a nearby health resort in Finland on December 24–27 and on New Year's Eve Krupskaya accompanied Lenin at a public appearance at a huge workers' party in the Vyborg district.

When the government moved to Moscow in March 1918, the couple lived temporarily in the Hotel National, close to the Kremlin; then they moved inside the walls of that ancient fortress. Their apartment, now preserved as a Lenin shrine, proved to be Krupskaya's home for the remaining two decades of her life. This was the only period in her entire life when she had a really stable residence, and she seems to have been much attached to the four modest rooms that were converted into living quarters for Lenin, his sister Maria, and herself. Though the Kremlin walls enclose a variety of ornate and ceremonial buildings, it had not been a residence of the tsars for a long time, and the apartment of the new chief of state was a cramped and partly improvised affair. Ironically, Lenin and Krupskaya may have had slightly more floor space in their quarters when they were the tsar's convicts, living in Siberia, than when Lenin became the tsar's successor, living in the Kremlin. Here they each had a cubicle of a bedroom with a metal-frame, single bed, a dresser, hard chair, and desk-table.

The apartment was a third-floor walk-up, though the high ceilings in the old buildings made this the equivalent of a five- or six-story climb, which caused Lenin some concern for his wife's heart. He talked of an elevator, but for several years none was installed. The dining room in the suite was a converted hallway. There was really no place to receive visitors with the slightest formality, which mattered little because only a few friends or colleagues and very few outsiders were admitted at any time. Often Krupskaya or Maria served tea for them, but she never faced the conventional task of playing hostess to a state reception or banquet. The years of Lenin's personal rule in Russia were lean ones, and an austere style of life was becoming to the head of state. But one suspects that Krupskaya especially would have preferred much the same austerity in any event. A degree of asceticism was a matter of moral principle with her, the more so since she had become a public personage. In matters of dress this principle seems to have required not merely frugality but downright scruffiness. Photographs of Krupskaya in the early Soviet years indicate that she did add to her wardrobe one moderately stylish belted overcoat and a modish hat, but mostly we see her in a light-colored, shapeless, long-sleeved dress reaching to her ankles or a very rumpled, striped, two-piece outfit with baggy pockets in a tunic and again a long skirt.

The new life did include some servants, although the only one of these to achieve any special place in the family was Lenin's chauffeur S. K. Gil', who often picked up Krupskaya at her office at the end of the day's work. He was a bodyguard of sorts, the only one continually attached to Lenin, though there were always military guards and chekists (political police) around Lenin's residence. For her part, Krupskaya seems never to have been especially protected. There must have been a cook or two somewhere near the apartment, and Krupskaya recollects having a Latvian woman as temporary household help in 1918; she was distinguished only in that she locked herself up and wailed during a crisis. According to Trotsky, he shared a dining room with the Ulyanovs when the government first moved to Moscow, and both families were served by an aged retainer of the Romanovs who reverently turned the plates so that the double-headed eagle on the crest faced the diner. But when Lenin's apartment was fully prepared, they left this anachronism, plates and all, with the Trotskys.

Only through her work did Krupskaya acquire a personal helper, a young woman named Vera Dridzo, who became her secretary in June 1919. The two were almost constantly together for the rest of Krupskaya's life, and Vera lived on through another generation, to become the chief curator of Krupskaya memorabilia at the Institute of Marxism-Leninism after Stalin died. There was real affection between the two, and Dridzo seems to have been as much companion as secretary. She was one of the few people to have dinner with the Ulyanov household from time to time. No doubt Vera helped with many chores, but she never seems to have taken on any serious responsibility, such as ghost-writing. The diligent Krupskaya never wanted a strong and capable assistant to whom she could delegate serious jobs. In photos Dridzo looks like an exceptionally hearty and cheerful sort, and seems to have been totally loyal to her mistress, which was quite enough.

There was one other companion in the Kremlin household, a cat (nameless to history), the Ulyanovs' first pet since they left Siberia. At least one American reporter, Lincoln Eyre of the *New York World,* maintained that Lenin had many cats, but when Louise Bryant, who was John Reed's widow, brought up this weighty matter (and not much else) in an interview with Krupskaya in 1920, assurance was given that there was but one cat. Therefore the scholar may safely assume either that Eyre was bent on *slandering* Lenin, or that the Ulyanov cat had been receiving visitors during Eyre's visit.[4]

Despite the informality of Krupskaya's life as first lady, there was one occasion in the early weeks of the Soviet regime when she did attend a state affair in a conventional ceremonial way. This was the long-awaited day in the mythology of the revolutionary movement — the time when a democratically elected body would meet to give Russia a constitution. The Bolsheviks had competed with other political parties in the election of this Constituent Assembly, which was held in November 1917. Krupskaya had been nominated by her party as one of their numerous candidates, but she had been put on the ballot in the Viatka district. The Socialist Revolutionary Party was predominant in this mainly peasant region, not far west of the Ural Mountains, so she had no real chance of election.[5] In fact, the assembly was dominated by the Socialist Revolutionary Party, and Lenin was prepared to dissolve it by force when it convened on January 18, 1918, in the Tauride Palace in Petrograd. At the same time he seems to have kept open until the last minute the option of salvaging something from this body, such as the passage of a resolution legitimizing his October Revolution. So it was that he attended the opening session of the Constituent Assembly, arriving with some pomp as head of the government, accompanied in a limousine by his wife and sister. Apparently he felt that this was essentially a "bourgeois-democratic" occasion, which should be faced in the style of a bourgeois premier, accompanied by his "first lady." Soon, however, Lenin led a Bolshevik walkout on the affair, not long after his opponents had taken control of the proceedings. The Bolshevik "guards" in the hall turned out the delegates late at night, and that was that. In the next few years, Krupskaya appeared very rarely with Lenin in such a ceremonial wifely capacity, the most memorable occasion being the opening of a rural electric power plant.

Her idea of an appropriate role for the "first *woman*" (Louise Bryant's variant on the phrase) was one of hard work in the service of the revolutionary state. Like most of the wives of leading Bolsheviks at this time, Krupskaya wanted to do her bit to support a regime that was based on a very small political party and, within it, an almost infinitesimal elite of experienced followers of Lenin. Also like the other Bolshevik women, she was content to allow the men to run the most important organs of power, such as the Council of People's Commissars, the Central Committee and the Political Bureau. Instead, she devoted herself primarily to the area that had been her interest for so many years and had been her main occupation in the summer and fall of 1917, education.

If the heavenly city of Communism could have been entered by dint of Krupskaya's labor, Russia would have become the world's first perfect society years ago. Despite chronic ill health, she hurled herself at a furious pace into the impossible task of designing and constructing a humane, cultivated, socialist system of education in a country that was economically ruined, racked by civil war, and ruled by an increasingly inflexible and dogmatic bureaucracy. And as she approached it, education included not only schools, but also continuing adult education, the "liquidation" of illiteracy, the emancipation of women, the development of libraries, the Communist youth movement, "proletarian culture," the elimination of religion, and the organization of political propaganda.

A great part of her energy was devoted to the spoken and written word. Krupskaya, who had written little for publication and had hardly ever spoken in public before the age of forty-eight, was a prolific author and orator in her remaining two decades of life. She felt a compulsion to sluice the flow of progress with a flood of words, and as an important personage she did not lack publishers or audiences. On the contrary, much of the most redundant droning in her almost ceaseless writings and speeches may be blamed primarily on zealous Communist officials who appealed to Krupskaya's revolutionary conscience for pot-boilers. Still, her emphasis was certainly on quantity rather than quality. The laborious, but incomplete, Soviet bibliography of her published writings shows about two thousand entries between the October Revolution and her death, and her much less complete *Pedagogical Works* contains over seven thousand mind-boggling pages of her output in the educational field alone. None of this was originally written in the form of a complete book, but the accumulation of articles on one subject or another eventually led to the creation of an assembly line of Krupskaya anthologies. Her official bibliography lists fifty-six book-size collections of Krupskaya's own composition published between 1918 and her death in 1939 and another twenty-eight between that event and 1967 (not counting separate editions of the same anthology or anthologies of someone else's work, compiled by Krupskaya, of which there are a number). Like many active evangelists, she had no compunction about repeating herself again and again and again. While Lenin ruled Russia, the subject matter was overwhelmingly education, and a large portion of it appeared in periodicals over which she had effective editorial control, such as *Narodnoe Prosveschenie (Public Education) Vneshkolnoe Obrazovania (Adult Education)* or *Kommunistka (The Communist Woman)* with a goodly smattering of articles in *Pravda,* the organ of the party, on which her sister-in-law Maria, held an important editorial post. These circumstances, not to mention her position as Lenin's wife, were assurance against any critical check on the compulsive flow of earnest, lifeless verbiage. Although much of it could be churned out without the slightest new thought, Krupskaya usually cannot be accused of writing from ignorance. Her numerous published book reviews testify to her diligent reading of an imposing number of professional works on pedagogy in Russian, German, French, and English. One luxury she did enjoy in her eminence was a personal library that eventually comprised twenty thousand books. Lenin also reveled in this privilege and had a personal librarian who also helped Krupskaya. Her reviews were not all pedagogical. On one occasion she took time off to whack a distinguished historian, Rozhkov, for writing "slanderous rubbish" about Lenin's *What Is to Be Done?* in a history of socialism, on another to praise John Reed's *Ten Days That Shook the World* (for which she also wrote an introduction), or even, once, to review a play that she had seen, or to write a short homily on the virtues of Soviet medical services.[6]

Her speeches were about as prolific as her writings. Her audiences in the Lenin years of Soviet Russia ranged from the august Tenth Party Congress (1921) and Fourth Congress of the Communist International (1922) down to the obscure "second conference of heads of adult education sub-offices of provincial offices of public education" (1919). In addition, she sat through many lengthy meetings without giving an address, including party and Comintern congresses and the Supreme Soviet.

While she was generally kept busy with the many meetings that were held in Moscow, Krupskaya on one occasion carried her evangelism into the countryside. This was a six- or seven-week trip by rail to Nizhnii Novgorod (now Gorky) and thence by river steamer down the Volga and up the Kama to Perm. This was no ordinary steamer but an *"agitparakhod"* (agitation steamboat) with a sizable crew of party workers headed by young Vyacheslav Molotov, no friend of Krupskaya, it seems. Towing a barge that was set up to show outdoor movies, they steamed by night and preached by day in July and August 1919. We are told that Krupskaya made thirty-four speeches during the trip, despite illness and oppressively hot weather. She was, in fact, supposedly taking a rest, but could not turn down a plea to speak to the masses. To her friend Zinaida Krizhanovskaya she wrote that she tried to rest, but then "they send me a note from the river transport workers: 'let her only say two words, and if she can't speak to us, let her only show herself.' Well, one has to go and speak."[7] On one occasion she agreed to speak to an artillery battery, but instead found an audience of six thousand Red Army soldiers, to whom she tried to say something without the benefit of sound amplification. It probably did not matter much. The ordinary listener in this backwater was impressed enough to have seen the wife of the great Lenin — impressed too by her careless courage, if he considered that part of the area she entered had been occupied by the Whites not long before and for a still longer time had been a stronghold of the Socialist Revolutionary Party, which had included a terrorist wing.

Her prestige no doubt helped to compensate for lack of rhetorical talent. Krupskaya has never been credited with a good speaking voice and rarely had anything new to say, but she *was* Lenin's wife and usually was brief by Soviet standards. Limited stamina and reticence on the platform, which she says she struggled to overcome in her early years as a speaker, may have been an asset after all.

However strenuous, this evangelical effort was only one aspect of Krupskaya's work. Much of her writing and speaking grew out of an active career as an administrator. The Bolsheviks had only a tiny handful of reliable personnel to spread thinly over an immense government apparatus. A person with Krupskaya's background could scarcely avoid a senior appointment, though she professed to wish it were otherwise. In a letter to her former publisher, the Tolstoyan educational-reformist, I. I. Gorbunov-Posadov, she wrote in November 1917, "It has come about that I am the directing commissar for adult education. I do not like centralist work very much, but personal taste cannot be one's guide today, and it was impossible to decline this work."[8] She was right, for the party could not find any other senior Bolshevik to take a leading post in the Commissariat (ministry) entrusted with reshaping education in the interests of socialism. This was "Narkompros," the Russian acronym for "People's Commissariat of Enlightenment" ("enlightenment" was a synonym for education already in common use in Russian administration). The "Narkom" or commissar was Anatole Lunacharsky, a cultivated, goateed, pince-nezed intellectual with fuzzy ideas on educational reform and little talent as an administrator. Lunacharsky proved remarkably durable in his office, which he held until 1929. Krupskaya and Lunacharsky worked closely in these years and fought a long, hard, and eventually futile battle for the reformist educational creed that they shared. A professional friendship based on mutual respect, despite some differences, grew up between them. The association began a few days after the establishment of the new regime, when Lenin saw his new-fledged People's Commissar of Enlightenment in the corridor at Smolny and told him to take on Krupskaya as one of his deputies. He did so, appointing her "directing commissar" for the adult education department and a member of the "collegium" or executive committee of the whole commissariat. Between March and November 1918, Krupskaya ran the whole affair. In this period the Soviet government had moved to Moscow, while Lunacharsky (with typical impracticality) preferred to remain in Petrograd. When the move to Moscow took place in March Krupskaya assumed the title of "deputy narkom," but in May she dropped this rank, apparently out of modesty.[9]

It is not easy to appraise her work as an active administrator. There is no question that she was diligent, arriving early in her Moscow office in the mansion that had been expropriated for the commissariat and sometimes leaving only after Lenin had telephoned from the Kremlin that he would not eat supper without her. Vera Dridzo recalls that it was only by deceit that the staff of the commissariat prevented Krupskaya from turning up for the weekly cleaning sessions at the office that were held in the guise of *subbotniki*. These were voluntary working Saturdays that the Soviet state encouraged in its early years. Krupskaya thought it her duty to pitch in and called her colleagues "conscienceless deceivers" when she learned that the work had been done in her absence.

Vera and other admiring memoirists recall Krupskaya's unassuming manner as a senior bureaucrat. One anecdote has it that a pompous official in her commissariat stormed in, demanding that he be supplied with a desk, to which Nadezhda disarmingly replied, "Take mine, I'll fix up something." She must have gained some reputation as a leading Bolshevik to whom supplicants might come. In at least one case she induced Lenin to advise the secret police to reconsider the case of a professor of geology whom they had arrested. Krupskaya had known him in the 1890's and vouched for his integrity. The son of one beneficiary of her help later published Krupskaya's letters, in which she went well out of her way to be accommodating. First Krupskaya found the supplicant, a girl of 19, a job in a major government office. Upon a further request she sent the help-seeker a requisition on the Moscow Soviet, signed by Lenin himself, for warm clothing, and still later, after the help-seeker had married and given birth to a son, Krupskaya made arrangements for the young mother to recuperate in a sanatorium. This, for the daughter of a man she had merely known briefly as a colleague in 1917. On other occasions she induced Lenin to write to the Tambov authorities to see that an old woman and her daughter who had once been acquainted with her were saved from starvation, and she attempted to obtain financial support for two of her old friends in the movement, Klasson and Kalmykova.[10] Lenin accepted her special role as an intercessor on behalf of the needy. When Krupskaya was cruising on the river steamer he wrote, "I read the letters asking for help that sometimes come for you and try to do what I can."[11]

But Krupskaya developed a tougher, more practical side, too. When she went to work at Narkompros, she was all for minimizing central authority. Again and again in 1917–18 she stressed that the control of schools should be in the hands of ordinary people on the local level. Her first official act on November 25 was to convene an open conference of persons interested in working in adult education. In her address Krupskaya told the meeting she planned on no strong central authority, and a voluntary "Society for Cooperation with Adult Education" was established (on paper only) as an alternative to bureaucratic activity.[12] In the same week she privately invoked the name of Tolstoy as a guide to her new work. ". . . It is such a pity that Leo Nikolaevich is not alive!" she wrote to Gorbunov-Posadov, little thinking what the pacifist anarchist would have said about Lenin's regime. Within the school system Krupskaya hoped to realize her democratic goals through a new body, the "educational soviet" (council), which would exist apart from the local Soviet government in each locality. The educational soviet was supposed to have much in common with the American system of elected boards of education. This fits in well with Krupskaya's pedagogical Americanism, which was at its peak in the early months of the Soviet era. She cited Horace Mann with admiration because he had taken education out of the control of the state in Massachusetts. In democratic America, she believed, teachers were elected by the people. "The new Russia needs schools of the American type."[13] To be sure, her educational soviets were to represent democratic interest groups, such as teachers and trade unions, rather than simply voters in general, but the ideal of local, popular self-rule in education was clear, even if Krupskaya's understanding of America was not.

Experience eroded such idealism. In the next few years Krupskaya became painfully aware that the people were not really fulfilling the desired reforms on their own (though she tended to blame officials and reactionary teachers). In the course of her trip on the agitation steamboat in mid-1919 she wrote to her friend Zinaida Krizhanovskaya, with urgent underscoring, that they needed to deal with the provinces with *"more authority, not fearing to interfere* [in provincial educational affairs] . . ."[14] By 1920, her main concern had shifted from local autonomy to the problem of efficiency at the center. In a draft on administrative reform in the commissariat, which showed sound concern for such matters as clear division of responsibility, Krupskaya called for the study of two possible sources of help: one was the American efficiency expert

Frederick W. Taylor and the other, "the experience of the old apparatus [tsarist bureaucracy]. Not everything in it was bad. For example, there were tables of organization (*shtaty*). The bureaucracy reduced these to something formal and senseless, but what are tables of organization in essence? They are the division of functions, and this is something very good."[15]

Only a rough education in the facts of life and power could have led Krupskaya from her Tolstoyan ideas of educational self-rule to the tsarist model of strong central authority. In the transition her character as a bureaucratic politician had hardened, too. In conflict with other Soviet administrators she had learned the necessity of trying to defend her own interests. Even though she was Lenin's wife, there were plenty of tough Communist bureaucrats who had no use for her ideas on education or challenged the authority of her particular office. They did not treat her with undue respect in debate (once she was called a *narodnik*) and she had to fight for the power she enjoyed. Only a Stalin could win the ultimate jackpot in such games, but Krupskaya learned to maneuver and attack with verve. She was not above using her special position to appeal directly to the Central Committee of the Communist Party on behalf of her commissariat (thus avoiding "proper channels"), or to try to bring Lenin in on her side (as will be seen, this could be disappointing). Opponents could feel the sting of her reproach; for example, "If O. Schmidt [not the polite "Comrade" Schmidt] even slightly interested himself in questions of the history of the labor school, he would know . . ." etc., etc. "But what has that to do with O. Schmidt!" This particular opponent lost his job with Narkompros by a decision of the Central Committee two days after Krupskaya's assault.[16]

It must be admitted, however, that her most ambitious play for expansion of her bureaucratic empire was a failure. This was an attempt to concentrate the entire Communist propaganda machine in the adult education department of Narkompros, which was, of course, Krupskaya's domain.

The original initiative for this power play came not from Krupskaya but from a party official named E. A. Litkens, who joined the Narkompros in the fall of 1920. He had no real interest in education and was assigned to Narkompros to reform its inept administration. In attempting this he dealt directly with Lenin on several occasions, which must have rankled Krupskaya. She retaliated by using her unique position to persuade Lenin that Litkens' over-all plan was unsuitable.[17] Somehow he failed to realize that this seemingly modest woman could and would react any time he crossed her. In late 1921, for example, Litkens tried to have one of her main assistants at the ministry, L. G. Shapiro, fired for alleged political unreliability. Again Krupskaya took the matter straight to her husband, who wrote a letter in defense of the man, warning against "intrigues."[18]

But this personal feud did not prevent Krupskaya from seeing merit in Litkens' plan to transform the "modest adult education section," as she later called it, into the kingpin of the whole Soviet propaganda system. Along with Litkens she argued for this proposal at a Politburo meeting and also campaigned for it in a series of articles.[19] With or without Lenin's forceful intervention on behalf of the scheme, it prospered. The adult education section, mellifluously renamed Glavpolitprosvet (Main Committee of Political Enlightenment), was increasingly regarded by the party authorities as the chief propaganda center, and in late 1920 or early 1921 they subsidized its budget to the tune of a million rubles.[20] At some point in 1921, Krupskaya later claimed, its organization comprised 475,000 people.[21] Best of all, she had kept that wretch Litkens from maneuvering her out of the top job in the agency. He must have tried something of the sort, for the "collegium" (executive committee) of Glavpolitprosvet had lacked a chairman from its creation in the fall of 1920 until March 1921, even though Krupskaya had an obvious claim to the job as head of the adult education section. By one means or another, however, she succeeded in getting the post in

March. Litkens apparently felt defeated at this point and wrote Lenin that he did not think that Krupskaya wanted him in Glavpolitprosvet. But she told Lenin that she was really *in favor* of his working there — a rather disingenuous attitude now that she was in charge.[22]

It was one thing for Glavpolitprosvet to get Central Committee support as the propaganda center, but something else actually to wrest authority away from powerful government agencies that had vested interests in the field, especially the trade unions and the army. Krupskaya tried to gain ground in this struggle at the Tenth Party Congress, which met in March 1921. It was her first real speech to a party congress, and the only she made in Lenin's lifetime at such an august gathering.[23] In it she argued for the need to eliminate duplication of effort by several agencies, to coordinate their work better. To do this the trade unions, army, youth movement, and other agencies should, in effect, subordinate their propaganda activities to her. True, she maintained that it was a question of coordination rather than subordination but it is pretty clear where the authority was to lie. Mindful that she was addressing not educational reformers but tough-minded party officials, Krupskaya presented Glavpolitprosvet as an ideologically militant body. It had a high percent of party members in it, she argued, it worked under the directives of the party, and it proffered *Communist* enlightenment to the masses.[24]

In this Krupskaya had to watch her step. Some rivals had argued that such enlightenment should be directed by the "agit-prop" section of the Central Committee itself, rather than a branch of the education ministry. Mindful of the threat, Krupskaya argued that her agency was better equipped with personnel and local organizations than the party itself, in this particular specialty.

As it turned out Krupskaya and Glavpolitprosvet were tackling too many powerful adversaries in the bureaucracy. Worse, Glavpolitprosvet was hit by a general tightening of the budget as part of the country's badly-needed attempt at economic revival (the so-called New Economic Policy) and in response to famine conditions in later 1921 and 1922. Krupskaya's agency, once rapidly inflated, collapsed abjectly. The staff shrank to 10,000 in the whole country and the party subsidy was cut off. Still worse, the masses, whom Krupskaya had long idealized, made no protest at the loss of the "enlightenment" — "a bitter lesson", she admitted (and one more blow to the old Tolstoyan-democratic ideal of letting the people administer their own education).

Admitting disaster, she bravely concluded a speech to the tattered remnants of her agency in 1922, "We know that our work is important, and a temporary defeat does not upset us."[25] Unfortunately, it turned out to be more than temporary. While Krupskaya continued to serve as head of Glavpolitprosvet until its dissolution in 1930, it remained a third-rate agency and her authority as a bureaucrat never recovered.

It is not surprising that Krupskaya's own education in bureaucratic politics should have brought out an increasingly tough-minded attitude toward civil liberties in general and intellectual freedom in particular. Despite her long years as a Leninist, she did not come to the October Revolution with a very realistic idea of "the dictatorship of the proletariat," but she learned.

There was no question in her mind about the rightness of exclusive Bolshevik rule, but she resisted the early signs of the police state that accompanied it. In the spring of 1918, for example, reports reached Krupskaya that local party officials were abusing the principle of election of teachers by local educational soviets, which had recently been decreed as part of the new, democratic order. Actually educational soviets scarcely existed, but local government officials were using the decree as an excuse to purge the teaching profession (albeit without physical violence). At a meeting of the Narkompros collegium Krupskaya complained that "The teachers are being cross-examined about their beliefs in a most detailed way, which is an inadmissible violation of freedom of conscience . . . a most unjust form of the principle of local re-election of teachers." Later in the year she again acted through the collegium to protest to the Cheka concerning the arrest of leading members of the non-Communist teachers' union, insisting either that definite charges be laid or that the prisoners be released.[26] This was an especially liberal step because Krupskaya, along with the rest of the Narkompros leadership, was definitely opposed to this union, which had been highly uncooperative. She had actively supported efforts to get rid of the anti-Soviet leadership of the union but scrupled to do this by police action.

At the beginning of 1919 Krupskaya continued to oppose the appearance of an intellectual dictatorship. It seems that Narkompros had been criticized in some official circles because it had published the complete works of the poet V. A. Zhukovsky, who had died in 1852 at a great age. These included the words of the hymn "God Save the Tsar," which some critics considered dangerous monarchist propaganda. With creditable commonsense, Krupskaya ridiculed this fear on the pages of *Pravda*. The people are not mere children, she argued, and it is foolish to say that they should be allowed to read nothing but "agitational literature, about the priest, the kulak and so on." It was simply "funny" to fear Zhukovsky's political influence. She ended by directly attacking no less a figure than the deputy chief of the Cheka, Ya. Kh. Peters, something few persons in Russia would have dared to do. She derided his alleged wish to destroy all the libraries because they contained the works of Pushkin, replacing such "bourgeois" culture with some kind of "socialist encyclopedia." As if this were not enough, she pointed out that Peters had recently prepared some didactic manuscript which had been rejected because of its low quality. Krupskaya preferred the classics to poor socialist literature, she said.[27]

As late as December 1919, she opposed the establishment of a literary section of Narkompros with dictatorial authority. In a memorandum to the collegium she maintained that the proposal would place "great power in the hands of a handful of men, power to strengthen their own literary tendency." It was impossible to determine what was good proletarian literature, she felt. "Only the reader may determine the significance of a writer. That is how it must be. . . . Organization is necessary, and let it [the collegium of the new literary section] be nine men, but they must have much less power. They cannot take under their monopolistic influence the unions, associations, clubs, and circles. All these organizations must have the right to self-determination."[28]

The trouble with freedom is that people persist in using it to do inconvenient things. Krupskaya seems to have been pressed to the conclusion that her scruples about intellectual liberty were getting in the way of the building of socialism. As early as her trip on the river steamer in the summer of 1919 she had reacted unsympathetically to teachers who had "shed crocodile tears about the Cheka, arrests. . . . [and] babbled on about freedom of the press."[29] By late 1920 her concern for the autonomy of diverse intellectual trends had yielded to the conviction that only a strong central authority could get things done the right way. Since 1918 there had existed on the fringes of Narkompros a non-party association called "Proletkult," inspired by various left intellectuals who sought to encourage real proletarians to invent new art forms. Krupskaya had never been very happy with this, but had generally avoided a major collision with Lunarcharsky, who was rather well disposed toward Proletkult. By 1920, however, she had had enough. She flatly stated that Proletkult had taken the wrong path. Forgetting her former skepticism concerning the possibility of bureaucratically defining proletarian art, she left no doubt that she expected Proletkult to subordinate itself strictly to her own agency, Glavpolitprosvet.[30]

But the most striking outcome of Krupskaya's deliberalization was in the field of library administration, which also fell under the authority of Glavpolitprosvet. Between late 1920 and early 1924 she signed three directives on the censorship of Soviet libraries.[31] These documents came pretty close to ordering the destruction of their "bourgeois" content, in the spirit of the Chekist Peters. The excuse was "the simple protection of the interests" of the masses. The range of intellectual pitfalls faced by the unenlightened now seemed vast. To cope with these dangers it was necessary to consider six broad categories (said the directive of 1923): philosophy; religion; social science; natural science; history-literary; history-geography; and belletristic and children's literature.

It is not surprising to find Krupskaya taking a hard line on religion. Anti-religious education was one of her specialties. In 1919 a proposal to readmit priests to peasant schools to give religious instruction outside of class hours aroused her to write directly to the Central Committee in anguished protest.[32] But it comes as something of a shock to find her advocating the removal of all belletristic and children's books "that may arouse, strengthen, or develop mean, brutal, egotistical, or anti-social feelings." Considering her previous scorn for the chekist Peters, it is also remarkable that the directive orders that the purge commissions include a representative of the secret police (now called GPU), if no representative of the Main Literary Administration is available. This would no doubt be the norm outside a few large cities. The whole directive is couched in such general terms that some specific illustrative guidance was plainly needed. For this purpose some official composed a list of books that had to go. In doing so he exceeded Krupskaya's wishes in some respects. Not only were Plato and Kant to be suppressed, but also Tolstoy, of all people. The supreme irony was that the list called for the removal of *all* books sponsored by *Posrednik* ("The Intermediary"), the Tolstoyan project for which the teenage Krupskaya had corrected the translation of *The Count of Monte Cristo*. The entire series of the supplement to the journal *Niva* was also proscribed. This was the principle publisher of inexpensive editions of Russian literary classics, and its removal would have denuded the humbler libraries. Word of this program against books caused an outcry abroad and even in Russia, and Krupskaya felt obliged to explain the directive to the readers of *Pravda*.[33] She squarely took responsibility for the directive itself, as its prime signatory (though not as author), while maintaining that the attached list had been a mistake and that she had withdrawn it as soon as it became known to her. Plato and Kant could be left alone, she explained — the masses won't read them anyway. Nor had she ever wished the suppression of Tolstoy, despite his religious errors. On that point, she went over to the offensive: the list was not tough *enough* on religious books, and the real mistake was not the overzealous list but the view expressed by one library administrator who had written that the party need not oppose "religion that is completely free of superstition, . . . that puts no opposition or traps in the path of science. . . ."[34]

The sequel to this directive was issued in 1924. Also signed by Krupskaya, it repeated the main themes of its predecessor and added a few new ideas on thought control. It ordered the removal of *Soviet* books that had become obsolete owing to a change in the party line. It made a superlative bureaucratic effort to put everything on a standard form, which was attached to the new directive. On this form all books removed were to be listed for the approval of a Central Library Commission, which might decide to permit the circulation of some of them. The main library of each province should, however, keep "no more than two copies" of each banned book in a special collection, having a separate catalog, for the use of approved persons. This entire scheme for intellectual control did not yet function very well. The 1924 directive complains that the earlier ones had not been adequately executed by local librarians, "and in some provinces the intervention of the GPU has been required."[35] But it is clear that Krupskaya had a hand in the formation of the Soviet system of intellectual dictatorship, even though she was later to complain of its constraints on her own activities.

There was one area in which Krupskaya's idealism did not yield, despite all difficulties. This was her faith in "polytechnical" education, conducted in the "single labor school." This had been the main vision sketched in her pre-revolutionary essay on "Public Education and Democracy," and she clung to it throughout her life. It was a noble ideal, an attempt to fuse the anti-technical, humanistic, Tolstoyan ideas of individual development with the technological, labor-oriented values derived from Marx and the industrial age. The basic gap between humanistic man and technological man is in any case hard to bridge, and Krupskaya's attempt to do this suffered seriously from one fundamental weakness: she never understood technology or industry. Hence, her numerous preachments about "polytechnicism" were invariably gaseous abstractions. Polytechnicism, she explained, forms "a person who understands all the interrelations between the different branches of production, the role of each, the tendencies of the development of each . . . , the person who knows what and why it is necessary to do at a given moment, in a word, a master of production in the present sense of the word."[36] This is achieved through the "labor" method, which is "an all-round study of the labor of the populace. . . . This all-roundedness of study is polytechnicism." No *single* trade or skill was to be taught, and all of this is supposed to be "close to life," avoiding the irrelevance of the old educational system.[37] It is also democratic, because every child goes to the single school through the secondary level; there are no privileged programs for either the rich or the talented.

Such abstractions are well and good for a professor of education, and have much in common with the western "progressive education" that Krupskaya drew upon. They are something else again when you are faced with the actual responsibility of operating the world's largest school system. Krupskaya's faith in these ideals carried the day in the first year of Narkompros. She found a ready collaborator in Lunacharsky, who had little background in pedagogy but held the sort of vaguely edifying ideas about the new society that fit in with polytechnicism and the single labor school. Not so the other leading member of the original Narkompros team, the eminent Russian Marxist historian, M. N. Pokrovsky, who was mainly concerned with higher education rather than with schools. At an important conference on education in the summer of 1918, at which his colleagues were advocating alternative versions of the single labor school, Pokrovsky acidly remarked, "Before we start thinking about the labor school, we need whatever kind of school there is now. . . . The labor school never existed and never will exist."[38]

But Krupskaya was insistent that it would exist, and on October 16, 1918, was rewarded by an official "Regulation on the Single Labor School," which in suitably vague terms made her ideal the model for the entire republic. This was a really revolutionary victory on paper, but in the next two years the new system floundered badly. In keeping with Krupskaya's early decentralist idealism, little was done by Narkompros to tell the local schools *how* to be polytechnical. They were supposed to work this out for themselves on the basis of exceedingly general pronouncements at the center. No definite curriculum was to be distributed for fear of crushing somebody's creativity. The existing corps of teachers was at a loss, most of them knowing little about polytechnicism and having scant love for the new government. Some did nothing new. Others made gestures toward reform, such as having the children clean up their own schools or knit mittens, which Krupskaya always considered a perversion of the true ideal. Some of the more reform-minded teachers were seduced by doctrines that were much more radical than Krupskaya's, such as the ideal of the "dying out" of the school, through its literal assimilation into the sacred factory.[39]

The disaster that swept over Russia's once-respectable system of public education in 1918–20 was not simply the result of half-baked reforms. The country was racked by civil war and economic collapse, and it was from this general disaster that the most serious challenge to polytechnical labor education emerged. The men concerned with the economic survival and revival of Soviet Russia were alarmed by the shortage of skilled industrial workers and found no sign of remedy in Krupskaya's program, which regarded the graduation of a competent lathe operator as a scandal to be avoided at all costs. The opponents of polytechnicism camped in an acronymic fortress called "Glavprofobr" (Main Administration of Professional — meaning vocational — Education), and from this strong point within Narkompros bombarded the government with demands that polytechnicism be dropped. Trotsky could well have been considered the general behind this campaign. He was in charge of an emergency program to revive the economy by quasi-military means, conscripting labor and giving vocational training on a crash basis. He did not tangle personally Krupskaya on this issue, but one of his close associates, Preobrazhensky, became one of the principle foes of polytechnicism within Narkompros.

Hard pressed, Krupskaya turned to Lenin for support in the last weeks of 1920. A special conference on education was to be held at the very end of the year under the sponsorship of the party, and she wanted very much to have her husband's prestige working for her and polytechnicism. We have two alternative, undated drafts of fundamental policy points that she was to present to the conference, both of which stress her customary, vague ideals. For example, "the task of the polytechnical school consists in the preparation of a new generation, people who may be considered as workers in production and masters of it in the full sense of this word."[40] In the past Lenin had generally approved of her educational writings, although he had not been able to give much attention to this area since the revolution. He now considered it against the background of profound economic crisis. The country was in ruins. With acute judgment Lenin, the ideologist, was urging his comrades to set aside ideology for the moment and concentrate on the practical question of reviving the economy. Not without reason, he had conceived an obsessive repulsion for fancy phrases and impractical visions. Krupskaya for her part had not been involved in the mainstream of her husband's work for the past few years and evidently failed to realize how untimely her idealistic preachments would be in his eyes.

Upon reading these theses, Lenin wrote some comments. It is a tribute to his personal tact that he headed them "Private. Draft. *Not to be published. I shall consider this again and yet again.*" Still, he seems to have known exactly what he could not accept in his wife's approach when he wrote his first line: "One must not write *thus* about polytechnical education: it [Krupskaya's draft] proceeds abstractly, for the distant future, *not* studying the existing, present, sorry actuality." "The extremely difficult condition of the republic," he continued, demands that the secondary level be converted into a "proftekhshkol" (vocational-technical school), though not merely a trade school, for it would be enriched with compulsory courses in such subjects as "communism, general history, the history of revolution, the revolution of 1917, geography, literature, and so on. . . . This is arch-important. We are paupers. We need joiners, metal workers *at once. Absolutely.* All [pupils] must become joiners, metal workers, and so forth, *but* with some sort of supplementary general education and polytechnical minimum."[41]

We do not know how Krupskaya reacted to this blunt dismissal of her treasured ideas and the substitution of an old-fashioned trade-school course (enriched with Communist propaganda). From her point of view it must have been all the worse that Lenin would demean the grand idea of "polytechnicism" by keeping it as a label for such pedestrian practical proposals. Having dealt thus with Krupskaya's attempt to win his support, Lenin went off for a rest in the country and did not attend the conference on education. Krupskaya too was forced to stay home because of an illness, and Lunacharsky read her theses to the conference.

In a subsequent article, which attacked the conference as unrepresentative, Krupskaya subtly reproached Lenin for its shortcomings. The Central Committee, she said, did not play a major part in the affair, leaving the anti-polytechnicists ascendant. The careful reader could easily guess who was primarily responsible for the actions of the Central Committee.[42]

What emerged from all this was a compromise in favor of the advocates of vocational education. The ideal of polytechnicism was retained on paper, but most so-called secondary education, beginning at age 15 in theory (often earlier in practice), was to be vocational. Supposedly this was a temporary measure, but to a considerable extent the trade-school approach still dominates almost fifty years later. All in all it must have been a crushing experience for Krupskaya.

Even without such disappointments, the sheer physical toll of the early years of the Soviet regime was heavy for both Lenin and Krupskaya. She seemed the unhealthy one, but hated to admit it, obliging Lenin to conspire to make her rest. The agitation steamboat trip was supposed to serve this purpose at a time when Krupskaya was in shaky condition. In practice, however, the ruse backfired, for she did as much on the river as in her office and under more trying conditions. Molotov reported to Lenin that she had a heart attack in July 1919, and Lenin sent her one of his typical comradely lectures on obeying the doctors and getting a good rest.[43] Whatever the nature of this heart trouble, it was still keeping her abed from time to time that fall. "My heart refuses to do its job. These days I am a lady all the time," she wrote ironically to an acquaintance.[44] Toward the end of the year Lenin plotted with their old friend Bonch-Bruevich, a physician as well as revolutionary, to persuade Krupskaya to spend a few weeks at a boarding school for homeless children at Sokolniki on the edge of Moscow.[45] This was a more successful venture. Krupskaya was persuaded that it was acceptable to be in bed at a *school* and stayed put for several weeks. Lenin came to visit her on New Year's Eve and other occasions, once meeting robbers on the road. They expropriated the expropriator of the expropriators, by taking his Rolls Royce car and his revolver.

Lenin had reason to carry a gun. His Cheka had given many people motivation for vengeance and Russia had a history rich in assassinations. On August 30, 1918, a young woman named Fanya Kaplan shot him with a revolver at close range. One bullet broke his shoulder, the other passed through his lung and lodged in the neck. Krupskaya, who had been at a meeting elsewhere in Moscow, was rushed back to the Kremlin by special car without any explanation. When she got there Lenin was in serious condition, though conscious. There was little Krupskaya could do, though she sat up through the night. Neither she nor anyone else insisted on taking the critically wounded man to a hospital, but this may have been more sensible than it now appears. There had been an abortive insurrection of the Left Socialist Revolutionary Party in July, starting with the assassination of the German ambassador. It would not have been unreasonable to fear a second effort in August, in which case the Kremlin was more secure than any hospital.

It soon appeared that Fanya Kaplan had acted alone. She had been captured at the scene of the crime, and the question of her fate became a sensitive one in the Ulyanov household. She was, after all, a young woman, just like Sofia Perovskaya, who had played an active part in the successful assassination of Alexander II and had gone to the gallows for it. Lenin, Krupskaya, and most radicals of their generation had grown up with the conviction that Sofia's martyrdom was proof of the immorality of the old regime. Angelica Balabanova, a radical Russian woman who spent most of her life abroad, recalls visiting Lenin and Krupskaya after Lenin was well out of danger and had moved to his country house to rest. When the subject of Kaplan came up, Lenin tersely said, "The Central Committee will have to decide," and changed the subject. But Krupskaya, in saying goodbye to Angelica, who was not a close friend, reacted differently. "Throwing her arms around me," Angelica relates, "she sobbed, 'A revolutionist executed in a revolutionary country! Never!' "[46] Lenin had known better. Fanya had already been shot and (unlike Sofia Perovskaya) without trial. For the benefit of Krupskaya and other tender-minded humanitarians this was concealed for many years. Very likely Krupskaya lived out her life in the consoling belief that Fanya Kaplan was alive in jail.

The night that he was shot Lenin thought that he was dying, but he pulled through the critical days without complications and was soon convalescing. His first visitor was an old friend—Inessa Armand. He must have asked for her especially, for he was being kept very quiet. Angelica Balabanova, whom Lenin did not know well, relates that even after he had moved into the country to rest, only a few people whom Lenin *asked* to see were being admitted. Inessa had been working in Moscow since April 1917, but it seems that neither Lenin nor Krupskaya had seen her in this hectic period. Now she reappeared, and while Inessa and Lenin talked, Krupskaya entertained Inessa's teenage daughter Varvara with photographs of the old days.[47] It was probably the last time Lenin saw Inessa, but in the following year or so he was highly attentive to her well-being. He wrote a letter on behalf of her son Alexander, who apparently wanted to become a Red Army aviator, but had to live down the fact that he had been a flying officer of the tsar during the World War.[48] When Inessa contracted pneumonia in February 1920, Lenin wrote an exceedingly solicitous letter, implicitly offering all of his influence if she needed help with such details as firewood and food. He ordered her "to insist without fail that your son call me every day (between 12 and 4)," a unique mark of concern. It even appears from the letter that Inessa had appealed to Lenin to have a telephone installed in her quarters — an impossible goal for most people in the turmoil of the Russian civil war.[49] By a cruel stroke of irony it was Lenin's unstinting concern for Inessa that brought about her death in September 1920. Her son, the flier, became seriously ill and Lenin apparently was asked to arrange for his recuperation, accompanied by Inessa, at a sanatorium in the Caucasus. The head of the Soviet state not only made the sanatorium reservations himself, but also sent two messages to his top man in the Caucasus, Ordzhonikidze, asking that he look after Inessa and her son.[50] They first settled at the mineral spa of Kislovodsk. A comrade who saw them there recalls the son as robust and Inessa as completely exhausted. She probably would have regained her vitality, but for Lenin's solicitude. A White guerrilla force threatened the town, and the local Red commander arrived with orders "from the center" to remove Inessa (nobody else was thus honored) from possible harm. He was even ready to carry her off if she was uncooperative. Although this crisis passed before the departure could occur, it was decided to close down the spa for the season in the interests of safety and to move the patients to Nal'chik, a less exposed town north of the Caucasus mountains. The party of ailing comrades had to travel by decrepit railroads and spent two days waiting at a filthy station in a little town called Beslan. It is likely that this is where Inessa contracted cholera, which was widespread in southern Russia at this time. She came down with it just after reaching Nal'chik, and died in the hospital there. G. Kotov, the memoirist of this sad affair, recalls that her body was so desiccated that it lay for eight days in the local mortuary, yet hardly smelled at all.[51] As a Russian, Kotov must have been well aware that this was generally considered a sign of sainthood among the Orthodox, but, writing in 1921, he could not have known that Inessa's great friend would also become a corpse that does not decay.

Finally her body was shipped back to Moscow for cremation, and her ashes were interred by the Kremlin wall, which was already the most honored cemetery for Bolsheviks. Lenin attended. He was "unrecognizable. He walked with closed eyes; at every moment we thought he would collapse," recalls Alexandra Kollontai.[52] Krupskaya contributed a formal eulogy to the numerous ones published in *Pravda*.

Lenin and Krupskaya continued to interest themselves in the Armands' children after Inessa's death. In May 1921, Lenin wrote to Kamenev to ask on behalf of the children that flowers and a small stone marker be placed on Inessa's grave. Later that year he arranged for Alexander and Varvara Armand to visit the Soviet mission in Iran. Neither had any diplomatic qualifications but apparently they wanted an interesting trip.[53] Krupskaya virtually adopted Varvara, who spent a lot of time in the Lenin apartment after her mother died, and at some time compiled, at Krupskaya's request, an album of Lenin's pictures in the press. According to Dridzo, this was a treasured possession that Krupskaya kept on her desk. When Varvara enrolled in a school of stagecraft in Moscow, Lenin and Krupskaya paid an unannounced visit to the dormitory one night to see how she was getting on.

The close companionship that Nadezhda cultivated with Varvara Armand was innocent enough, but the whole Lenin-Armand story sufficiently embarrassed some Soviet editors that they found it necessary to distort the inconsequential report that John Reed's widow, Louise Bryant, gave of her visit with Krupskaya. In the original account of the conversation, which was conducted in English, one reads, ". . . a pretty girl of eighteen came in and Krupskaya said, 'This is my niece. She is usually with me. I love her and want you to know her.' "[54] No further identification of the girl appeared in this account. But when the Soviet magazine *Novyi Mir* reprinted the article in Russian translation in 1964, we find Krupskaya's companion drastically changed. The "pretty girl of eighteen" is a "kindly-faced woman" (*milovidnaia zhenshchina*) (no age given) and she is called "my kinswoman" (*rodstvenitsa*) rather than "niece." The Soviet editor adds a footnote stating that the person was Lenin's sister Maria.[55] This is no technical slip but an amusing deception to avoid the whole problem of the Lenin-Krupskaya-Armand relationship. Maria was forty-three at this time and not even John Reed's widow could have considered her pretty and eighteen. Varvara was about eighteen at the time, reasonably pretty judging from photographs, and was the only person whom Krupskaya ever called "my beloved daughter," as she did in letters to Varvara at a slightly later date.[56] It is natural enough that the aging Krupskaya, whose maternal feelings had never been satisfied, should adopt Inessa's daughter, at least in her own mind.

This intimacy continued for several more years. Her letters are full of affection and concern for Varvara's fragile health. "Well, it's good that you [thou—*ty*] are resting," wrote Nadezhda to her at a spa on the Black Sea in June 1924. "Perhaps at your favorite sea your nerves will mend themselves and you will get well. . . . Only, please, sleep more and go bathing in moderation, and not like a Komsomol."[57] In 1926 Varvara lived in Moscow and visited her foster-mother regularly — "I give an account of my activities every Sunday to Varyushka, who spends a lot of time with me, an old woman," Krupskaya wrote to Varvara's sister Inessa.[58] Her correspondence with the young Inessa, who married a German Communist and moved to Berlin, was also extended, but less intimate.

By the close of the twenties this filial relationship had dwindled. It may be that Varvara was a bit embarrassed or found Krupskaya dull. She recalls that she was rather bored by the old lady's talk about the glories of Nekrasov. Then, too, Varvara seems to have been more or less neurotic. Krupskaya's letters express solicitude for her nerves. In 1929 Varvara Armand must have been physically or psychically ill, for Krupskaya asked a mutual friend, Ya. D. Romas, "Is Varyushka alive, or is her suffering at an end?"[59] Clearly she was out of touch. In fact, Varvara lived on for over thirty years more, and in 1932 must have visited Krupskaya once again (there is a photograph of them together at this time.)

It would be perverse to doubt the sincerity of Krupskaya's affection for Inessa's daughters, but it is possible that she had somewhat more complicated motives in keeping a picture of Inessa on her desk in the Kremlin after 1920, beside one of Lenin and one of her mother — and no others[60] — or in editing and contributing to the memorial volume that was published for Inessa in 1926.[61] As will be seen, there is reason to think that the shade of Inessa Armand pursued Krupskaya in the catacombs of Kremlin politics after Lenin died.

Lenin's recovery from his wounds seemed excellent, and he kept up a terrific pace of work in 1919 and 1920. He took only a few short vacations and hunting trips, ranging as far as Smolensk province once, but never to the famous curative resorts of the Caucasus Mountains or the Crimean seashore, as many of his comrades did, sometimes on his orders. Lenin was much better at handing out medical admonitions than at taking them. The nearest that he came to arranging some kind of regular place to rest was the acquisition (not as personal property, of course) of an estate of a one-time mayor of Moscow at Gorki, close to Moscow. (Not to be confused with Nizhnii Novogorod, which was later renamed for the writer Maxim Gorky.) Here Lenin and Krupskaya spent a number of weekends or short holidays in the early Soviet years.

By late 1921 Lenin developed ominous symptoms. He complained to his brother Dmitri, the doctor, that he was suffering from insomnia and lack of interest in work — a most unusual complaint for him, which Dmitri correctly considered a sign of arterial sclerosis. Over the winter of 1921-22 Lenin was not himself. He took several short vacations, and in April began to plan on a trip to the Caucasus in June, accompanied by Krupskaya. He corresponded with Sergo Ordzhonikidze, the top Communist in the Caucasus, about a suitable place, one that would be quiet, with walks, not too rainy, but not at too high an elevation for Nadezhda Konstantinovna's heart.[62] Meanwhile his doctors decided to remove one of Fanya Kaplan's bullets from his neck. It was not considered a major operation, and was performed under local anesthetic in a Moscow hospital on April 23, 1922. Lenin returned home the next day. All went well and on April 27, Lenin was already able to attend a meeting of the Politburo. But he still felt exhausted and on May 23, went to Gorki for a rest. There, on May 25-27 he suffered a serious cerebral hemorrhage. Lenin was speechless and his right arm and leg were paralyzed. He was entirely out of action for four months and was never again fully in possession of his physical powers. Or his political powers. Lenin's lieutenants knew that he had little future, and the unspoken question of succession was never far from their minds for the rest of his life. Krupskaya, after twenty-four years as Lenin's wife, suddenly found herself in the unfamiliar and precarious role of widow-designate.

CHAPTER VIII

Widow-Designate

Between his first stroke in May 1922 and the fall of that year Lenin made a seemingly good recovery, and even returned to work for a bit over two months. This phase of his illness was not so hard on Krupskaya, who gave up most of her accustomed overload of work in order to be with Lenin. Until October 2 they stayed at Gorki, but by midsummer Lenin could receive visitors and speak for himself, so there was no special burden on his wife politically.

In various photographs we see them sitting outdoors during the summer of 1922, Nadezhda in flowing, ankle-length summer dress, tired but not ill in appearance, Lenin in high-laced orthopedic shoes, with a squinty, paralytic smile. In one photograph they have a rather large, tripod-mounted telescope on a table before them along with some books. Have they been bird-watching? In another they are joined by two children, one the six-year-old son of Lenin's brother Dmitri, the other a child of "a worker" in the neighborhood. The nephew, Victor by name, and his sister Olga were the only offspring of Lenin's generation of the Ulyanov line. In later years they played little role in Krupskaya's life, although there is a photograph of Victor with his illustrious aunt and other relatives around 1932, when he was a handsome, strapping teen-ager. During Lenin's recuperative stays at Gorki his brother Dmitri and sister Anna came to visit, but only sister Maria remained a member of the household throughout the illness.

Although the months at Gorki kept Krupskaya from her usual administrative work in Narkompros and all but a few public appearances, she did manage to keep in touch with Soviet education through visits from colleagues and by continuing to turn out her tracts, at a much-reduced rate. When Lenin returned to Moscow on October 2 to attempt resumption of his work, Krupskaya did the same. In the nine weeks before Lenin's next collapse she managed to address the Fourth World Congress of the Communist International (a routine survey of Soviet education), the All-Russian Congress of the Communist Youth organization (more on the same lines), and the All-Russian Congress of Political Education Workers, her old personal bastion in the state machinery.[1] If anything is particularly notable in this, it is a shift of her interests from schools to the politicized youth movement, the "Russian Communist Union of Youth" or Komsomol. Krupskaya had been interested in this field in 1917, but had given it little serious attention until 1922. At the opening of the year she had published a piece on "The Russian Communist Union of Youth and Boyscoutism," based on some solid study of the Scouts. While reproaching their "bourgeois" and "monarchist" character, she spent most of the article advocating the imitation of such techniques as tests and merit badges. All very useful, she maintained. Her speeches at the Youth Congress in October were on the whole rambling banalities (everyone should get to work at six in the morning, like Zola, she said), yet just possibly colored by a premonition of the future without Lenin. Toward the end of the session she submitted to a question-and-answer period, appearing as a guru-at-large, and taking pains to present Lenin as the ideal man, a legend that she could interpret to youth. Was there in Krupskaya's swing toward youth work in Lenin's last months a realization that the power to mold the next generation of party members would determine the fate of his ideals?

Certainly Lenin was deeply concerned with the fate of his goals when the second round of strokes put him off his feet in mid-December 1922. The founder of the Bolshevik party and Soviet state had become gravely displeased with the drift of these institutions in 1922. At the heart of the matter was the personal character of the top leaders, none of whom he considered fit to take his place. He found them responsible for the rise of "bureaucratism" in the system, the failure of the party-state inspectorial agencies to check this trend and the emergence of "Great Russian chauvinism," which treated the minority nationalities tactlessly. It is highly unlikely that he had discussed his misgivings with Krupskaya at any length during their long rest at Gorki in 1922. It was only toward the end of his stay there that they had taken shape in his mind. A crucial step in Lenin's disenchantment with his system was an acrimonious exchange of letters with Stalin, who in April 1922 had assumed the post of General Secretary of the party, and in the fall openly opposed Lenin on the question of minority nationalities. Lenin had won his points on the particular constitutional issue that was involved, but friction continued over the treatment of the Georgian communist leadership by Stalin and his crony Ordzhonikidze. The evasiveness and obstructionism that Lenin encountered in October-November 1922 in dealing with this situation increased his irritation over Soviet "bureaucratism" and the leaders who encouraged it. He had hopes that Trotsky would assist him in putting the Bolshevik house in order, and, according to Trotsky, the two agreed on a "bloc" against bureaucratism. Trotsky was in some ways a natural choice, for he was a brilliant man and the political enemy of the politicians whom Lenin wished to reduce in power. As matters turned out, however, Trotsky could not be relied on for the task. He had no real solution to "bureaucratism" except the substitution of his own authority for that of alternative leaders, and he proved to be weak and vacillating in the prolonged political struggle that developed. From Krupskaya's point of view Trotsky was far from an ideal ally. She had not had much personal contact with him since the days of emigration in London, before he broke with Lenin in 1903, and she felt far closer to Kamenev and Zinoviev, who were friends in the last years of emigration. They were now aligned with Stalin, forming a "troika" to take up the power that was slipping from Lenin's hands.

Lenin had only barely started his reform campaign when the new wave of strokes began. From mid-December 1922 until March 9, 1923, he was not totally incapacitated but was confined to his room in the Kremlin and cut off from the outside world. He suffered from severe headaches, loss of memory, partial paralysis of his right side, and general weakness, but he still struggled heroically to reform the Soviet political system.

Total rest seemed the obvious prescription, and Krupskaya no doubt recollected that in bygone years Lenin had regained his vitality after severe nervous attacks by hiking in the Alps and forgetting politics as much as possible. But this time Lenin refused to cooperate, sensing that he had only a little time left and fearing that the party leaders would use medical excuses to forestall his efforts.

Krupskaya was in the most excruciating dilemma of her life. There had been a brief foretaste of it when he was recovering from the bullet wounds. At this time, too, the doctors had ordered rest and no excitement. Krupskaya was responsible for reading Lenin the news of the civil war, and he sensed that she was not telling him everything. According to one of the nurses, he challenged Nadezhda on this and asked, "Which is dearer to you, me or the party?" She evaded this painful question by replying, "The one and the other. You are dear and the party is dear."[2] Lenin's recovery was good in this case, and the dilemma evaporated, only to reappear with renewed keenness in his final illness.

Her husband was still dear to her, and she no doubt wanted to spare his strength as much as possible in keeping with the doctors' orders, especially since their opinion was that Lenin had no irreversible illness. On the other hand, he was determined that the party was now in critical need of his leadership, even from his deathbed. Krupskaya probably understood very little of Lenin's last political vision, but she no doubt wanted to help him and also realized that his tensions had to be appeased to some degree if he was to have any chance of recovery. At times, then, she conspired with Lenin against the medical-political regime, at other times against Lenin for his own good. "The one and the other. You are dear and the party is dear" — Krupskaya could never bring herself to make a definite choice.

Shortly after Lenin's severe attack of December 13, she telephoned Lenin's secretary, Lidya Fotieva, and asked her to "phone (Emil) Yaroslavsky *conspiratorially*" to request him to copy down some of the speeches at the forthcoming Congress of Soviets. Lenin had asked her to do this because he feared that the true report on the issue of the state monopoly on foreign trade would be concealed from him.[3]

At the opening of the century Krupskaya had helped her husband conspire against his political colleagues — the future Mensheviks from whom she had concealed part of her secretarial correspondence. Now the Bolshevik leadership was the adversary, and she was at it again, but Stalin was no trusting friend like Martov. On December 18 Stalin was chosen by the Politburo to be "personally responsible for the observance of the regimen that the doctors had prescribed for Lenin," and he was not about to be outmaneuvered by a sick man and his wife.[4] While never again admitted to the presence of the living Lenin, Stalin no doubt had ways of watching the pathetic conspirators. In fact, it is possible that Lenin and Krupskaya were completely isolated in an environment of informers, willing or otherwise. Stalin's own wife was a member of the secretarial staff. The senior secretary, Fotieva, was not above

Lenin's suspicion. "First of all," he told her on January 24, 1923, "concerning our 'conspiratorial' business, I know that you are betraying me."[5] Krupskaya never had any warm recollections of Fotieva, who later survived the Stalin purges in uncommonly good health. Lenin's sister Maria, the person closest to Lenin (except Krupskaya) in this period, was an intimate friend of Fotieva and also a coworker and close friend of Bukharin, a Politburo member who might well have been willing to pass information to Stalin. Throughout the illness, security guards were much in evidence around the household. While Lenin was in his Kremlin bedroom the chief guard, Pakaln, called every day with a dog named "Aida," to which Lenin was much attached. These guards, mostly Latvians, like many members of the political police at this time, mixed with the Lenin family in a friendly manner. This gave them an excellent opportunity to know what was going on, and it is fair to assume that they reported regularly to the head chekist, Dzerzhinsky, who was on very good terms with Stalin at this time. He had, in fact, been an active supporter of Stalin's side in the controversy about Georgia, and by the end of 1922 Lenin considered Dzerzhinsky one of his chief opponents. Finally, the medical staff that attended Lenin reported directly to Stalin, according to the Politburo decision of December 18, 1922.

Small wonder that on December 23, 1922, Stalin already knew that on the previous day Lenin had dictated to Krupskaya a letter intended for Trotsky. It was merely a note of congratulation concerning the latter's success in defending the state monopoly on foreign trade at a Central Committee meeting, but its existence implied that Krupskaya was willing to conspire with Lenin against the Stalin group in the Politburo. Actually, the note was dictated with the doctors' permission,[6] but it gave Stalin a pretext for disciplinary action. He called Krupskaya to the telephone and gave her a crude, intimidating dressing-down that has never been recorded. As Stalin's daughter recollected many years later, he had a fine store of obscenities, and he seems to have used it to upset the very proper Krupskaya. It is clear in any case that he threatened her with action by the Central Control Commission, the party's disciplinary body.

But if he thought to cow her into submission, Stalin underestimated his opponent. Not wishing to upset Lenin with this episode, Krupskaya at once dispatched a letter to Lev Kamenev, her long-time friend and now one of the top three active leaders of the party:

Lev Borisovich!

Because of a short letter which I had written in words dictated to me by Vladimir Ilyich by permission of the doctors, Stalin allowed himself yesterday an unusually rude outburst directed at me. This is not my first day in the party. During all these thirty years I have never heard from any comrade one word of rudeness. The business of the party and of Ilyich are not less dear to me than to Stalin. I need at present the maximum of self-control. What one can and cannot discuss with Ilyich — I know better than any doctor, because I know what makes him nervous and what does not, in any case I know better than Stalin. I am turning to you and to Grigory [Zinoviev] as much closer comrades of V. I. and I beg you to protect me from rude interference with my private life and from vile invectives and threats. I have no doubt as to what will be the unanimous decision of the Control Commission, with which Stalin sees fit to threaten me; however, I have neither the strength nor the time to waste on this foolish quarrel. And I am a living person and my nerves are strained to the utmost.

N. Krupskaya[7]

What Kamenev did is not wholly clear, but Krupskaya's counterattack seems to have been partially successful. A few months later, when Lenin did learn of the affair and wrote an angry letter to Stalin, he remarked that Krupskaya had "agreed to forget what was said" (by Stalin on December 23). In other words, Kamenev induced his colleague to apologize after some fashion, and Krupskaya had accepted the apology. Unwittingly, Lenin simultaneously brought up some heavy artillery of his own. On December 24, 1922, he threatened to refuse all medical attention if he was not allowed to dictate for at least a few minutes a day.[8] After a short conference, Stalin, Kamenev, and Bukharin handed down new rules for the sick man and, implicitly, Krupskaya, too. He was granted "five to ten" minutes per day for dictation (later extended until it reached two daily sessions of forty minutes each), but nobody was to "communicate to Vladimir Ilyich anything from political life, so as not to provide materials for misunderstanding and anxiety."[9] This put Krupskaya, and the secretaries, very much on the spot. While his ability to talk remained, Lenin would continually try to wheedle information out of them, which could easily subject them to the wrath of the leadership. He also wheedled extra time out of Krupskaya, who did make an effort to enforce the doctors' orders. On January 22, for example, she told the secretary that Lenin had "illegally taken still a few more minutes to review the article" that he was writing.

From the last week in December 1922 until March 1923 Lenin, partly with Krupskaya's connivance, succeeded in working on a series of articles that were published, a speech that he optimistically hoped to give in the spring at the Twelfth Party Congress, and some more or less testamentary material in case his health did not improve. It was the latter material that placed the greatest burden on Krupskaya. During the last week of December Lenin dictated a series of critical observations on the various leading figures in the party, finding none of them really suitable to carry on his work. He also dealt with the nationality question and especially the handling of Georgia, for which he blamed Stalin. His cumulative feelings about the General Secretary took their final, but somewhat ambiguous form on January 4, 1923, when Lenin added the last bit to his political testament. He castigated Stalin for rudeness, which made him unfit for his high responsibility, and urged his comrades "to find a way" to depose and replace him.[10] While Krupskaya did not tell Lenin about Stalin's rude behavior toward her at this time, it is possible that the subject of his personality came up in their conversation, and she may have influenced Lenin's attitude toward Stalin, intentionally or otherwise. Even if she actually played no role in shaping Lenin's opinion on this issue, Stalin was justified in suspecting that she had, as he later intimated.[11] It seems highly unlikely, however, that Krupskaya wanted to be burdened with the kind of testament that Lenin entrusted to her. In it he did not give his blessing to any new system or to any particular successor (s) , but had something offensive to say about almost everyone in power. And if Lenin himself could only recommend to the comrades that they "find a way" to reduce Stalin's authority, how was his widow to solve this problem?

Five copies of the testimony writings were typed, and the original manuscript was then burned. Lenin kept one copy, presumably in his Kremlin room, the secretaries kept one, and three were marked for Nadezhda, as if extra copies would better enable her to cope with this impossible task.[12]

According to M. A. Volodicheva, the secretary who handled this matter, Lenin asked that all five copies be placed in envelopes sealed with wax. He asked that they be marked with instructions that they be opened only by himself or "after his death by Nadezhda Konstantinovna." Volodicheva, by her own admission, omitted the dreaded words "after his death."[13]

How much did Krupskaya know about the content of her husband's political testament and the way in which he wanted her to act on it? It is not certain that she ever read or heard the text of the secret dictations until she was a widow. After December 24, 1922, the secretaries, rather than Krupskaya, took dictation from the sick man, and it seems clear from Fotieva's memoirs and the secretaries' journal that they did this privately, without Krupskaya's presence. Lenin could have discussed the entire matter with Krupskaya before March 9, but it seems doubtful. He was using his waning strength sparingly, saving it for his dictations, and Krupskaya was almost certainly trying to avoid discussing political topics that would upset her husband, not only because Stalin, Kamenev, and Bukharin had ordered it but also because she thought she knew what would and would not upset him. And certainly the question of Stalin and bureaucratism was ultra-upsetting.

To be sure, part of Lenin's final, critical view of the Soviet political system was published and well known to Krupskaya.[14] The trouble was that what he said was perplexing to old Leninists, conditioned by his familiar ideas of centralism and elitism in the party and state. Alienated from his own *"apparatchiki"* (professional administrators), Lenin looked to ordinary "workers from the bench" to reform the system, and he wanted to impose large numbers of these imaginary proletarian paragons on the chief organs of government, making them voting members of the Politburo, for example. The majority of the Politburo held up publication of one such article for almost a month, wishing to protect orthodox Leninism from the sick and capricious Lenin.

While more devoted to her husband than any of his lieutenants, Krupskaya, too, must have had grave difficulties in fathoming the final stage of Lenin's thought. Of course, she opposed "bureaucratism" — so did Stalin and everyone else — in words. But her whole life in the party, and especially her practical experience as a bureaucrat in Narkompros, confirmed her understanding of Bolshevism as the command of the working class movement and government by an elite drawn largely from people of her own type — the intelligentsia. It was precisely because Stalin did not conform to this cultural style that he was so odious to her.

All in all, Krupskaya was poorly equipped to attempt to become the executrix of her husband's political estate. She was prestigious but not a powerful political figure in her own right. She had no reliable allies in the Politburo. She probably did not read the contents of the sealed envelopes until Lenin ceased to be able to explain his ideas about his heirs. And she did not really understand the high-minded and impractical hostility that the dying Lenin felt toward the political apparatus that he had worked all his life to create.

At the opening of 1923 the whole situation seemed to depend on the Twelfth Party Congress, which was to meet in April. After dictating the secret testamentary notes, Lenin felt somewhat stronger and began to work on published articles, as mentioned above, and then a strongly anti-Stalin speech for the congress.

This seemed to absolve Krupskaya from immediate political action on her husband's behalf. She was almost constantly at Lenin's service, calling in secretaries when requested, getting books and other material that he wanted, more or less "illegally," and on one occasion reading one of her own works to him for comment (an innocuous tract on the liquidation of illiteracy). But she seems to have hoped that his health would permit him to carry out his political campaign with little reliance on her.

This was not to be. The comparative tranquility that had settled on the Lenin apartment in January and February 1923 was broken on March 5. Feeling worse, Lenin sent Trotsky "all the manuscripts that were to make part of his bomb [against Stalin] for the twelfth congress," and a request that Trotsky "undertake the defense of the Georgian affair."[15] The invitation was declined, but Trotsky craftily kept copies of the material — a fairly good indication of his reliability as an executor of Lenin's campaign. On the same day, how it is not clear, Lenin learned about Stalin's row with Krupskaya back in December. Deeply angry, Lenin dictated a letter to Stalin, in which he implied that Krupskaya was his alter ego in politics:

> To Comrade Stalin.
> Copies for: Kamenev and Zinoviev.
> Dear Comrade Stalin:
> You permitted yourself a rude summons of my wife to the telephone and a rude reprimand of her. Despite

the fact that she told you that she agreed to forget what was said, nevertheless Zinoviev and Kamenev heard about it from her. I have no intention to forget so easily that which is being done against me, and I need not stress here that I consider as directed against me that which is being done against my wife. I ask you, therefore, that you weigh carefully whether you are agreeable to retracting your words and apologizing or whether you prefer the severance of relations between us.

Sincerely,

LENIN

March 5, 1923[16]

Lenin delayed sending the letter until March 6, evidently mistrusting his stormy emotions, then ordered it dispatched by hand to Stalin, who was to reply at once through the courier-secretary. Krupskaya was alarmed. If, as seems possible from Lenin's wording, she had let slip the story of the quarrel, she surely had not intended to evoke such a reaction. Nadezhda plainly wanted to avoid a new encounter with Stalin, and she attempted to dissuade Volodicheva from obeying Lenin's orders, a desperate move that in effect put her on the side of the conspiracy *against* Lenin. But on March 7 the secretary insisted that she must follow his orders, and Krupskaya had to give in. She had a hurried conference with Kamenev, her erstwhile mediator with Stalin.[17] We do not know what was said. Trotsky, who talked to Kamenev afterwards, wrote that Krupskaya asserted firmly that Lenin had decided to crush Stalin politically.[18] This harmonizes very poorly with her well documented efforts to avert a collision and does not reflect the wording of Lenin's letter, which left Stalin a fairly easy way out.

In any case it was decided that Volodicheva should carry out her mission, with copies of the letter going to Kamenev and Zinoviev. Like Trotsky, they were less interested in obeying Lenin's wishes or defending Krupskaya than in storing up ammunition for use after Lenin died.

The episode ended in futility. Stalin dictated an apology to Volodicheva, but it was never seen by Lenin, whose condition was worsening.[19]

Nor was the apology ever published, despite the efforts of party researchers to support Nikita Khrushchev's anti-Stalin campaign with archival documents from this period. They did, however, turn up the record of Krupskaya's efforts to prevent the sending of Lenin's ultimatum to Stalin. It was in code — Volodicheva's shorthand, which only she could decipher, and did in 1956. Why had this record not been transcribed into plain Russian like the rest of the journal kept by Lenin's secretaries? To protect the secretary from criminal charges that she had conspired with Krupskaya against Lenin? To save for posterity the only written record that Stalin humbled himself on this occasion, a record that he would have burned (like his letter of apology), if he could have read it in the journal? Perhaps for both reasons. In any case it seems that Stalin never learned of Krupskaya's efforts to stop Lenin's ultimatum, and on the contrary had fresh reason to think that she was trying to turn Lenin against him.

On March 10 the third serious onset of cerebral hemorrhages paralyzed Lenin more completely, depriving him of speech and effectively ending his last political campaign. Encouraged by the somewhat obtuse optimism of the doctors, Krupskaya continued to hope that Lenin could still recover sufficiently to carry out his political plans, and she probably desisted from opening the sealed envelopes, if they had been given to her at this point. When Fotieva decided on her own initiative to attempt to place Lenin's testamentary writings before the Twelfth Congress in April 1923, Krupskaya took no part in the ensuing crisis. All the political leaders backed away from the idea that the material should be put on the agenda of the congress. Stalin, the chief victim of Lenin's wrath, succeeded in pointing out Trotsky's evasion of Lenin's wishes and managed to extract from Maria Ulyanova a statement that the testamentary writings could not be made public, although they could be discussed informally among congress delegates outside the plenary sessions.[20]

The implication is that Maria knew what was in the secret material, but this may not be wholly true. She served as Lenin's link with the *Pravda* editorial offices, where she worked before and after his final illness. When Lenin wanted to send a completed article from his sickroom to the newspaper, he would do it through her.[21] Thus Stalin was able to approach the matter of the testament as if it were an incomplete newspaper article, and the statement that he extracted from Maria was a matter of general policy (no publication of materials that were "not ready for the printer") rather than a comment on the content of the testament. This approach also had the advantage of bypassing Krupskaya, who might have felt called upon to act if invited to by the party leadership. In the absence of such a call, she seems to have been content to remain inactive, participating in neither the secret exchanges of communication before the congress nor the speeches at the meeting itself. She attended as a delegate with a consultative vote, but kept her peace while some fragmentary descriptions of Lenin's testament were circulated among at least some of the delegates.

Her life was now devoted to her husband's convalescence rather than his legacy. "I do not belong to the ranks of the optimists," she wrote to Lunacharsky at the end of July, referring to Lenin's health. But the doctors assured her that everything was coming along very well, and Krupskaya felt duty-bound to do what she could despite her doubts. As for Lenin's political legacy, it would hardly be surprising if she were reluctant to attack this problem.

On May 15, 1923, they moved once more to Gorki, where Krupskaya patiently played the role of nurse, physiotherapist, censor, and companion. There were no secretaries and no dictation. Krupskaya described the temper of their life in a letter to Varvara Armand, dated September 13, 1923:

I don't know what to write. Things aren't bad with us, although at times it seems that one only deceives one's self. In any case it is all moving much more slowly than one would want. Of course, time will tell. . . . We go in the car deep in the woods to look for mushrooms, we read newspapers. They have definitely called off the sister. The doctors' supervision is at a minimum. We live not badlý, really, if I don't think too much, and so I try to occupy myself with this business [of illness] as little as possible. Well, that's all there is to my business.[22]

The terse comment on "the sister" is interesting. It could not refer to Maria, who was still with the household according to other witnesses. But sister Anna came to visit at about this time, and it seems likely that she wanted to stay on and help nurse her brother. Krupskaya never did get along with Anna, and the wording of her comment suggests that there had been a short scuffle in the family which ended when "they" (the doctors) were persuaded, probably by Krupskaya, that Lenin's nerves could not stand Anna.

They also could not stand doctors, and Krupskaya tried to do her best to fend off the attentions of the large medical corps that the Politburo had assigned. Writing (in German) to Klara Zetkin, who was living in Moscow and had become quite a good friend, Krupskaya noted on June 19 that:

Lenin did not sleep yesterday night and was exceptionally nervous and upset. In such circumstances it was impossible to examine him [medically]. A whole crowd of doctors, Russian, German, etc. had already examined him earlier. This upset him so that once again a severe worsening of his condition came on. Therefore one must be very careful and undertake no new examination except in dire necessity.[23]

The sick man could not speak or read normally, but by summer he could hobble around with the help of a male nurse, then with only a cane. He was still struggling to keep in touch with politics, and Krupskaya was supposed to see that he was kept isolated from such anxieties. A guard, A. B. Belmas, recalls one crisis that Krupskaya smoothed over:

> Once, in the summer of 1923, it seems, my negligence brought about an incident which, fortunately, ended all right. I received newspapers in the mail. Absorbed in reading a feuilleton in the newspaper *Bednota* [*The Poor Peasants*], I didn't notice that Ilyich, leaning on the shoulder of the feldsher Comrade Casimir Zor'ki, was approaching the table in the [guards'] day room. His eyes lit up when he saw the newspapers on my table, which I consequently tried to hide in time. Ilyich came up to the desk, greeted me and demanded all the newspapers [no doubt by gestures, facial expression and grunts — he could not speak.] I stood in terror, not knowing what to do. Maria Ilyinichna shot annihilating looks at me, as if to say, what kind of a mess have you made? But Nadezhda Konstantinovna, with her wonderful restraint and tact, smiled at Ilyich and said caressingly to him, 'All right, Volodya, we will read the news right now.' She took all the newspapers from the table, went off a little way right beside the main house, sat down with him on a bench and began to read the newspapers. Nadezhda Konstantinovna knew well what could be read to him. She read of the construction of a factory, the arrival of a supply train of potatoes in Moscow, of the improvement of the way of life of the workers in one of the plants, and so on. She knew how to avoid the tense aspects of international relations, and to make up something herself at these points.[24]

By August 10, Krupskaya recalled later, they undertook a daily ritual with the newspapers that continued until the end. Lenin would scan *Pravda* and *Izvestia* and point out the articles that he wanted her to read to him. Apparently the strokes had affected his vision in such a way that he could manage headlines, illustrations, political cartoons, and an illustrated wall calendar given to him by a Comintern representative, but he usually had to depend on a reader for ordinary print.[25] This, of course, left Krupskaya room to exclude the upsetting and to invent cheering news. It is a fine irony that the man who founded the system by which the Soviet populace is deprived of unfit news and fed endless stories of toilers' victories should have been condemned to just such treatment in his last months — and at the hands of the former secretary of his first newspaper, *Iskra*.

No doubt this kind of creative reading was a great strain on Krupskaya. Reading works created by others, such as poetry by Demian Bednyi, stories by Jack London, and Gorky's autobiography, imposed less tension, but any kind of extended reading aloud is tiresome. It also must have been a great trial to attempt daily lessons to try to help Lenin speak. This involved a highly complicated kind of physiotherapy in which Krupskaya had no training. Perhaps she did it herself because Lenin was hostile to most medical practitioners. It is hardly surprising that they made little progress, although it does seem that Lenin learned to say *"tak"* ("so" — meaning yes) fairly clearly, and Krupskaya seems to have been able to make something out of his other inarticulate sounds. Understandably, she was glad to see Lenin go off by himself for occasional jaunts in a carriage or sleigh to watch others hunt, accompanied by a medical assistant. "He wanted to be without a nanny," she told Zinoviev, acknowledging that the relationship was a strain. She also found some outlet in a more or less weekly trip to Moscow, visiting a few friends, such as Klara Zetkin or Varvara Armand.

By October Lenin felt strong enough to want to join her on one of these outings. Nadezhda and the doctors tried to dissuade him, but on October 19 he simply limped to the garage, sat down in the car, and indicated that he was bent on going. His nanny capitulated and they went to the Kremlin, where Lenin paid a last visit to his apartment. In memoirs that were secret until 1968 Krupskaya recollects that he gathered his "notebooks" and three volumes of Hegel, and that after spending the night in town he was in a great hurry to return to Gorki.[26] Perhaps this simply expressed Lenin's vain hope that he could resume his philosophical studies while convalescing, or perhaps the "notebooks" included material on his last political campaign. Krupskaya seems to have thought that in these months Lenin was more sympathetic to some of the pre-revolutionary comrades with whom he had quarreled than with his current Bolshevik colleagues. If she did not know how the old-timers were, he sent her to the telephone to find out. He asked about "Aksel'rod, Stanislav Vol'sky, Bogdanov. In connection with Askel'rod he asked about Martov. I signified by my expression that I did not understand. On another day he went downstairs to the library and found in an emigrant newspaper the report of the death of Martov [on April 4, 1923] and reproachfully showed it to me."[27] He also asked about Gorky, who had left the Soviet Union as a critic of the regime.

Was Krupskaya not intimating — writing in the reign of Stalin — that in Lenin's last months his thoughts were with the men whose humanitarian qualities had helped to make them losers, rather than with the new "bureaucrats" whom he wished to attack?

This perspective came to Krupskaya only years later, if at all. At the end of 1923 she took quite a different view of the succession crisis that was taking form in the party. As it had become increasingly clear to the party leaders that Lenin was finished, two main factions had emerged. On one side stood the party establishment, which controlled the administrative machinery of Bolshevism. It was headed by the troika of Stalin-Zinoviev-Kamenev. Against them stood Trotsky, supported (and urged on during his frequent periods of inaction) by a variety of second-rank figures, many of them talented.

In January 1924, Krupskaya committed her prestige and implicitly, Lenin's, to the troika, which was organizing a campaign against the opposition. Her old friends Zinoviev and Kamenev probably recruited her for this service, but it is clear that her interventions were her own words and reflected her own thinking at this time. There is a uniquely Krupskayan flavor to her two works of January 1923: soft-spoken but confident, modest in a preachy way, conciliatory in tone but armed with polemical daggers.

Krupskaya's first article was a rebuttal of the two main opposition statements at this stage: the "Declaration of the Forty-Six" and Trotsky's essay, "The New Course," which she mentioned specifically. Writing in *Pravda* (January 3, 1924) under the title "Closer to the Worker Mass," she denied the charge that the party was becoming alienated from the working class. It was not a question of the percent of the party membership who were actually workers, but of maintaining close links between the worker mass and the higher levels. Trotsky also erred in talking about the distinction between old and young party members, for the old Bolsheviks were as vigorous as anyone in the party. As for charges of bureaucratism, she tartly observed that the opposition had no practical solution unless they intended the substitution of Pyatakov and Ossinsky (signers of the "Declaration") for existing officials. The point was well taken. Pyatakov was himself a bureaucrat and became one of Stalin's leading officials later on — before he was purged.

The next venture was a speech at a conference of the party organization of the Bauman district of Moscow on January 8, 1924. This was a tactically important occasion because the main support for the opposition was in Moscow and the election of delegates to the Thirteenth Party Conference was about to take place there. Published in *Pravda* on January 11, the speech was a shrewd political appeal on behalf of the ruling troika and her own right to interpret true Leninism. She achieved this without mentioning her husband's name, relying on her prestige and references to the tradition that Lenin (and she) represented. She recalled the early years of the party, when it had been necessary to establish firm discipline for the struggle, to prevent factionalism. The question "What is to be done?" faces the party in every epoch, she said, alluding to the title of Lenin's famous centralist tract of 1902, and "This question stands before us right now." The analogy between the new oppositionists and the Mensheviks of 1903 was obvious, and the implication that Trotsky was on the anti-Leninist side both times was clear.

Still without mentioning names, except a word of praise for Zinoviev, she went on to stress the difficult position of the Soviet republic and to imply that the oppositionists were coming close to endangering national security with their factions and their criticism of centralized authority in the party. "In a moment of battle," she argued, "everyone understands very well that the party needs the *part-apparat* [the bureaucratic machine]."

Here she was coming right into Stalin's domain, providing an imposing Leninist blessing for the whole hierarchical system that served the General Secretary. She chided comrades who worried because party officials were being appointed from above, rather than elected from below. "Formal election yields very little in the end," she said. Improvements were of course necessary, but "All sorts of talk about bureaucratism in general, about the good or ill intentions of these or those "apparatchiks" only complicates this important question [i.e., reform]." For Stalin, the chief apparatchik, this was sweet music.

At the time Krupskaya could not have seen things this way. Very few Soviet politicians had the insight at the beginning of 1924 to see Stalin as the potential successor to Lenin. Zinoviev was commonly considered to be Trotsky's chief rival, and Krupskaya regarded him as a friend, who, with Kamenev, had helped protect her against Stalin a year earlier. Trotsky, on the other hand, had seemed a very unreliable Leninist, not only between 1903 and 1916, but during the early part of 1923. It would not have been hard for Zinoviev to persuade Krupskaya that the cause of party unity was at stake, that true Leninism stood on the side of the troika, who were defending the party against the latest heresy.

The campaign against the opposition that she had supported bore fruit at the Thirteenth Party Conference (not Congress) on January 16-18. Led by Stalin, the troika overwhelmed the opposition in an imposing show of "unanimity" — that is, the troika and especially Stalin's political machine, had excluded all but three voting opposition delegates (some others attended as delegates without a "deciding" vote). Trotsky was absent because of illness. Krupskaya remained with Lenin in Gorki during the meetings, but probably was well satisfied with the success of her work. Thinking, one may surmise, that Lenin would be heartened by the show of unity at the conference, she read him the newspaper accounts of the conference in *Pravda* on January 17-20, and in particular the resolutions passed by the delegates.[28]

Perhaps Krupskaya omitted Stalin's lengthy speech on "Trotsky's Six Errors," which would have shown Lenin who was delivering a "bomb" against whom. But if she read the resolutions with even moderate accuracy, Lenin would have learned that the new opposition had been castigated as a "petit-bourgeois deviation." At some such point in the reading of the resolutions the old fox, though mortally wounded, caught the scent of what was happening to his last political campaign. "When, on Saturday, Vladimir Ilyich became visibly alarmed [while listening to Krupskaya read a resolution from the conference], I told him that the resolution was taken unanimously."[29] This was a lie. If Krupskaya did not know it, Lenin, the old expert in producing spurious majorities, surely did.

It is hard to say if Krupskaya realized fully at this time the seriousness of her indiscretion. Her fragmentary recollection about the reading of the resolution continues blandly: "We spent Saturday and Sunday reading the resolutions. Vladimir Ilyich listened very attentively, sometimes asking questions."[30] Quite possibly Lenin cunningly suppressed his anxiety so that Krupskaya would not deprive him of this insight into the succession struggle. On another occasion Krupskaya recollected that on the same days, January 19 and 20, she read to him from Jack London, one of his favorite authors. Was this an attempt to distract him from the upset caused by the resolutions of the conference?

For several months prior to this point Lenin's condition had been improving steadily, and the doctors, even Krupskaya and Maria, were all predicting eventual recovery. There were tentative plans to move Lenin to the balmy Crimean coast in the spring to help the process. But the day after Krupskaya read Lenin the last installment of the resolutions of the Thirteenth Party Conference, that is, on January 21, 1924, he suddenly took a turn for the worse, suffering convulsions, high fever, and loss of consciousness. Krupskaya was with him, caressing his hand. It was all that anyone could do. At 6:50 p.m. Lenin died.

Some writers, including Trotsky, have tried to suggest that Stalin murdered Lenin to save himself. It is impossible to offer conclusive negative proof concerning conjectural poisons and the like, but the whole theory is implausible. There is every reason to believe that Lenin really did have irreversible cerebral arterial sclerosis, as the official medical evidence maintains. The partial remission that he had in late 1923 and the first weeks of 1924 is not a medical miracle, nor is it surprising that he died of a new stroke on January 21. There is no way of knowing precisely what triggered this, but if one wishes to embark on any theorizing on the matter, one need not start with Stalin or poisons. Lenin's fatal stroke is far more likely to have been triggered by Krupskaya's soft voice reading from the resolutions of the Thirteenth Party Conference.

CHAPTER IX

The Widow and the Legacy

The death of her husband, six months after her uncele-
brated silver wedding anniversary, was a great blow to
Krupskaya. She was devoted to Lenin, and her life had
been inseparably attached to his both personally and politically. She was bereaved not only of her husband but also
of her political guide, left to puzzle out her own understanding of true Marxism, or Marxism-*Leninism* as it had
now become. For Krupskaya this was far from being a
purely personal concern. It was the key to the success or
failure of the whole cause of Communism, hence her life.
Although she never aspired to high political office for herself, she was convinced that nobody understood her late
husband and his goals as well as she. In his absence she
bore the crucial responsibility of interpreting Leninism to
the party and the masses, and this obliged her to enter into
the main arena of Soviet politics, regardless of her personal
wishes.

This sense of duty helped Krupskaya to live through
the weeks just after Lenin died, bearing her along on the
certain conviction that she had a job to do. But in the
longer run Nadezhda had neither the power nor the per-

ception to fill the role that she attempted to play. Even before he died, the founder of Bolshevism and the Soviet Union had become a mythic figure. While he was still alive, in October 1923, the party had established an "Institute of V. I. Lenin," the opening of which Krupskaya had attended. It was inevitable that the various party leaders who were contending for succession to supreme authority in Russia would seek to legitimize themselves and their policies as being true to Leninism. Krupskaya's great prestige as Lenin's closest comrade could therefore be a valuable political asset, and her approval would be sought. But the rivals for power would want to use her, not listen to her ideas on Leninism, and for several years after Lenin died Krupskaya was to be buffeted by the turmoil of the succession struggle.

Who could say what Lenin would have wanted in this essentially post-Leninist situation? Krupskaya no doubt tried to answer this question, but could not arrive at a consistent answer of her own. In the end she supported Stalin's answer, not because she liked him better, but because he seemed to represent the will of the party, Lenin's party, outside of which there could be no Leninism.

This outcome was not at all what she or others expected at the time Lenin died. The widow correctly saw the funeral as a political event of the first magnitude, and she attempted to use it to establish her moral authority. On January 23, 1924, she accompanied the coffin on the funeral train from the station nearest Gorki to Moscow. All the members of the Politburo were there save Trotsky, who was stranded in the Caucasus where he was taking a rest-cure for a persistent fever. According to one witness, Krupskaya was the only dry-eyed person at the station in Moscow. The body then lay in state in the Hall of Columns, the building which had already become the Bolsheviks' principal funeral parlor. Elena Krylenko recorded her impression of the scene in a letter to her future husband, Max Eastman: "And his wife is standing there, looking at his face. She is standing there all the time. Nobody can replace her." The representatives of the Central Committee, on the other hand, took ten-minute turns standing by the bier, Krylenko said.[1]

This could not have been literally true, for Lenin lay in state from January 23 to January 27, but the important point is that Krupskaya made her presence felt before all others. Her real devotion to Lenin and her sense of mission on behalf of his cause required this pre-eminence.

These same days witnessed other events that in the long run proved more important to the fate of the Lenin myth. The day after Lenin died his funeral arrangements were entrusted to a special commission headed by the police chief, Dzerzhinsky. In view of his close ties to Stalin, this was a bad sign for Krupskaya. The most important political ceremony that the commission arranged was a special session of the All-Russian Congress of Soviets to hear eulogies from the principal political leaders of the country. Stalin's was a famous incantation that invoked Lenin's departing wishes and the General Secretary's authority to interpret them. A short excerpt illustrates its tone:

> For twenty-five years Comrade Lenin tended our party and made it into the strongest and most highly selected workers' party in the world. . . . *Departing from us, Comrade Lenin enjoined us to guard the unity of our party as the apple of our eye. We vow to you, Comrade Lenin, that this behest, too, we shall fulfill with honor!*[2]

It was unknown until 1964 that Krupskaya had drafted a strikingly similar, perhaps better speech. A fair copy of it in her own handwriting shows that she had given the matter considerable thought since the night Lenin died. Like Stalin's speech, it is notable not for intellectual content but for ritualistic significance:

"LENIN"
"LENIN was the foe of tsars, landlords and capitalists, the foe of oppressors.

"LENIN was the closest friend of the working men and women, peasant men and women, the friend of all toilers.

"LENIN was the friend of the oppressed nations, called them to battle.

"LENIN all his life led the millions of workers and peasants to battle against oppression, for freedom, for land, for a better lot.

"LENIN all his life worked for the creation of the Communist Party, which must show all workers and peasants the path to struggle, to go into battle in the first ranks.

"LENIN raised the fight against the predatory world war which the tsars and capitalists started. He called on the toilers of all the warring countries to form a fraternal union. He called on them to arise against those who started the war.

"LENIN helped the workers and peasants of his own country to take power, to achieve peace, to take the land, factories and plants. He helped the republic of workers and peasants defend itself against enemies.

"LENIN called the toilers of all countries to come together, to organize around the militant international union of workers, the Third International.

"LENIN called on the workers and peasants who had taken power together to build a life of abundance, health, education and light — socialism.

"LENIN BEQUEATHS [the commands]:

"1. To strengthen further the fraternal union of workers and peasants.

"2. To strengthen and improve their power — Soviet power.

"3. To unite more closely around the Communist Party.

"4. To be true to the international union of toilers.

"5. To struggle with darkness, to fight for knowledge.

"6. To raise the economic level of the country by every means.

"7. To unite its small farms through cooperatives.

"8. To organize everything jointly in the best way.

"UNSWERVINGLY FORWARD TO THE LIFE OF LIGHT,
TO SOCIALISM, TO COMMUNISM!
"FULFILL LENIN'S BEHESTS!"[3]

Why was this consigned to the archives for forty years? Most probably because all speeches had to be cleared with Dzerzhinsky's commission, which decided that only Stalin was to be permitted to interpret Lenin's legacy. Krupskaya was, however, permitted a speech at the session of the Supreme Soviet on January 26 — a rather exceptional act for a widow at her husband's funeral. She spoke briefly of her personal knowledge of Lenin's love of the workers, of his belief in the alliance of the peasants and workers.[4] It was a rather unimposing speech, totally lacking in the tightly structured, ritualistic form of the suppressed version. Probably it was composed in great haste and exhaustion. Nevertheless, various Communists present have recollected that hers was the most moving of all the speeches, and this could be, considering who she was, and how dignified.

The day after the funeral orations Lenin's coffin was carried by prominent Bolsheviks from the Hall of Columns to a hastily erected wooden mausoleum, standing above the ground on Red Square, a long stone's throw from Lenin's apartment, now occupied only by Krupskaya and Maria. Lenin still lay in state for the public, but this did not displease Krupskaya. On January 28 she wrote to Inessa Armand's daughter Inessa, "Yesterday we held Vladimir Ilyich's funeral. . . . They have not yet prepared the tomb [*grob,* which could mean either "grave" or "coffin"] now, and *for a while it will still be possible to look at Ilyich.* His face is peaceful, peaceful. He rested in the House of Unions [Hall of Columns], everything there was very fine and ceremonious and special. Night and day the people went past, looked on Lenin, and wept. . . ."[5]

Obviously Krupskaya expected that a grave would be prepared soon, the body would be removed from the temporary mausoleum, and the lying in state would be decently terminated.

But to this day Lenin's body is the most remarkable tourist attraction in Moscow. Apparently Krupskaya learned of the decision to keep him on display, or the probability of this decision, by January 29, for the next day she had an open letter in *Pravda* which was a veiled protest. "I have a great request to you," she wrote, addressing herself to all the workers and peasants. "Do not permit your grief for Ilyich to take the form of external reverence for his person. Do not raise memorials to him, palaces named after him, splendorous festivals in commemoration of him, etc.: To all this he attached so little importance in his life, all this was so burdensome to him. . . ." But the workers and peasants were mute, and continued to flock to the mausoleum.[6]

Although she lost this fight, Krupskaya never publicly mentioned the mausoleum or its contents in her voluminous works glorifying Lenin, never visited it nor stood atop it during party festivals. In the same spirit she persisted in referring to the city of *Lenin*grad by its old nickname, "Piter," in her own correspondence.

As one would expect, Krupskaya received an enormous flood of condolences, from the Central Committee of the party down to innumerable obscure individuals. Although it was impossible for her to acknowledge any large number of these, she did take time quite soon after Lenin's death to write some personal notes on the occasion, her own condolences to some special people. One letter went to Gorky, living in exile in Italy. He had left Russia on poor terms with Lenin, whose regime he found brutal. Krupskaya, who seems to have admired the great literary man from afar, wanted him to know that the dying Lenin retained warm feelings for him, having asked Nadezhda to read Gorky's *My Universities* shortly before the end.[7]

Another went to Klara Zetkin, the German Communist leader, who was in her homeland. Krupskaya had become well acquainted with Klara during her extended visits to Russia after the revolution. Lenin probably did not attach such exceptional importance to Klara as a friend or leader, but Krupskaya thought of her as an intimate and wished to commune with her.

Still another, which was quoted above, went to Inessa Armand's daughter Inessa, who was married to a German Communist leader and living in Berlin. It has never been published in full, perhaps by chance, perhaps because Krupskaya, in this emotional hour, was embarrassingly honest concerning Lenin and the elder Inessa.

The fourth letter that Krupskaya wrote when Lenin died was to Trotsky, who had made no serious effort to rush from the Caucasus to appear at the funeral. Krupskaya, writing two days after that event, was far from reproachful. Instead, she tried to bridge the gulf that existed between herself and Trotsky, whom she had publicly attacked a few weeks before:

> Dear Lev Davidovich,
> I write to tell you that about a month before his death, as he was looking through your book, Vladimir Ilyich stopped at the place where you sum up Marx and Lenin, and asked me to read it over again to him; he listened very attentively, and then looked it over again himself. And here is another thing I want to tell you. The attitude of V. I. toward you at the time when you came to us in London from Siberia has not changed until his death. I wish you, Lev Davidovich, strength and health, and I embrace you warmly.
> N. Krupskaya[8]

When Krupskaya made this overture to Trotsky, she probably had in mind the awesome burden that Lenin's testament imposed on her — not her own or Stalin's fictionalized "behests" of Lenin, but the dictations in the now-unsealed envelopes. Since it was now certain that Lenin himself could not act on his last political wishes, his executrix was obliged to see to it that his thoughts were properly transmitted to the next party congress. Lenin himself had called his final dictations not a "testament" but "Letters to the Congress." Clearly this transmission would not be easy, as the fiasco of Fotieva's attempts to disseminate the material at the congress of the previous spring had proved. Although Krupskaya knew that Trotsky had failed to act on Lenin's behalf at this time, she also knew that he had the most to gain by Lenin's attack on Stalin and that it was he to whom Lenin had turned in his last articulate period.

In later years Trotsky, understandably, took pride in Krupskaya's letter to him, as evidence that the Stalinists were wrong in calling him a bad Leninist. But in early 1924 he seems to have taken no slight step to accept the proffered reconciliation, or even to acknowledge the note — a remarkable and even rude oversight that could only have alienated Krupskaya.[9] The reconciliation that he spurned in 1924, he was to plead for, in vain, three years later.[10]

Krupskaya attempted to resume her normal activities as soon as possible after the funeral. On February 5 she was back at Narkompros and in the coming weeks resumed her heavy schedule of public speaking at various conferences on education and youth. She also sought to establish her place as an authoritative interpreter of Leninism by addressing a large party audience on March 21, 1924, on "How to Study Leninism."[11] In this she had a rival. The next month Stalin delivered a series of lectures on "The Foundations of Leninism," which he made sure soon became far more widely disseminated than Krupskaya's talk.[12]

But her numerous articles and speeches could not fulfill the mission that Lenin had bequeathed to Krupskaya: the transmission of his final words to the party congress. Only on May 18, 1924, five days before the opening of the congress, did she act, and then in uncertain fashion. She gathered up all of Lenin's papers of December 23, 1922–January 23, 1923, and (excepting one on the nationalities problem) sent them to Kamenev. In her short covering letter she noted that Lenin particularly wanted the next party congress to hear his comments on the leading political figures, implicitly including the suggestion that Stalin be fired as General Secretary.[13]

Kamenev proved to be a poor ally, but it was hard for Nadezhda to know where to turn. Stalin, whose office made him the correct person to deal with the agenda of the congress, was the last person for Krupskaya to approach. Trotsky had ignored her overture after Lenin's death. If she thought of gaining the tribune at the congress as a delegate and unloading Lenin's testament as a bomb, she probably concluded that this might be too dangerous for party unity. Kamenev at least still appeared to be a personal friend, and was one of the three top leaders. He accepted the documents, and gave signs of compliance with Lenin's intention, but in a devious fashion that had the effect of suppressing the testament. On May 19 he submitted the material to a group of six Bolsheviks which called itself "the Central Committee Plenum Commission," although no such body had any legitimate status in the party. Dominated by the Stalin-Kamenev-Zinoviev troika, this "commission" made the pretence of acceding to Krupskaya's request, and decided to "submit them [the documents] to the nearest party congress for its information."[14] What the "congress" turned out to be was a special gathering of about forty "senior" delegates who met on May 22, the eve of the actual congress.[15]

Kamenev read the documents, or at least the testamentary ones dealing with personalities. Then the personalities in question vied to find ways of burying the unpleasant subject. Trotsky recalls that Stalin referred to the Lenin who dictated the testament as "a sick man surrounded by womenfolk" — a direct dig at Krupskaya. Zinoviev hypocritically assured everyone that Lenin's words were sacred, but that he was at least wrong about Stalin and the danger of disunity. Trotsky was perhaps still less honest. Krupskaya, he recalled years later, argued "with gentle insistence" that concealing the testament was "a direct violation of the will of Lenin, to whom you could not deny the right to bring his last advice to the attention of the party."[16] But Trotsky kept completely silent. Krupskaya's plea won her a vote of about ten against thirty, a rather large minority opposition by Bolshevik standards. Still, she had lost. The documents were partially disclosed to delegates at a special meeting, with the explanation that Lenin had been ill and misinformed by those around him (meaning Krupskaya above all) at the time of his last dictations. The testament was not read into the published record. Immediately following the congress Stalin went through the motions of offering his resignation to the newly elected Central Committee. He had selected this body to the best of his ability, and it responded loyally.

This was a serious defeat, and one that left Krupskaya seemingly isolated. A less determined person might have withdrawn from political activity, discouraged. Krupskaya, however, took a more active part in the Thirteenth Party Congress than in any of its predecessors. She dutifully accepted various formal honors that were offered her as Lenin's widow: election to the presidium of the congress, to its committee on agitation and propaganda, to the committee on press affairs, and to the Central Control Commission. This inspectorial body had an important political role in the next few years, meeting jointly with the Central Committee itself. She also was assigned the task of delivering, with Mikhail Kalinin, the report on party affairs on the countryside, one of the major, routine speeches. Hers was a long one, stressing the great difficulties that Soviet education and political education encountered in rural areas, and appealing for more money for this branch of the bureaucracy, her own.[17]

All of this was much less important, however, than her dramatic and unexpected intervention in the midst of the critical political issue of the day — the troika's attack on Trotsky and his supporters. As Lenin had feared, the party seemed to be splitting on factional lines, pitting Stalin against Trotsky. The General Secretary had succeeded in packing the congress with his supporters (by means of the political machine that Krupskaya had supported four months earlier) and sought to trap Trotsky in a dilemma: either recant your errors (admitting your unworthiness) or declare yourself an opponent of the party. Trotsky would do neither, although he did lay down the principle that was to guide many Bolsheviks in future capitulations to Stalin: "None of us wishes to be right, or can be right, against his party. The party is in the last resort always right."

Stalin's rejoinder was to reject this formula (much as he might later use it) and carry home the attack with a column of speakers on the theme: "Recant or admit your factionalism."

After a good deal of this Krupskaya asked for the floor and was recognized. She was greeted with enthusiasm by the delegates: "The whole congress rises. Prolonged applause, an ovation." Many of the delegates, and probably the ruling troika, expected her to enter into the spirit of the anti-Trotsky campaign as she had in January 1924. But her brief address was something else again. Frustrated in her efforts to put Lenin's testament before the congress, she could at least try to use her inherited moral authority to avoid the kind of open split in the party that he had feared. She rejected Trotsky's dictum that the party is infallible, but called for an end to the "duplication" of speeches on the whole subject and especially the demand that Trotsky admit his guilt. This, she said, was "psychologically impossible." The whole business "introduced superfluous bitterness into relations between the former opposition and the main body of the party." It interfered with the obligation of the party to cope with current problems, "And this obligation is stronger than ever because Vladimir Ilyich is not with us," she said, playing her trump card.[18]

It was the most effective speech Krupskaya ever made. The troika could not easily challenge her moral authority on this matter, and perhaps they were even a little worried that she might decide to read Lenin's testament to the congress. Stalin replied somewhat defensively that it was not he who had started the debate on the opposition, and the attack on Trotsky was allowed to subside without any conclusive action.[19]

With this the turmoil in the party subsided temporarily, and with it the protracted period of extreme tension that had afflicted Krupskaya since Lenin's last days. Her own health now showed the strain, though she tried to keep to her routine at Narkompros and resisted the doctors' attempts to make her rest. On June 14, 1924, we find her writing to Varvara Armand:

"Today they unleashed the doctors on me as well [as Maria, who was ill], and I only agreed to drink any amount of abominable filth [mineral water, beloved by most Russians, the stronger the better], but I said in advance that I would not drown myself in their regimen. I already told [Dr.] Pogasian today that I won't submit even if some politburo says so."

In July, however, the doctors won out and ordered her to the North Caucasian spa of Kislovodsk, and Krupskaya, who had been dry-eyed at Lenin's funeral, broke down and wept. By the time she arrived there, however, she had recovered her spirits enough to vent her feelings on the incompetent arrangements: "It's all an abomination," she wrote to Varvara. "They hustled me from hotel to hotel to hotel [looking for a room]. In the evening there was some sort of rumble of voices all around, around one in the night it was replaced by the furious barking of a dog and then by the crowing of roosters. It wasn't worth going three tenths of the way around the world to sleep for three hours in twenty-four. . . . Well, what an abomination."[20]

Her opinion of the trip improved, typically, after she was able to get down to some useful work — the beginnings of her memoirs of life with Lenin. By September 5 she wrote Varvara that she could be leaving for Moscow except that Maria, who was with her, was not getting better and yet would stay only if Nadezhda did. Soon they did return and Krupskaya resumed her accustomed, exhausting round of speeches and writings on education. By the opening of the new year, 1925, she had developed "serious heart trouble" and a new attack of the thyroid disease, followed in February by a bad case of grippe.

To recuperate she was sent to the Crimean seacoast resort of Mukholatka. "It's good here: mountains and the sea, there are places for walking, which I do. . . . But even though it's good here, all in all I don't like cures and am already thinking of Moscow." After a rest of about three weeks she did return, along with Maria and her secretary-companion Vera Dridzo. She boasted to Varvara Armand that she had gained "a kilo a day" and was "black as a jackdaw," but admitted that her heart still bothered her.[21]

Only rarely during this year of precarious health had Krupskaya re-entered the political struggle, which Trotsky had reheated in October 1924 with an attack on the ruling troika. In an essay on "The Lessons of October" he harked back to his own heroic role in the revolution, which contrasted so strikingly with that of the three. Stalin, Kamenev, and Zinoviev responded in a series of counter-articles, and induced Krupskaya to add her prestige to their cause. In an article "On the Question of the Lessons of October," published in *Pravda* (December 16, 1924) and reprinted in an anti-Trotsky anthology, *For Leninism,* she criticized Trotsky for weakness in "Marxist analysis" and in taking "a purely 'administrative' and utterly superficial" view of the party's role as the leading staff of the movement. This point was a sly reference to Lenin's testamentary criticism of Trotsky ("excessively attracted by the purely administrative side of affairs"). But otherwise the essay was not a very passionate polemic. It relied on irrelevant and vague talk of the party "as an organization cast in one piece" and the like, and carefully avoided the troika's hard line against Trotsky. "I do not know whether Comrade Trotsky has actually committed all the deadly sins of which he is accused — the exaggerations of controversy are inevitable," she said, making a sarcastic dig at Stalin's earlier listing of Trotsky's "six errors." And in her peroration: "Comrade

Trotsky devoted the whole of his powers to the fight for Soviet power during the decisive years of the revolution. He courageously stood by his difficult and responsible post. [This was meant as a dig at Kamenev and Zinoviev, who had opposed the October coup, as Lenin also noted in his testament.] He displayed colossal energy, enormous forcefulness to secure the victory of the revolution. The party will not forget this."

In all this Krupskaya further developed the stance that she had adopted at the Thirteenth Party Congress: support for the "general line" of the party against Trotsky, while remaining above factions, retaining her respect for the opposition and keeping open the possibility of reconciliation with it. Her readiness to lean toward the opposition was enhanced by the debate on the peasant question that developed in 1925. Stalin was maneuvering to dump Kamenev and Zinoviev, and to do this he joined with Bukharin, who advocated a soft line on peasants in general and the prosperous ones ("kulaks") in particular. Krupskaya, like Trotsky, Kamenev, and Zinoviev, held that too much socialism was being conceded to capitalism in the name of economic recovery. She first broached her criticism of Bukharin–Stalin, without mentioning names, at a session of the Central Control Commission on January 21, 1925. In a short speech she took a hard line on concessions to "kulaks, traders, and exploiters" on the countryside and stressed Lenin's desire for more peasant cooperatives, excluding prosperous peasants.[22]

In June this issue flared up in a new way. Bukharin, as editor of *Pravda*, sought to undermine his critics by publishing some of Lenin's private writings (*not* the sickbed dictations of 1923–1924) that suited his point. Outraged that anyone should use unpublished Lenin papers on behalf of erroneous policies, while she had been unable to publish the testament, Krupskaya wrote a sharp polemic against Bukharin. It must have hit home because the Politburo, over the pleas of Zinoviev and Kamenev, voted to suppress her article. The idea of gagging Lenin's widow was justified by arguing that Bukharin had written a reply which also would be suppressed.[23] This affront must have gone some distance in persuading Krupskaya that she really stood with the opposition. It is hard to put a date on her entry into this status because the "opposition" lacked any definite organization or any formal membership, thanks to the Leninist tradition of unity and discipline in the party.

In July 1925 this tradition no doubt helped to induce both Trotsky and Krupskaya to deceive the public about the nature of Lenin's testament. The cause of this grotesque episode was the publication by Max Eastman, the pro-Trotsky American writer, of a book called *Since Lenin Died*. Relying on what Trotsky had told him previously, Eastman gave a generally accurate description of the testament, along with various observations on the supposed decline of true Leninism in Russia. The book never appeared there, but Krupskaya received a copy and could scarcely have liked it. Eastman carried on the kind of vague talk about bureaucratism in the party that she never really accepted, and his idea of Trotsky as Lenin's alter ego and proper successor was deeply offensive. In a public letter, dated July 7 1925, she tackled these points with sincere feeling. To satisfy Stalin and his allies she also went beyond her real beliefs and maintained that Lenin did not express any "distrust" of any of his colleagues in his final letters to the party congress.[24] This sorry deception must have burned on her conscience, even if it was supposedly for the good of the party.

While appearing to be an ultra-orthodox Bolshevik at this time, Krupskaya was in reality coming round to the one step that definitely could mark her as a member of the opposition: signing a manifesto of protest against official policy. This document was the work of Zinoviev, who was by the summer of 1925 the focus of anti-Stalin politics. Krupskaya's personal friendship with him had suffered during his alliance with Stalin, but it was still there, and in the summer of 1925 he thanked her for reading (and implicitly approving) his long book called *Leninism*. On

September 5 he, Kamenev, Krupskaya, and Sokolnikov (the commissar of finance) jointly signed a "platform" attacking the Stalin-Bukharin leadership. The issues at stake were peasant policy and administrative methods.[25] This document was never published, but in October 1925 it was circulated among members of the Central Committee and Central Control Commission, which were meeting jointly. Krupskaya, as a member of the Central Control Commission, attended and added her voice to the other oppositionists present to demand that the issues be openly debated.

Such ideas of political pluralism might be considered contrary to Lenin's insistence on unity and the subordination of the minority to the party leadership. On the other hand, if *he* had been in the minority, he undoubtedly would have fought for his position or, failing in that, would have withdrawn at the head of his own "true" party.

Krupskaya was not up to this, but she did struggle valiantly to persuade the representatives of the party of the rightness of opposition. The trouble was that Stalin's political machine controlled most of the key organizations, except in Leningrad, Zinoviev's stronghold. In Moscow Krupskaya had no noticeable success in winning over the delegates to the regional party conference preceding the Fourteenth Party Congress in December 1925. Following Bukharin and other luminaries, she noted that illness had prevented her speaking out sooner, and went on to appeal to the ordinary party member against the propaganda of the leaders. Their speeches, she complained, attempted to create an atmosphere of "panic, doubts about the party, liquidationism" (Lenin's term for opponents who allegedly wanted to end the underground party in pre-war days). Actually, she said, the opposition supported the Central Committee and merely wished to modify its soft policy toward kulaks and exploiters. She specifically attacked Bukharin and his claim that he was following Lenin's line on peasant affairs. Pathetically assuming that her authority as the interpreter of Lenin was still unchallenged, Krupskaya recounted that she had on several occasions *told* Bukharin that Lenin wanted co-ops rather than kulaks.[26]

The Fourteenth Party Congress itself was the pinnacle of Krupskaya's public career in the opposition. With shrewd political timing she had published the first installments of her memoirs of Lenin at about this time, stressing their common struggle with early un-Leninist deviations, as if to suggest that this was the fight she was still carrying on. At the congress she was elected to the presidium and her suppressed article against Bukharin's peasant policy, as well as the Platform of the Four (Kamenev, Zinoviev, Krupskaya, Sokolnikov), were privately circulated among the delegates. Most important, it was left to her to begin the opposition's critique from the rostrum. Zinoviev, their nominal leader, did not choose to deliver a polemic, either from timidity or the belief that it would be more useful to seem statesmanlike. Kamenev made a sharp attack on Stalin, but only after Krupskaya had opened the campaign.

In some ways her speech was powerful and acute, especially in its conclusion, invoking the name of Lenin to good effect.[27] She skillfully used examples from his life (and her own) to justify the position of the opposition against the majority: "One cannot soothe one's self with the thought that the majority is always right. In the history of the party there have been times when the majority was not right. Let us recall, for example, the Stockholm Congress [1906]." At this point there were "voices," the record states: "That is a gentle hint on a weighty matter." Without saying so, Krupskaya had projected the comparison of the Stalin-Bukharin leadership, which was "soft" on kulaks, with the "soft" Mensheviks of yore.

Proceeding in the same subtle tone, she noted that Lenin himself had written of the fate of revolutionary leaders who, after their deaths, became "harmless icons," which deflected attention from their revolutionary teachings. This should warn the delegates against labeling "this or that one of our views as Leninism." For those delegates with the wit to understand, and they were few enough, this was a damning comment on the Stalin leadership, which could sanctify Lenin's body and use this inert image, like an icon, to prove the validity of their un-Leninist creed.

Despite her denial that anyone should claim to speak for Lenin, Krupskaya was trying to do just this in the main part of her speech. This was less imposing than its finale, a bit rambling and redundant, aimed principally at Bukharin's peasant policy, while Stalin himself was ignored. He was shrewdly letting Bukharin appear as the chief policy formulator of the current leadership, decoying most of the opposition into polemics against an expendable ally. Despite her long personal antipathy to Stalin, Krupskaya fell for the ruse, continuing her insistence that Bukharin's peasant policy was insufficiently socialist.

Only briefly and obliquely did she come to the key question of dictatorship within the party, under Stalin. Alluding by implication to the fate of her own suppressed article against Bukharin, she complained that the party press had not permitted open discussion of all the issues, which meant that dissenting ideas appeared as a shock at the congress. In particular she objected to the "shameful" heckling that Zinoviev had encountered. This, she said, was contrary to the traditions of the party. Perhaps, but this very tradition included ruthless suppression of "deviations," and Krupskaya seriously undermined her own moral position by recalling the harsh tactics that Lenin had encouraged in dealing with Mensheviks and Socialist Revolutionaries. One could not act so ruthlessly, she protested, *within* the party. Here she fell into a trap. If she compared the situation in 1925 with that of 1906, why shouldn't deviators of the later year be treated like Mensheviks? Why shouldn't Stalin crush deviations, as Lenin always did if he could? This contradiction in Krupskaya's major speech for the opposition summed up her personal dilemma: true Leninism or the party? In her husband's lifetime the two had always been inseparable in her eyes. Now, with Lenin dead, and her understanding of Leninism rejected, there was a terrible choice between Leninism (as she saw it) and the party. The dilemma expressed in her words to Lenin — "You are dear and the party is dear" — had revived in a new form.

Stalin, too, understood something of Lenin's career, and would not suffer a heresy to live, even though weak in numbers at the moment. He organized an effective counter-attack, part of which was aimed personally at Krupskaya. A variety of speakers rebutted her, generally keeping to fairly dignified criticism of her version of Leninism. Stalin himself skillfully picked on her definition of the New Economic Policy which she had called essentially capitalism. This, he said, was "unmitigated nonsense," adding mockingly, "and may she pardon me."[28]

Perhaps pardon could be compelled. Stalin admitted that Krupskaya's article against Bukharin had been suppressed, but he menacingly asked, "and why should it not be suppressed if the interests of party unity require this of us? *And what, in particular, distinguishes Comrade Krupskaya from any other responsible comrade?*"[29] To dispose of the obvious reply that she was Lenin's closest comrade, Stalin produced a remarkable speaker: Maria Ulyanova. She opened with an implied but obvious rebuff to her sister-in-law: "I take the floor not as Lenin's sister, thus pretending to a better understanding and interpretation of Leninism than all the other members of our party. (Applause.) I think that such a monopoly of better understanding of Leninism by Lenin's relatives does not exist and cannot exist. . . ."[30] Bukharin, who was a good friend of Maria's through their work on *Pravda,* no doubt helped to arrange this dig. How the political tensions between Nadezhda and Maria at this point reacted in their private lives in the small apartment in the Kremlin, one can only guess.

That Krupskaya had no special privileges, or even the right to be heard, was driven home more brutally when she tried to enter the debate once more on December 25. Stalin's hecklers were waiting for her, taunting her re-

peatedly for having signed the oppositional declaration of
the four, and on several occasions forcing her to plead for
a hearing. It was quite a change from the reverent audiences she was accustomed to. This was the one speech in
her career in the opposition that came right down to the
question of democracy within the party and the dictatorial
control that the Secretariat and Organizational Bureau ex-
ercised — meaning Stalin. She spoke of "the establishment
of intra-party democracy" as if it were something for the
future and castigated the ability of the ruling organs to
silence dissenters by transferring them out of the way. It
was a serious appeal for intellectual freedom, and it is revealing that it was one time when Krupskaya could not
support her case by citing Lenin's authority — intellectual
freedom was not his specialty.[31]

Krupskaya remained in the opposition for ten more
months — until October 1926 — but it was difficult for her
to find an effective form of struggle. The leading core of
the opposition gained strength and determination with the
formation of a Trotsky-Zinoviev alliance in the spring of
1926, but Nadezhda seems to have had little or no direct
role in this, or in the formation of a rudimentary underground network. She signed the major political manifesto
that the Trotsky-Zinoviev opposition produced in this
period, the "Declaration of the Thirteen," which was submitted to a joint meeting of the Central Committee and
Central Control Commission.[32] Its main theme was the
growth of bureaucratism and alienation of workers — not
exactly the kind of criticism that appealed to Krupskaya.
But sign it she did, along with another protest against
Soviet policy in the English General Strike of 1926. At the
Central Committee plenum itself she probably did not
speak out, risking further heckling by the large Stalinist
majority, but she did vote against one of the major resolutions of the meeting and signed a statement along with six
other opposition leaders who cast negative votes.[33]

As for the party membership or the public at large,
she was unable or unwilling to air her criticisms of the

leadership. She spoke and published very frequently in these months, still enjoying great eminence, but she skirted the real issues of the day. While her health did not prevent her from keeping to a vigorous pace during most of 1926, it probably undermined her combativeness. In February she had another round of grippe with a high temperature, and was cut off from all visitors and even the phone. It must have been serious enough, although Krupskaya wrote to an old friend at Narkompros, Alisa Radchenko, that her condition was not so bad and "the nurse will tell you how I had hysterics when they began to care for me." For recuperation she went to Gorki, not the south, and then at the end of July took a three-week vacation with the Radchenko family at their summer cottage on the Volga not far from the ancient city of Tver. The Radchenkos, incidentally, were good friends of Stalin's young wife, as well as old revolutionary comrades of Lenin and Krupskaya. At their simple retreat Nadezhda was cut off from all except members of the family and was able to rest, to enjoy country walks, sometimes hunting mushrooms, or simply to gaze at the Volga. It was a time of recuperation and reflection which not only improved her health (as she wrote to young Inessa Armand) but also strengthened her determination to make one desperate act of revolutionary defiance on behalf of Lenin's memory.

His testament and her obligation to him, the obligation of a revolutionary to risk self-sacrifice for the cause, seems to have been much on her mind during this vacation. Alisa Radchenko's diary recounts Krupskaya's continual talk of Lenin, which was fairly normal for her, but especially of the recollection of the police persecution that they had faced — life in Siberia, searches, arrests, "the anxieties and dangers."[34] The presence of the Radchenkos, tested comrades in the underground, also may have helped to rekindle this spirit. The Volga itself reminded Nadezhda of her past as a harried enemy of the state. In a letter written at this time she recalled how she had sailed on the great river by steamer with Lenin and his mother, when she was still a political prisoner. In a nearby hamlet Krupskaya visited a peasant cooperative that had been founded years before by Sofia Perovskaya, the regicide girl who sacrificed herself willingly on the gallows. Just before returning to Moscow at the end of August 1926, she spent three days on a "triumphal march," as Alisa Radchenko called it, through the city of Tver. The cheering crowds that followed her car knew little if anything of the intra-party struggle, but their enthusiasm excited Krupskaya (she described herself as "whirling like a madwoman") and raised the old revolutionary ardor in her. On the way out of Tver she even declaimed "The Storm," a poem by her beloved Nekrasov, evoking the spirit of revolt.[35]

The outcome of this rededication was a conspiracy in the old style — smuggling an illegal message across the closely guarded Russian border by a secret agent. The message was Lenin's last dictations about leading party members and the suggestion that Stalin be demoted. It was dispatched by a secret courier, a member of the opposition who was going abroad to attend a conference on international debts. He transmitted it to the French oppositionist Boris Souvarine, who arranged with Max Eastman for its publication in *The New York Times* on October 18, 1926.

This was a bold gesture of defiance, but futile, serving better to gratify Krupskaya's self-sacrificing zeal than to affect Soviet politics. The document was a sensation of sorts in the West but was easily kept out of the Soviet Union, and most foreign Communists were by this time too well disciplined to make trouble for Stalin in the Communist International. It is hard to know just what practical effect Krupskaya expected from this, her last revolutionary act. Perhaps she merely wanted to be put in jail, for it was at about this time that she is said to have told Kamenev, "If Lenin were alive today, he would be in jail."[36] Certainly martyrdom would have ended her responsibility for the fate of the revolution.

But Stalin was not about to give Krupskaya this satisfaction. He had other ways of bringing about her submission. Above all was the icon of the party and its "unity." The opposition always insisted that they were as much for unity as anyone else, and were always vulnerable to pressures to stop splitting the sacred vehicle of the working-class revolution. Squeezed by this logic and the threat of expulsion, Zinoviev, Trotsky, and others, on October 16, 1926, signed a recantation of their dissent and promised to give up factional activity. Although this did not in fact end the opposition, it must have destroyed Krupskaya's confidence in her allies against Stalin. It must have occurred to her that Lenin would never have surrendered, would never have admitted that he was the heretic. Trotsky, Zinoviev, and company had demonstrated, and not for the first time, that they could not carry on Lenin's work and were unworthy allies for his widow.

By the time this had happened, Stalin had also brought to bear some other, lower forms of pressure on Krupskaya, The details of his campaign are uncertain, much of it consisting of rumors, whispers, and innuendo. Yet its main drift is clear: Stalin threatened to discredit Krupskaya as Lenin's true consort and political intimate.

Stalin is supposed to have said, "I shall make someone else Lenin's widow." In some versions of the story he even specified his choice. Elena Stasova, R. S. Zemlyachka, and even one Artiukhina have been among those nominated.[37] Quite possibly Stalin did drop various names at one time or another, or possibly they were added to the story as it passed around the grapevine. Surely the most credible selection would have been Inessa Armand. If in fact her name was not being mentioned in this connection, it may be that Stalin was tormenting Krupskaya by circulating some less plausible names as a starter, and reserving Inessa's name for an open attack, if it came to that.

In any case, there was a nasty whispering campaign at this time, as Trotsky discreetly recalls in his obituary for Krupskaya:

". . . within the ranks of the apparatus they systematically compromised her, blackened her, degraded her, and in the ranks of the Komsomol spread the crudest and most ridiculous scandals."[38]

Krupskaya seems to have been trying to fend off this threat when she edited a new collection of memorial essays on Inessa in 1926.[39] Her esteem for Inessa was no novelty, but it is peculiar that Nadezhda should have found it necessary to interrupt her many tasks of the day to produce a memorial for a comrade who had already received extensive eulogies at the time of her death. Of course, this book never hinted at romantic connections, and suggested that Inessa and Krupskaya were simply the best of comrades. But this high-mindedness could not have offset the kind of low, sniggering stories that Trotsky mentioned. Nothing could have been more odious to Krupskaya, nothing more unworthy of rebuttal in her eyes, but the menace was real. If she proved too annoying to Stalin, he could dispose of her without resorting to prison.

Abandoned by her allies, pressed by the claims of party unity, threatened by Stalin, Krupskaya quit the opposition during the Fifteenth Party Conference. She must have communicated this to Stalin on about November 2 or 3, 1926, because he slipped the news into his concluding speech on the 3rd. Trotsky, Stalin noted, said that the opposition would grow stronger, but it was falling apart. "Is it not really a fact that Comrade Krupskaya, for example, is leaving the opposition bloc? [Stormy applause.] Is this accidental?"[40]

No, not accidental. Stalin was applying pressure to deprive the opposition of the prestige of Lenin's widow, which he wanted for himself. But had he completely succeeded in early November of 1926? There is almost no information on Krupskaya's thinking on this matter during the fall and winter of 1926–1927, but there is persuasive evidence that she did not capitulate quickly, completely, or without compensation. She was silent in public concerning the whole business for about six months after Stalin's announcement, neither confirming his statement nor supporting the opposition. The latter apparently did not consider her definitely lost, for Trotsky wrote Nadezhda a long letter, dated May 17, 1927, drafting it himself on his own typewriter.[41] In it Trotsky did not consider Krupskaya a Stalinist, but implied that she had adopted a neutralist position. He referred to some recent incident when she had dismissed the debate on world revolution (particularly the English General Strike of 1926 and the suppression of the Chinese Communists) as a "fuss" (*buza*). Her position on the opposition, Trotsky said, was to distinguish between "self-criticism" in the party, which she approved, and "partisan criticism," which she did not.

Knowing that both he and Krupskaya were watched, Trotsky indicated that he was trying to send the letter to her through "G. E." (Zinoviev), assuming that he was still in touch with Krupskaya. We cannot be sure that this was so or that the letter was delivered, but it was disseminated to some extent as a mimeographed, underground tract of the opposition, entitled "On the Question of Self Criticism." Trotsky's desire to use the letter to appeal to a wider audience seems to have undermined his potential appeal to its addressee. Trotsky showed remarkably little sense for Krupskaya's self-esteem, preaching to *her* on the necessity of observing Leninism. At one point he even implied that *she* had failed to speak out on a current issue *"po leninskii"* (in a Leninist way). Such exhortations were doomed, and undercut the effect of the one good argument in the letter: who is correct, Stalin or the opposition? Knowing her feelings for Lenin's testament and for Stalin personally, Trotsky came close to the bone in reminding her that they had previously agreed that "we have an unhealthy regime, crude and disloyal." The last adjectives were lifted from Lenin's critique of Stalin in the testament. The letter ended with a warm, handwritten farewell: "From my soul I wish you good health and an equally invincible confidence in the truth of the line that you will defend."

No reply from Krupskaya exists in the Trotsky archive, but she did respond in a fashion. On May 20, 1927, three days after Trotsky signed his letter, *Pravda* carried a short, undated note from Krupskaya to the editor. In it she gave the party and public at large the first confirmation that she had left the opposition, noting that she had done so in the previous year. Unlike all other oppositionists, when they were driven back into the fold, Krupskaya did not recant or repent. Her letter is full of ambiguity. On one hand, the opposition "went too far," "quantity was transformed into quality, comradely criticism became factionalism," "the broad mass of the workers and peasants understood the statements of the opposition as statements against the basic principles of the party and Soviet power," the present times demand "the maximum unity in action" — all the classic arguments for submission to the ruling group. But at the same time she insisted that it was "fundamentally mistaken" to think that the opposition really was attacking the basic principles of the party. "A more restrained and comradely form of polemic" was needed, she said, implying that some form of criticism of the existing leadership was still in order. There was no word of repentance on any specific issue, nor a word of support for Stalin.

This could hardly have satisfied him, and the pressures on Krupskaya were not yet withdrawn. At some point in 1927 Alexandra Kollontai's novella *A Great Love* was published, popularizing in barely concealed form the rumor that Inessa had been Lenin's real soulmate and Krupskaya more of a burden than a comrade. One can only speculate what went through Krupskaya's mind, what angry exchanges may have occurred in the first half of 1927, but by summer of that year she actively joined Stalin's last drive against the Zinoviev-Trotsky opposition. At the August plenum of the Central Committee and Central Control Commission she raked the opposition for all of its principal doctrines, and was interrupted repeatedly by the applause of the Stalinist claque, a sure sign of her acceptability to the General Secretary. The value of Krupskaya's moral support probably compensated Stalin for her refusal to repent. At the conclusion of her speech she even explained her membership in the opposition as if it had been quite correct. At that time, she said, the situation of the USSR had been stable enough to tolerate criticism, and "The danger of certain developments that were taking place" (mainly the pro-kulak policy, no doubt) justified the opposition of that time. Now, in mid-1927, she maintained, there was a danger of war, and the country needed maximum unity.[42] This was hokum in a Europe that was disarmed as it rarely has been in this century, but the war menace in the USSR was widely believed and probably did not strain Krupskaya's credulity. With her usual earnestness she even wrote a pedagogical article at this time which urged the schools to prepare for war.[43]

In November 1927 she resumed the same theme during Stalin's anti-Trotsky finale, which drowned out the feeble efforts of the opposition to stage rallies on the tenth anniversary of the October Revolution. Speaking at a meeting in Moscow's Bauman district, she still held that the 1925 opposition had been "natural" and that it had been necessary to "verify" that "there was enough socialism in our structure."[44]

In adhering to this unrepentant line Krupskaya enjoyed special dispensation from Stalin. It also seems that she had won a concession on a more sensitive point. Apparently Stalin or his representative promised to publish, at last, Lenin's testament. When the Fifteenth Party Congress met in December 1927, publication of the testament was proposed by Sergo Ordzhonikidze. Very likely Sergo served as Stalin's emissary to Krupskaya in this period and perhaps for several years afterwards. He was a Georgian like Stalin and one of the leader's closest colleagues. Unlike Stalin, he could approach Krupskaya on fairly friendly terms, for she had known him since 1912, when he had come to Paris as one of Lenin's disciples and a student at the party school in Longjumeau.[45] In her memoirs Krupskaya singled out Sergo for his intimacy with Lenin. When Ordzhonikidze's fiftieth birthday was publicly celebrated in 1936, Krupskaya contributed a short letter of congratulations that is more suggestive of genuine personal respect than most of the ceremonial greetings that she published — and she did not honor any other Stalinist dignitary with such a note. "You loved Lenin," she said, and this simple tribute, far from the usual rhetoric of such occasions, could have served as the link between Krupskaya and Ordzhonikidze.[46] At any rate it was Ordzhonikidze who presented the motion to publish Lenin's testament, an un-Stalinist step that is hard to explain except as fulfillment of an understanding with Krupskaya. The motion was carried unanimously, but it appears that Stalin cheated in its execution. While the resolution originally specified publication in the scholarly series *The Lenin Collection (Leninskii Sbornik)*, the testament was actually placed in the *Bulletin* of the party congress, which has never been seen by the outside world and was unknown to all but a few party members.[47] Still, this represented the official communication of Lenin's testamentary message to some party congress, and Krupskaya's conscience could take comfort in this. Apparently she never again raised the question of the testament.

Nor does it seem accidental that, during her remaining years, little more was heard of Inessa Armand. Lenin's letters to her remained unpublished until shortly after Krupskaya's death, although they must have been known to party archivists much earlier. Kollontai's novella vanished from sight by 1928, and has not been seen since in Soviet writings on literature or the life of Kollontai, who remained alive and politically acceptable until her death in 1952. Krupskaya had failed to influence Soviet policy or leadership, but she had retained her status as Lenin's revered widow.

CHAPTER X

Mother of Her People

Krupskaya lived on for eleven years after her reconciliation with the mainstream of Bolshevism in 1927. These were tumultuous, heroic, creative, cruel, and even retrogressive years for the Soviet Union, a trying time to be Lenin's widow. She, more than any other person, faced the question that has bedeviled historians of Russia: was Stalin carrying on the main precepts of Leninism, or was he their nemesis? There is no simple answer to this question. Who can doubt that Lenin would have been gratified to know that the Soviet Union made enormous strides in industrialization, that agriculture became relatively mechanized and consolidated into large, collectivized units, that the armed forces gained prowess, that mass illiteracy was largely overcome, that the party survived his death and the rivalry of his heirs? On the other hand, who can doubt that Lenin would have been horrified by the deification of Stalin, by the increased concentration of power in the hands of this man, by the use of this power to make Trotsky and countless thousands of humble Soviet citizens into "enemies of the people"? And who is not entitled to doubt concerning Lenin's hypothetical attitude toward a host of other issues

in the age of Stalin: the handling of "kulaks" during collectivization, the revival of Russian nationalism, the
growth of the party far beyond its size at Lenin's death,
the introduction of increased wage differentials and social
class distinctions, the development of "socialist realism"
in the arts, among others.

One cannot know how Krupskaya resolved, or avoided,
all of these questions. It is at least clear that she did not
avoid them by sinking into senility. On the contrary, she
remained vigorous and involved in public life until her
ailments and age finally finished her in early 1939. Super-
ficially she was a living advertisement for the official doctrine that "Stalin is the Lenin of today," Lenin's widow in
support of Stalin's regime. There was no room for her to
criticize the leader or his policies, and in post-Stalin Russia
sensitivities about the whole era have continued to inhibit
discussion of her doubts about the regime. Nevertheless,
Soviet publications have revealed enough to make possible
a sketch of her situation, fairly clear and detailed in some
areas, blurred and half-conjectural in others.

One essential is obvious. Krupskaya was convinced
that the continuation of Lenin's work required a clear understanding of Lenin. A major part of her strenuous activity from the time of his death until her own was devoted
to this cause through writing, public speaking, and attempts to influence the contribution of others to the stream
of propaganda that constituted the Lenin cult. True, Krupskaya would have rejected the word "cult," as she rejected
the mummification of Lenin's body, and at her best she
rose above the banal, inflated reverence that has character-
ized Soviet presentations of the Lenin image. Her best was
the series of personal sketches that she wrote between 1925
and 1933, which first appeared separately in *Pravda* or
Bol'shevik, and then were gathered into a book, *Memoirs
of Lenin (Vospominaniia o Lenine)*. The first version
appeared in 1926, followed by a fuller and somewhat doctored edition that emerged in installments in 1930, 1932,
and 1934. In 1957 some of her additional memoirs of Lenin

were added when the book was revived after Stalin's death. It was by all odds her most widely-read work, not only in the Soviet Union, where it was translated into all the major languages of the national minorities, but also abroad, appearing in English, Mongolian, and other editions.

As a narrative of life with Lenin, Krupskaya's memoirs are informative and generally accurate. She not only relied on her memory but also did a fair bit of checking with other sources. A few slips did occur. Lev Deich, one of the first Russian Marxists, heatedly protested to *Pravda* about the factual content of her somewhat critical treatment of his role in émigré life. Krupskaya was obliged to admit that she was wrong on certain particulars, although she defended herself ably on the main issues, citing archival materials that she had used.[1] A slightly more consequential matter is the date that Krupskaya assigned to Lenin's return to Petrograd, incognito, in the weeks preceding the seizure of power. Here she evidently relied on memory, which may have been accurate insofar as she had ever known the true facts, but is now held by most Soviet historians to be a week or two late. There are some other minor errors, but as memoirs go her record is good, and as Soviet memoirs about Lenin go, stupendously good.

Naturally, *Memoirs of Lenin* is a partisan book, taking for granted that he was invariably right in his struggles on both sides of the barricades — against tsar, provisional government, White generals and imperialist predators; against narodniks, "economists," Mensheviks, Vperedists, and all the other revolutionary deviants. But Krupskaya assumed this partisanship with little personal acrimony or exaggerated polemics. Nobody emerges as an "enemy of the people" in the Stalinist sense, and the numerous Social Democrats who at some time strayed from Lenin's line, such as Trotsky, Zinoviev, and Kamenev, are forgiven. Martov, the chief Menshevik leader, is portrayed in quite a sympathetic light, and Plekhanov's deserved status as the father of Russian Marxism is steadfastly respected. Compared to the Stalinist historical treatments of the party, especially the *Short Course* that appeared under Stalin's sponsorship in 1938, the memoirs are admirably honest and detached. If it seems that Lenin is the dominant figure in the history of Russian Communism, a man whose qualities distinguished him from all the rest, this is the conclusion that most historians outside the USSR have also reached.

Krupskaya tried to convey these qualities, and her simple descriptions of Lenin at close range are one of the best available projections of his personality. This was not easy, for Lenin was marked by an inner distance, to use André Malraux's expressive comment on his impression of both Mao Tse-tung and De Gaulle. While Krupskaya had an unmatched opportunity to know Lenin, it appears that his inner life remained inaccessible even to her. She describes how he wrote *What Is to Be Done?*, the seminal work on the idea of the party, shut up with her in a small room in Germany, whispering to himself, and notes that this was typical and that she never "spoke to him or asked him any questions" at such times.[2] True, she goes on to recollect that after these sessions they would go for walks and Lenin would tell her what he was thinking about, that "this became as much a necessity to him as whispering his article over to himself before putting it down in writing." But the reader of her memoirs never learns much about these revelations, and one wonders if Lenin did share with his wife the calculations, the doubts, ambitions, fantasies, and fears that stirred within him. The memoirs provide a good close-range picture of the image that Lenin turned to the world, but no approach at all to what went on behind the surface. It would, of course, be pointless to expect the reserved Krupskaya to go into her husband's psychic life, and it may be that Lenin really was the perfect one-dimensional political man. But his relationship with Inessa, whatever its true character, suggests that there was something here beside revolutionary intelligence and will. Even in politics there must have been much more than Krupskaya said, or probably knew. What, for example, of

Lenin's calculations concerning the question of war and peace in 1917? Although he was outwardly anti-war to a degree that seems to have surprised Krupskaya when they first returned to Russia, Lenin was far from committing himself to buy peace at the Kaiser's price in April 1917, and his fertile and wide-ranging mind must surely have been constantly churning over a multitude of variables when he wrote "The April Theses." Of this Krupskaya says nothing, nor does she say that Lenin shared his thoughts with her as they made their way from Switzerland to the Finland Station.

The moral side of Lenin remains equally withdrawn. The deathbed doubts that assailed him concerning the moral validity of the revolutionary state that he had founded seem to have mystified Krupskaya at the time, probably because she was never part of Lenin's inner world. She described him as she saw him — a hero incapable of self-doubt. The well-springs of moral concern that disturbed the dying man were separated from her by that inner distance, and the memoirs do not prepare us for this tragic and perhaps admirable finale to Lenin's life. To be sure, Krupskaya never wrote of this period, nor is it likely that Stalin would have permitted her to publish on the matter.

Compared to *Memoirs of Lenin,* Krupskaya's other writings about Lenin, numbering over one hundred, are a sorry lot. She could fruitfully describe her own experiences and observations as Lenin's wife, but her sermons, such as "Lenin on the Organization of the Cause of the Construction of Socialism" or her preface to the anthology *What Lenin Wrote and Said about Libraries,* are enough to set even the most dutiful party member yawning. In a considerable number of her later works, such as *"Capital* in the Works of Lenin," it is painfully clear that Krupskaya, like any hack propagandist, had merely culled some suitable quotations from the collected works of Lenin, which she kept close at hand, her secretary recalled. Dridzo stoutly maintains that none of Krupskaya's works were ghosted, but it is true that she had a librarian who served as a research assistant and compiled packets of material on various subjects, which probably accounts for some of her dullest tracts on Lenin.[3]

If her own standards for writing about Lenin declined with the passage of years, Krupskaya remained a severe critic for many of the other writers, painters, sculptors, actors, and directors who devoted themselves to the Lenin image. Although she had no copyright on this topic, the Soviet propaganda and artistic bureaucracy often asked her opinion and frequently took her advice. It was often negative.

She opposed publication of one memoir because the writer had Ilyich playing the card game "vingt," another because he was made to start for work as early as nine in the morning, while still another was "imprecise" and contained too little about Lenin. An unknown author of a biography of Lenin, based on memoirs, was told that most recollections proved to be "subjective" and unreliable. "We receive many purely fantastic letters, many facts are mistaken even by comrades who knew Lenin well." This writer was compounding their errors, and the result was "terribly false," unpublishable.[4]

Writers who sought the license of historical fiction to try to humanize the austere Lenin did not escape Krupskaya's wrath. What she disliked most was *"meshchanstvo,"* petit-bourgeois vulgarity, the cultural style that was above all others repugnant to the Russian intelligentsia (but characteristic of much in Stalin's Russia). One form of *meshchanstvo* which Krupskaya detested was the sentimental romantic spirit. In her later years she occasionally amused Vera Dridzo by singing the romantic songs that had been popular in her youth, by way of parody: "Under the silver moon on the golden sand I long searched for the dear footprints of the young maid," and others. But it was a serious matter when any writer introduced romantic love into a narrative involving Lenin. One hapless author evidently alluded romantically to Lenin's and Krupskaya's sojourn in Siberia in a manuscript that never was published. Krupskaya was outraged. "We could not stand *meshchanstvo*," she said in her crushing critique, "nor could Mama, and there was nothing Philistine in our lives."[5]

Another variant on this error which kept cropping up was the attempt to use Lenin "as some kind of incarnation of *meshchanstvo* morality," for example, exhortations to "see how nice and clean Lenin is . . . you should be nice like Lenin. . . ." "Better not to say a word about Lenin than to talk such nonsense. I know that often it is done without bad intentions, but really this will badly hinder an understanding of what Lenin really was," she wrote.[6]

The one writer of historical fiction whose work on Lenin ever pleased her was Marietta Shaginian. Sending her compliments concerning the novel *A Ticket to History*, Krupskaya explained that she was generally against "novels, stories, scenarios from the life of Ilyich. Try as they will the writers usually end up not with the image of Ilyich, the living Ilyich, but the image of some sort of different person. . . ."[7] Although Shaginian was complimented that time, her other efforts suffered the usual fate of historical fiction about Lenin, as far as Krupskaya was concerned. "I very much dislike this tale," she said at the opening of an extended dissection of Shaginian's *Volodya Ulyanov*. Here, as in many other critiques, Krupskaya stressed the author's failure to appreciate the historical epoch that they were dealing with.[8]

The same kind of dissatisfaction with other persons' portrayals of Lenin came out in her review of the major Soviet film "October." She considered the whole work an important advance for the Soviet cinema, but "The portrayal of Lenin is unsuccessful," because it made him appear "somehow very jumpy. Ilyich was never like that." If you can't do better than this, she said, it would be better not to put him in the film.[9] The particular problem of jumpy movement bothered her about other actors who attempted to portray Lenin, and she concluded that they were misled by primitive documentary films of Lenin.[10] Perhaps, but one memoirist, who was quite unaware of Krupskaya's annoyance about this problem, said that when he knew Lenin after the revolution he was struck by the man's rapid, jerky walk.[11] (This writer, Sabaneev, thought that this indicated syphilis, a popular notion among anti-Bolshevik emigrants, for which there is no good evidence.)

The visual arts fared no better. She advised an aspiring painter to study only photographs of Ilyich, because most paintings were poor likenesses of him. As for sculpture, they were all "ugly." The only good one in her estimate was Lenin's death mask.[12]

Of all the contributions to the Lenin cult that Krupskaya found wanting, her *bête noire* was a story for children which said that "Grandpa Lenin told all children to study, study and study and to brush their teeth every day." Thereafter, she would say whenever some new work on Lenin was given her, "If this one also says 'Grandpa Lenin says to brush your teeth every day,' I won't read it."[13]

This may be creditable taste, but it also is curious, because Krupskaya herself contributed no end of edifying preachments for children, and in one of them she even wrote, "A camp of Young Pioneers [Soviet boy and girl scouts]. Two hundred children in ordered ranks march to the river, each one has a toothbrush in his hand — Pioneers brush their teeth."[14] Evidently the point was that Lenin should not be involved in such mundane things, but it was appropriate for Lenin's widow, for she had become the mother of her people. "I was always very sad that I did not have children," she is supposed to have said, "but now I am not sad. Now I have many of them — Komsomols and Young Pioneers. All of them are Leninists. . . ."[15] And Krupskaya, the stern and reserved young *intelligentka,* had come to fill the maternal role with the passage of years. By the nineteen thirties she looked rather like an archtypal Russian *babushka* — rumpled, rotund, and suitable for hugging small children, a symbol of kindness and stability in a hard world. Many photographs show her with delegations of Pioneers, and Dridzo maintains that she developed a penchant for lustily singing "The Young Guard" and other pioneer songs during her walks in the country, sometimes to the amazement of the peasants.

She also wrote copiously about and to children, going over and over the same fundamentals: the need for better food, camps, day-care centers, libraries, and especially books in a suitable Soviet spirit. There is no need to doubt her goodwill in this, but these exercises came to smack of empty ritual, and there is little left in them of her former concern for Tolstoyan and progressive educational ideas about fostering creativity and individualism. Her most famous contribution in this area was an anthology of *Correspondence with Pioneers,* published in numerous editions from 1932. The letters are permeated with the most stultifying kind of Soviet didacticism, treating children as little party members. In a "letter" entitled "How to Struggle with [the problem of] Absentees and Latecomers," she began:

"Surely you all have read the resolution of the Central Committee of the All-Union Communist Party (Bolsheviks) on elementary and middle schools, surely you have already discussed among yourselves how you, Pioneers, can carry out the decisions of the Central Committee of the All-Union Communist Party (Bolsheviks) in life. . . ."[16]

Of course, what else would ten-year-olds talk about? Not football, Krupskaya hoped. While she was all in favor of organized physical culture for children, she deplored the rising popularity of soccer among children.

"In football roughness is certain," she wrote. But some people give children the idea that "you can't live without football." As for movies, children shouldn't go often because movies are bad for the nervous system.[17] She had a point. Anyone who has read many party resolutions can testify that they are a sedative, compared to football, movies, or almost anything.

Krupskaya often wrote about the need to improve the facilities for orphans, who were very numerous in Russia, thanks to the wars and other upheavals that the country had suffered since 1914. In 1936 she even wrote a letter to A. A. Zhdanov, who was then one of Stalin's main lieutenants, appealing to him for assistance to one group of orphans in Rostov-on-the-Don who were unable to continue their education because of the workings of Soviet bureaucracy. The care of orphans remained an acute problem, she wrote. "Can we not treat these children as human beings, really care about them?"[18] There is no indication that Zhdanov replied.

For those children who had parents, however, Krupskaya favored the traditional family over state guardianship. In an article entitled "The Strong Soviet Family" (1936) she took heart that the government was abolishing legal abortion and establishing financial aid for families with numerous children.[19] While some Bolshevik women had regarded legalized abortion, easy divorce, and other measures that undermined the family as an important step toward socialism, Krupskaya had always held conservative views, which were in harmony with Stalin's social policies in the thirties. According to her, the radical policies of the twenties concerning the family had merely been emergency measures to cope with the dislocation of the times, which were now happily past.

Naturally this conservatism came out in her continuing pronouncements on the status of women. Krupskaya was not only the mother of her people but also the party's first writer on the liberation of women. The situation in Stalin's Russia was mixed in this area. Women had obtained equal legal rights, as Krupskaya proudly observed, and had been able to move into a variety of occupations that had been closed to them before. On the other hand, there were still important male preserves, including the higher reaches of politics, and the ordinary pattern of male-female relationships in society was not so basically changed. Krupskaya observed that women bore the brunt of housework and child-rearing, and that sheer exhaustion kept many women out of political activities. (Ironically this was partly a result of the fairly complete employment of Soviet women. Having achieved more or less equal rights on the lower levels and in certain professions, many Soviet women were free to add these demanding jobs to the job of home-making.) For this situation Krupskaya could only repeat such limited and practical suggestions as expanded day-care facilities and inexpensive public dining rooms.[20] No all-out attack on male chauvinism for her, either in the family or in high-level politics, where she and a few others served as tokens of the party's traditional belief in equal rights for women. In reality they were symbols of the by-gone society of the radical intelligentsia, which had been a more open society for women than the socialist order that it created.

Of course, there was always school teaching. Krup-skaya once wrote that it was a natural profession for women because of their maternal role, and she continued to regard it as her own specialty. Her work in the Commissariat of Education continued to her death, but it declined in importance as the causes and organizations that Krupskaya supported were discarded by the Stalinists. Glavpolitpros-vet, the organization dealing with education and propa-ganda for adults, never really resumed the status that it had before 1922. Krupskaya remained its head, but it did not occupy much of her time in the twenties. In 1930 it was abolished and replaced by a "Political-Educational Committee of the Republic," which was supposed to unify all activities in this field. Krupskaya seems to have been pretty dissatisfied with the whole affair, and in 1931 called the situation "a violation of all of Vladimir Ilyich's di-rectives."[21]

This, however, was a minor defeat compared to the one suffered by her dearest cause — labor polytechnical education. Through the middle twenties there was little action on this, and Krupskaya had plenty of other preoccu-pations. But at the end of the decade she attempted to re-vive polytechnicism as a corollary of the Five-Year Plan for industrialization. The trouble was that the advocates of old-fashioned vocational education were trying the same thing, and a period of confusion and controversy began around the end of 1928. For a time two educational bureaucracies exchanged salvos, the "Scientific-Scholarly Section" of GUS (State Learned Council), headed by Krupskaya, and TsIT (Central Institute of Labor), headed by one A. K. Gastev, who advocated vocational education and was personally detested by Krupskaya. At sixty she still had a sharp tongue, and in one letter to a colleague spoke of the need to keep certain schools out of the hands of the "big and little Gastevs," whose policies were "medieval, reactionary."[22] He was one of the few people whom she never called "comrade," despite his high rank. She was particularly incensed toward the end of 1928, when the anti-polytechnicists proposed that the system of "Factory Schools" (FZU), the nearest existing approach to polytechnical education, be transferred from the Commissariat of Education to the Supreme Council of the National Economy.[23] Although the details are obscure, it must have been in connection with this whole conflict that Lunacharsky, Krupskaya, and Pokrovsky, the three original commissars of education, submitted their resignations in April 1929. Those of Lunacharsky and Krupskaya were not accepted, although Lunacharsky, Nadezhda's friend, was replaced in September 1929 by A. S. Bubnov, a tough Stalinist who had served for some time as the director of political propaganda in the Red Army.[24]

This was a bad omen, but at the opening of the thirties the prospects for the labor polytechnical idea seemed brighter. Bubnov included it as one of his objectives in the "Cultcampaign" or quasi-military drive to end illiteracy and improve schools. It seemed possible that his toughness would do for Krupskaya's program what Lunacharsky's intellectual charm and political weakness never could. In August 1930 the commissariat held a large conference on polytechnical education, chaired and addressed by Krupskaya. Soon she was busy drafting a program and even a law on polytechnical schools.[25]

But the drive for industrialization demanded the fastest possible training of workers with minimal literacy and a basic vocational skill, and Krupskaya's vague idealization of an all-round, integrated understanding of modern science and technology appeared to be an impractical luxury. Worse, there were people around who were saying that Soviet schools were not up to pre-revolutionary standards, that the basic subjects were badly taught. Stalin, for one, liked order, discipline, even school uniforms, and had little use for Tolstoy's or Dewey's theories. Beginning with a party resolution of September 5, 1931, there was a gradual retreat from the whole idea of labor polytechnical education.[26] At first the term was retained, but its content was steadily eroded, as something resembling the pre-revolutionary schools took shape. Krupskaya, who was a deputy commissar of education, complained bitterly. Bubnov was not impressed, and relations between the two became rather strained. One Soviet memoirist recalls that in 1935 (about the time that polytechnicism was going down the drain) Bubnov once jumped to his feet and interrupted a speech Krupskaya was making in the collegium (executive committee) of Narkompros, accusing her of changing her position on the issue at hand. She handled him rather effectively on this occasion by softly saying, "Andrei Sergeevich! What I think, I say," and going on with her speech without changing her intonation.[27] She tried appealing to higher authorities, first to Ordzhonikidze, her friend since 1912 and perhaps her contact with Stalin.[28] Perhaps on his suggestion, or perhaps in sheer frustration, she sought an interview with A. A. Zhdanov, a secretary of the party and one of the men closest to Stalin at the time. The Krupskaya archives contain a still-unpublished list of fourteen questions that she prepared for the interview, but it seems that Zhdanov would not receive her, for on February 9, 1937, she sent him a letter, protesting that current policy represented *"not the reorganization of labor* [in Soviet schools], *but its liquidation."* The letter began with reverent reference to the authority of Karl Marx, a name that Zhdanov probably did not hear very often in policy debates, and it ended with the statement that Soviet schools would "of course" remain labor polytechnical schools in the end, an unconvincing attempt at tactful salesmanship.[29]

At a time when Stalin's purges were in full swing, it is doubtful that any sane person except Lenin's widow would have dared to voice dissent so clearly and gratuitously. Perhaps she was warned to stop bothering party leaders. In any case, she was not permitted to make a public disturbance about the matter. In 1937 the editors of *"The Teacher's Newspaper"* (*Uchitel'skaia Gazeta*) would not print an article that she submitted, which argued that Lenin had considered productive labor an essential part of Communist education.[30] She could only vent her feelings in notes for her own files. In May 1937, for example, we find her characterizing a Soviet school on the basis of an inspector's report that she had seen: "A typical old school, in which there is nothing at all apart from the most boring studies. . . . Dead studies, with which we fought from the first, installed anew in full measure."[31]

If it was bitter for Krupskaya to accept Stalinism in education, there were still more painful adjustments to be made in other areas. The brutally rapid collectivization of the peasantry in the winter of 1929–1930 must have been a shock to her. Although she had consistently favored the development of collective agriculture, especially in the form of cooperatives, and at one stage had criticized the government for favoring the kulaks, she had never thought of enforced, overnight collectivization as Lenin's path to socialism on the countryside. Never an economist, she did not attempt to spell out the means by which Russian agriculture would be transformed, but her writings took it for granted that a gradualist (but not too gradualist) path to socialized agriculture existed. This was the drift of an article entitled "Ilyich on Kolkhoz Construction," which was written in early 1929 when official policy favored a moderate rate of collectivization.[32] Krupskaya appears to have been pleased with this approach and happy to do her bit as a propagandist.

By June 1929, however, she could see that matters were taking a different turn, as Stalin increasingly blamed the kulaks for the country's economic problems and prepared the party for civil war against them. Krupskaya reacted to this in an article that was supposedly concerned with education, but actually advanced arguments concerning the whole process of collectivization. In it she approved the necessity of class struggle on the countryside and accepted the official line that kulak violence was to blame if the struggle was sharp. Yet its real point is a plea for restraint: "But there is class struggle and class struggle. There is elemental, blind class struggle and there is conscious, organized, fully considered class struggle. . . . The working class in our country now has the enormous, powerful party, constrained by internal discipline. . . . It hardly needs to be argued that the class struggle that is now being conducted must be strictly thought through, molded into suitable forms."[33]

This was not so obvious to Stalin, and in a few months the countryside was in a turmoil as party, Komsomol, police, and military expeditions forced millions of peasants to give up their traditional ideal of the small family farm and sign up with more or less imaginary collective farms, which lacked equipment, cattle, seed, or management. Hundreds of thousands were branded as kulaks and shot, deported, or merely expropriated and moved to submarginal land. Nobody was allowed to protest in public, and, as Lenin's widow, she must have been under pressure to produce suitable blessings for Stalin's policy. In March 1930, while the turmoil was in full swing, she completed a popular pamphlet entitled "What Lenin Said about Kolkhozes and Small Peasant Farms," which confined itself to the dead man's writings and the general notion that collective agriculture was better than private farms. What is most significant in the tract is the complete absence of reference to any of the catch-phrases of Stalin's collectivization drive, such as "liquidation of the kulaks as a class" and "complete collectivization," or reference to the Leader himself.[34]

In public Krupskaya could do no more than protest by omitting explicit praise, but in one letter (published only in 1959) a short, sharp note of rage breaks through. She was writing to Bubnov, the commissar of education, and the immediate issue was one that she repeatedly tackled — the exclusion of children of kulaks and other dispossessed groups from educational opportunities. This form of class oppression seemed "medieval" to her, pointing toward the establishment of a new social hierarchy, and she protested against it a number of times. After objecting once again to such treatment of children, her letter to Bubnov cited a particular case and then burst out: "Here is your 'liquidation of the kulaks as a class on the basis of complete collectivization!' "[35] The little touches in this one sentence convey more about Krupskaya's attitude toward Stalin's method of collectivization than all her other works: the use of the word "your" to convey her sense of alienation, the contemptuous inverted commas around the sacred slogan of the campaign, even the exclamation point.

The general drift of Krupskaya's thinking about collectivization shares something with the ideas of the Right Opposition to Stalin at this time, headed by Bukharin, Rykov, and Tomsky. These sometime members of the Politburo had been defeated as a major force by the opening of 1930, but they were the only possible source of hope for any Communist who wanted to see more moderation in the process of collectivization. Krupskaya had been very well acquainted with Bukharin in her later years in emigration, and in 1930 she made an effort to defend him. There are few data on the details of this final venture by Krupskaya in the opposition to Stalin, but it is clear that it was too little, too late. Her one known sally in this combat occurred in late May 1930, when she attended the conference of the party organization of the Bauman district of Moscow. It was probably not anticipated that Krupskaya would suffer a relapse into her old heresies, for she was elected to the presidium of the conference. This no doubt helped her to gain the tribune, from which, Khrushchev tells us, she defended Bukharin and his ally Rykov from the attacks that were standard at this point. After her experiences in the previous decade she must have realized that it was a futile gesture. The press did not even mention her speech, and Khrushchev says that she "came under attack from most of the delegates at the conference."[36]

Krupskaya was isolated and paid the price for her indiscipline. "Without any publicity the word went out to the party cells to give her a working-over," says Khrushchev. "She was avoided like the plague . . ., was kept under close surveillance . . . , everyone was slinging mud at Nadezhda Konstantinovna." This treatment, and especially the renewal of low threats about her status as widow, which Khrushchev also recalls, seems to have brought her round to agreement again. She was permitted (or ordered) to deliver a speech at the Sixteenth Party Congress in July 1930, and it was in the main a rehash of the current party line, including the liquidation of kulaks as a class on the basis of complete collectivization. The record suggests, however, that Stalin was dissatisfied that she did not specifically attack Bukharin, or for that matter praise the name of Stalin, As in her retreat from opposition a few years before, Krupskaya did not yield everything.

The result was that a number of anonymous hecklers, who certainly would not have bothered Lenin's widow without orders, tried to get her to dwell specifically on the errors of Bukharin, Rykov, and Tomsky.

When she evaded them by saying that her point of view on Rykov's and Tomsky's speeches to the congress followed from what she had already said, the voices objected: "How does it follow?" "Speak more precisely, more clearly." "Not clear." "Extremely unsatisfactory." She tried to go back to her prepared text, but in a minute they were at her again, demanding an attack on the Rightists. This time she obliged to the modest extent of stating that she had not been satisfied with the speeches of Rykov and Tomsky, but she still evaded any general dissection of their errors during the collectivization campaign and ended her speech with a verbal smokescreen about the need for party unity. Stalin obviously was in control, but Krupskaya would not give him full satisfaction at this time.[37]

If she at first sought to register her objection to the disagreeable sides of Stalinism by ignoring them in her writings, she was foiled. By 1932 reverent references to Stalin began cropping up in her published works, as in those of all Soviet political writers in this age. The proper style for any essay was to open and close with suitable references to Stalin, whose works should be cited frequently. In many of her writings after about 1931 Krupskaya observed this formality. For example, an article of 1937 celebrating the new Soviet constitution, the "Stalin Constitution," concluded in the typical fashion of the day, ". . . let us go forward to Communism under the leadership of the party, under the leadership of the beloved Leader of the broad mass of the people, Comrade Stalin."[38] In some cases her reverential expressions embarrassed post-Stalin editors, and had to be doctored. For example, a passage that originally read, "When Lenin died his cause was carried on by his former helper in all things, Comrade Stalin . . ." reappeared in 1959 as, "When Lenin died the party carried on his cause."[39] Her major speech to the Seventeenth Party Congress in 1934 mentioned Stalin's name thirteen times in three pages, a moderate but acceptable showing, and a number of her works were dotted with suitable quotations from the great man.[40] In 1935 she even wrote a piece entitled "The Articles of Marx, Engels, Lenin, Stalin which Every Teacher Should Know."[41]

But her heart was not in this. In the essay just cited there were embarrassingly few articles by Stalin, and she never gave him an unduly prominent place in her memoirs of Lenin. They never substantiated the Stalinist myth that he had been Lenin's closest comrade for many years preceding the World War and in particular did not include the tale that the October Revolution was directed by a "Revolutionary Center" under Stalin.[42] Physical threats may have been implied, but subtler pressure could also be used. Krupskaya had become a compulsive publisher and no doubt felt it her duty to keep producing homilies as long as she lived. By 1930 she had already encountered the willingness of editors to suppress her writings, if they did not meet the current ideological norm, and it is reasonable to suppose that she accepted something like occasional conformity to the cult of Stalin as the price of having her works published at all.

At least this explanation can cover Krupskaya's humiliating little references to the great Stalin, but is it enough to cover her published statements in support of his purges? True, she had written a few words in 1931 in support of the trial of some non-party economists and engineers who were accused of trying to wreck Soviet industry, but these were ex-Mensheviks and perhaps Krupskaya actually found it credible that they had worked for foreign powers.[43] But what emerged in the years following the assassination of the high-ranking Stalinist Sergei Kirov, in December 1934, was something else for her. Many thousands of persons great and small were arrested and shot or imprisoned after secret pseudo-trials, while three highly-publicized trials of former party leaders provided a mythological explanation of it all. These three great trials, or public confessionals, took place in 1936, 1937, and 1938. In the first Krupskaya's former friends and political allies Kamenev and Zinoviev were the star culprits, and in the 1938 trial Bukharin was the main attraction.

Whatever Krupskaya swallowed of the Stalin line, it is impossible that she could have believed the fantastic charges and fulsome confessions of conspiracy to kill Lenin and Stalin, among others, to partition the USSR among the imperialist predators, and to restore capitalism in whatever was left. Her principal Soviet biographers, who had access to her papers and the recollections of her surviving friends in the post-Stalin era, write: "It was unbearable pain [for her] to see how many honorable and devoted leaders of the party and the people were shot. Krupskaya had been linked with some of them even in the period of the preparation of the revolution, and then in Soviet times."[44] Except for Trotsky, who was by now in foreign exile, the accused represented what was left of the cream of the old Bolshevik intelligentsia, the men who had been close to Lenin and, sooner or later, unsuccessful opponents of Stalin. Krupskaya herself deserved a place in the dock as richly as any of them. She had been Stalin's first declared enemy in Lenin's circle of intimates, condemning him as early as 1912, and as late as the collectivization drive she was still opposing him.

But Stalin was no irrational madman. Krupskaya was more useful to him as a propagandist than as a victim — and even the credulous Left of the western world might have had trouble believing that Lenin's widow was an old lady out of *Arsenic and Old Lace,* preparing to do in Stalin with a glass of wine. (Poisoning did figure prominently in the public confessions.) Krupskaya was left unharmed but was induced to add her prestige to the tumult of Stalinist voices that heaped abuse on the victims. To be sure, she did not contribute extensively, but contribute she did.

The longest of her published comments on the purge trials was in support of the verdict on the two victims who had been closest to her, Kamenev and Zinoviev. Entitled "Why the Second International Defends Trotsky" (who was always regarded as the arch-conspirator) , it appeared in *Pravda* on September 4, 1936, shortly after the trial, and was reprinted in a brochure with similar fabrications by other writers.[45] "Trotsky, Zinoviev, Kamenev, and all their band of assassins made a pact with German Fascism, concluded an alliance with the Gestapo. That is why the country has been so unanimous in demanding that the mad dogs be shot." Such is the spirit of this essay from the hand of the woman who had once written to Leo Tolstoy to see if there was anything she could do to help humanity.

Or was this cruel diatribe from her hand? Trotsky, in an obituary for Krupskaya, asserted that articles had been published over her name without her consent.[46] It is possible, but Trotsky had no way of knowing, and it may be pertinent that the Soviet bibliographers who compiled an exhaustive list of her works in the nineteen-*sixties* included this article.

One explanation of the article seems to lie in a story related by Elisabeth K. Poretsky, the wife of a Soviet intelligence operative. At Christmas in 1937 she was walking on Red Square with an old friend, a Red Army officer with important party contacts. They saw Krupskaya, wearing dark glasses, come out of a building. "I am sorry for her," said Mrs. Poretsky. "Why be sorry for her? [said her friend] She didn't have to do what she did. You know she begged HIM on her knees for the lives of the Sixteen [including Kamenev and Zinoviev] in the first trial. He insulted her and forced her to sign a statement condemning Lenin's old companions as counter-revolutionaries, spies and mad dogs. She didn't have to do that. What could HE have done to her now?"[47]

This, too, is possible, although it seems unlikely that the speaker was in a position to know what really happened. At least it was widely believed in party circles that direct police pressures had been brought to bear on Krupskaya. Sources that must remain nameless relate that she was subjected to various kinds of police harassment such as searches and was at length ordered to come to some police headquarters for a talk. According to the story Krupskaya met this threat by going on foot, alone (presumably she still had access to a car and chauffeur), carrying a small bag of personal effects such as people in those days generally kept if they feared arrest. This public display of her willingness to be a martyr is said to have made its point; the police harassment stopped.

If overt threats failed to force her capitulation, why did she write the vilification of Kamenev and Zinoviev? Her whole life and its meaning to her supply the most plausible explanation at this point. Could she accept the idea that Lenin's cause had failed, that the revolution was a cruel mockery? More likely her frame of mind was similar to that of the accused Bukharin, as he described it in his final plea:

"I shall now speak of myself, of the reasons for my repentance. . . . For three months I refused to say anything.

Then I began to testify. Why? Because while in prison I made a revaluation of my entire past. For when you ask yourself: 'If you must die, what are you dying for?' — an absolutely black vacuity suddenly rises before you with startling vividness. There is nothing to die for, if one wanted to die unrepented. And, on the contrary, everything positive that glistens in the Soviet Union acquires new dimensions in a man's mind. This in the end led me to bend my knees before the party and the country."[48]

Krupskaya did not endure jail or interrogation, but the psychology of the situation was much the same. She was old and ill, and could not expect to live long. The party required her "confession," although not in the same form as Bukharin's. She hated Stalin, but without the party what was there? That black vacuity. Better to write what they wanted and have faith that Lenin's truth was bound to conquer in the end.

The fate of Krupskaya during the purges was in some ways more pitiful than that of her friends who perished in the cellars of Lubianka Prison. When they had made their repentance, it was all over, while she was obliged to live on in helplessness, reading the pathetic appeals from the relatives of hundreds or thousands of the humble victims of the purge. It would be a great mistake to assume that most Soviet people were cynical about the cults that the regime propagated. Lenin really was regarded by millions as a great champion of mankind, not only in the officially inspired myth that "Stalin is the Lenin of today," but also in its unofficial opposite: Stalin and all his evil works would have been avoided, if only Lenin had lived. His widow was alive, and was not only widely known as Lenin's closest comrade, but also was the great maternal figure of her people: "Our beloved, tender, and solicitous mother," as one letter from Pioneers called her. As husbands, fathers, wives, mothers vanished in pre-dawn arrests, it was natural that many simple citizens would appeal to Lenin's widow, the one person in the Kremlin who understood Lenin's ideals and was known for her kind heart. Probably the effective help that she had rendered at least a few people in the early days of Soviet power had become widely known in legendary form, too.

Thus it was that at the peak of the purges in 1937–1938 she received four hundred to four hundred and fifty letters per day. Many of these probably were the routine greetings from Pioneers, inquiries from schoolteachers, and so on, but this peak in letters received is far above the average for the first five months of 1934 (about sixty per day) and corresponds with the peak of terror.[49] Dridzo also hints at this in noting the addresses that the simple folk often put on these letters: "To Lenin's wife," or "Moscow, the Court of the RSFSR [Russian Soviet Federative Socialist Republic], to the chairman of personal affairs Krupskaya," or "Moscow, to Babushka Krupskaya," or merely "Moscow, to Krupskaya." Krupskaya never held any judicial post, but there must have been some kind of popular legend that she sat in a court where individual amnesties could be granted.[50]

The same kind of pathetic popular feeling for her is illustrated by a poem about Krupskaya that, according to her Soviet biographers, was popular at this time:

> We go to thee
> With grief and tears.
> Thou meetest us with tenderness.
> We are warmed by thy tenderness.
> We will not forget those kindly eyes.

Some survivors of that era told Roy Medvedev, the dissident Soviet historian, that she carried her pleas into the June 1937 plenum of the Central Committee on behalf of the old Bolshevik I. Piatnitsky, in vain; that she approached the police boss Ezhov during a Lenin memorial meeting in the same year to try to save some others, but he ignored her; that she "tearfully begged Stalin" for the life of the man who had helped Lenin hide in 1917. In this case the victim's life was spared, though he remained in prison. Still better luck awaited the man who had issued

Lenin a party membership card in 1917. Thanks to Krupskaya's intercession, he was set free.[51]

On the whole she was powerless to affect the course of the terror. Her situation was all the more pathetic because of the formal honors that she held. Since the Fifteenth Party Congress in 1927 she had been a member of the Central Committee of the party, a reward no doubt for defecting from the opposition. In 1929, the year of her sixtieth birthday, she received the order of the Red Banner of Labor, to which was added the Order of the USSR and the Order of Lenin in 1933. In 1935 there was a ceremonial meeting in honor of her sixty-fifth birthday, with speeches by various dignitaries. In 1931 she became an honorary member of the Academy of Sciences, and in 1936, just as her educational ideas were being shoved aside, she was given an honorary doctorate of pedagogical science. In 1935 she was elected to the All-Union Congress of Soviets (the legislative assembly of the USSR), and in 1937 to its successor, the Supreme Soviet, which elected her to its presidium. In 1936–1939 she attended meetings of the party's Organizational Bureau, just when it was least possible for her to affect the fate of party members, the usual business of that body.[52] These honors were but baubles, signifying only that Lenin's widow gave her blessing (and his) to the regime of Stalin, who had arranged it all .

True, he did see to it that the material conditions of her life were tolerable in her final years. She retained the family apartment in the Kremlin. Apparently she and Stalin's own household were the only survivors in this residential compound of Bolshevism, and Nadezhda must have been far from cordial toward these neighbors. Svetlana Allilueva does not mention Lenin's widow in her published memoirs of these years, and it is reported that she recalls meeting the old lady only once, at the Bolshoi Theater. "Are you doing well in school?" Krupskaya is supposed to have asked Stalin's daughter, and that was the extent of the acquaintance of the youngest and oldest female residents of the Kremlin. She was not, however, under house arrest.

In 1931 she paid her last visit to her native Leningrad, still "Petersburg" in her mind. Her secretary recalls that in 1935 when her apartment was under repair Krupskaya went to stay with Dridzo and her husband in their relatively humble two-room apartment in the city. On the eve of the anniversary of the October Revolution they had a party for some neighbors. There was singing and a declamation of Mayakovsky's poetry. Then dancing, and Krupskaya even consented to waltz with a guest at the party. When she was willing to relax, there were rest homes available. In 1931, 1933, and 1937 (at least) she visited North Caucasian spas. For shorter holidays there was a sanatorium for old Bolsheviks at Arkhangelsk near Moscow, which she preferred to the villa at Gorki where Lenin had died. At the sanatorium she could chat with Klara Zetkin until her death in 1933. Maria Ulyanova also went with her, until she died in 1937, and her old friends the Krizhanovskys were there. While the purges wiped out most of the old Bolsheviks, the survivors at Arkhangelsk could still take walks along the Kaluga road, which they called the "Nevsky Prospect" in recollection of their youthful revolutionary days in St. Petersburg, looking for mushrooms. There was talk, too, but in Krupskaya's presence it could not be vulgar. If anyone brought up anything "Philistine," recalls Dridzo, Nadezhda would at once say "I have left," and would do just that.

During her last years Krupskaya did not meet many people outside of this circle or the staff at Narkompros. Her contacts with the Armand children appear to have dwindled. Although she was a Soviet celebrity and often received delegations or addressed meetings, her international contacts were pretty limited. A few American educationists, including John Dewey, paid short and inconsequential calls, at Krupskaya's invitation. In 1931 G. B. Shaw toured Russia with Lady Astor, and requested an interview with Krupskaya, which took place on July 30 at the villa in Gorki. Nadezhda had grumbled at the prospect of the interview, and it lived up to her dismal expectations. Shaw presented her with a box of chocolates and some of his books, there was some talk about plays. Then G. B. S. asked how Lenin had provided for them financially. Krupskaya was baffled, and had the question repeated in French. Annoyed, she tartly replied, "He didn't provide in any way" (*nekak ne obespechil*). Shaw, baffled in his turn, tried to suggest that he meant that we all have to think of our old age — "But you are not so young." "I do not consider myself old." Shaw made a quick aside to Lady Astor: "In the land of the Soviets it is also forbidden to talk to a woman about age — write it down."

Krupskaya sought to escape by giving Shaw a copy of her memoirs of Lenin. G. B. S. remarked that you can't find the truth in the biography of a man by his wife, which struck Krupskaya (she later said) as a terrible remark in the circumstances. Lenin and she were both primarily party members, she said, and she had written of their common struggle. "But people always remain people," replied Shaw. At about this point the interview was mercifully concluded. Shaw had his revenge by announcing to the world that he had found Krupskaya "lovable" and that she was one of the two ugliest women in the world, the other being Mrs. Booth of the Salvation Army.[53]

Another literary giant, Maxim Gorky, was in touch with Krupskaya, but only by correspondence. Even after his return to Russia from Italy in 1932, the two never met, despite their status as senior celebrities and close comrades of Lenin (at least that was how Gorky's relations with Lenin were represented). In 1930 he had written a glowing letter of appreciation to her for her memoirs of Lenin, and she had replied that this had lifted "a stone from my soul," because she had previously felt that "you did not like something about me." Probably she had heard something of the indignation with which Gorky had received reports of her censorship of library holdings in the early twenties. Living in exile then, he had even suggested that he would drop his Soviet citizenship "if this atrocity turns out to be true." Although Gorky assured her in 1930 that her apprehensions concerning his feelings toward her were groundless, he never took the trouble to drop in on her in Moscow, and they merely exchanged letters on anniversaries and in connection with her continuing memoirs of Lenin.[54]

These were her last consolation — the thought that the spirit of Lenin could at least be passed on to future generations through her memoirs. Yet even here there were difficulties. As early as 1932 Krupskaya had been obliged to alter her references to Trotsky in the memoirs.[55] Worse was to follow. Stalin never banished the Lenin cult, but in the later thirties he began to reduce the volume of publication about Lenin. Her memoirs were not reissued after 1934, even though she extended her coverage of Lenin's career in the form of articles, which she no doubt wanted to include in a new edition. As late as January 6, 1939, she was still adding to her memoirs of Lenin. In these years she was also attempting to write her autobiography, collecting material on her father's revolutionary activity and even drafting some of the book, none of which has been published.[56] It is unlikely that she had been told that in August 1938 Stalin had issued secret decrees which, in the words of a later party resolution, "actually led to the imposition of a ban" on works about Lenin.[57]

The seventieth birthday of Nadezhda Konstantinovna Krupskaya fell on February 26, 1939; she was looking forward to this less than to the Eighteenth Party Congress, scheduled for the following month. Despite a recurrent heart problem during the later thirties, it seemed likely that she could receive the ceremonial greetings and take part in the meetings.[58] She was still able to arise at about five or six in the morning and put in a long day quite regularly. On February 23 she read twenty-five letters and attended a meeting of the Council of People's Commissars of the Russian Federative Republic, and in the evening was driven out to Arkhangelsk for a routine day off. On the 24th the old-timers there held a modest birthday party for her, and there was much reminiscing. That night, however,

Krupskaya fell ill, was rushed to the Kremlin hospital, and soon lost consciousness. She revived once the following evening and declared, "Do as you please, but I am going to the congress." The Soviet press duly celebrated her birthday on the 26th with dozens of empty, ceremonious congratulations, which Krupskaya never saw. She suffered an abdominal embolism in connection with general arterial sclerosis, and there was nothing to be done. She died at 6:15 a.m. on February 27.[59]

CHAPTER XI

Epitaphs

Stalin gave Krupskaya a decent funeral.[1] She died early on February 27, 1939. At ten p.m. the next day her body was lying in state in the Hall of Columns, her three medals pinned to her dress. Stalin, Voroshilov, Molotov, Kalinin, Kaganovich, Mikoyan, and Andreev came first to pay their respects, then the public was admitted. For twenty-four hours ordinary Soviet citizens, an estimated half million of them, filed mutely past. The account in *Pravda* stressed the number of children who came. Following the departure of Stalin and his colleagues, various groups of her friends, colleagues, and others took turns standing by the coffin: first the Krizhanovskys, who, like Nadezhda and Lenin, had been married in Siberian exile, and some other old friends; then Lenin's brother Dmitri, his family, and Krupskaya's secretariat; then a variety of persons from different branches of the regime, few of whom had had any special ties with Krupskaya, excepting the widow of Sergo Ordzhonikidze, who had died in suspicious circumstances in 1936. Neither of her long-time superiors in Narkompros was there. Lunacharsky had died of natural causes in 1933, while Bubnov had been arrested in 1937 as an enemy of the people. (How had Krupskaya reacted to this? with terror? with anguish? with grim satisfaction?) An honor guard from the various branches of the armed forces was also on duty.

Shortly after the doors of the hall were closed at eleven p.m. on March 1, the body was cremated, and the urn containing the ashes was returned to the hall so that mourners could file past it from 7 a.m. until 3:30 p.m. Then twelve Stalinists, mostly of second- or third-rank status, carried the urn the last quarter-mile to Red Square and the Lenin mausoleum, which Krupskaya had so long avoided. From this podium three suitable Stalinist funeral orations were pronounced — by N. M. Shvernik, A. S. Shcherbakov, and O. F. Leonova. The first two were politicians, the latter a female educator who must have been chosen to do justice to Krupskaya's role as woman and pedagogue. Shvernik and Leonova noted Krupskaya's devotion to Stalin, while Shcherbakov praised her hatred for the "enemies of the people, the Trotskyite-Bukharinite spies," and her appeal to the people for "merciless struggle with them." The orations finished, Stalin and others carried the urn a short distance to the Kremlin wall, where it was buried, indicated only by a small marker, alongside many other heroes of the Soviet Union.

The Soviet press was for days filled with eulogies and messages from all quarters of the country. The only noteworthy one was a short recollection by Rosa Plekhanova, the aged widow of the father of Russian Marxism, who had died in 1918. It is surprising that she should have been permitted to contribute, for the name of Plekhanov had nearly vanished from Stalinist versions of party history. But it was highly appropriate that Plekhanova should wish to pay her respects to Krupskaya, because Nadezhda had never ceased to do justice to the historic role of Georgii Plekhanov in her memoirs and other writings, Stalin or no Stalin.

But the Leader had no intention of permitting the establishment of a feminine sub-cult of the Lenin myth.

Although he retained the Lenin cult, in somewhat reduced form, as the foundation of his own glory, Stalin had no further need of Lenin's wife. According to one Soviet intellectual who was employed by an educational publication in 1939, the word went out shortly after the funeral: "Do not print another word about Krupskaya."[2] This rule was not totally observed, but until Stalin's death in 1953 very little was heard of Krupskaya in the Soviet Union. Her memoirs of Lenin, which did so little for Stalin's image, were not reprinted, nor her other writings on Lenin. What little was kept alive of her literacy legacy was the work of educators, who at least dared to publish such useful non-political pieces as an essay on "How to Read a Book on Your Own."

It was not Stalin's biological death in 1953, but Khrushchev's assault on his political image in 1956 that liberated the shade of Krupskaya from the Stalinist purgatory. The Lenin cult was being refurbished to compensate for the deflation of Stalin, and the rightful place of honor of the first Leninist was recognized by the new leaders. Her works on Lenin, now reissued, were useful to the new dispensation, and her presence beside Lenin in party history to 1917 was useful now that Stalin was no longer considered Lenin's closest comrade.[3] Moreover, Krupskaya's life after the death of Lenin implicitly provided a moral justification for Khrushchev. If she, Lenin's closest comrade, remained true to the party throughout the worst years of the Stalin terror, it was surely justifiable for Khrushchev to have done the same. Of course, Soviet publications were careful to avoid extended discussion of Krupskaya's, or Khrushchev's, own compromises with the Leader.

A large body of Krupskaya writings emerged, including two short biographies (in general biographies of political figures are not extensive in Russia, nor are there more than one or two about a given person) ; two volumes of memoirs about her; and her *Pedagogical Works in Ten Volumes,* which actually comprises eleven volumes.[4] (This is called "overfulfilling the plan.") A bibliography of writings by and about Krupskaya, containing 528 pages and 5,117 separate entries, appeared in time for the centennial of her birth in 1969. This event was hailed with due solemnity the year before Lenin's centennial temporarily surfeited even Soviet propagandists with this kind of exercise.[5]

Her place in the Soviet pantheon is secure, below Lenin and nobody else. Krupskaya remains the symbol of the liberated woman, the devoted spouse, the loving mother — in sum, the bride of the revolution.

It should be her epitaph, but in a more tragic and ironic sense than Soviet writers can openly admit. As a girl Krupskaya determined to devote her life to humanity, and while still youthful determined that nothing could be accomplished without power, hence revolution. She was already espoused to the revolution when she married Lenin, who embodied it as did no other man in his time. It took toughness to live beside Lenin for twenty-five years — a willingness to be hard on one's self and on others. Despite some waverings concerning Lenin's tactical line in 1917, Krupskaya was tough enough to be his mate.

Although she lived in the shadow of her great husband, Krupskaya's life is marked by a sternness and integrity that is her own. If necessary, she could and did suffer imprisonment, break with Menshevik friends, accept Inessa Armand as a dear comrade, suppress undesirable books, and risk the consequences of smuggling Lenin's testament abroad. Above all she was tough enough not to be personally corrupted by the power that her husband and his party had won, against very long odds.

All this is impressive, and yet Krupskaya was a pathetic figure at the end of her life — a puppet of the dictator whom she hated, bearing witness on behalf of his utmost cruelty and lies. Ironically, this painful conclusion to her life's work is bound up with the unlimited devotion with which she started it. She was devoted to an abstraction — to an ideal revolution that existed for her beyond the realities of history. Like all such ideals it was unqualified and indivisible. This was equally true of her devotion, which would have been adulterated if it had made room for more than one doctrine, one party, one leader. Rejecting the plurality of truth, Krupskaya had no real alternative to continuing her self-sacrificing devotion to the revolution through all vicissitudes. Power could not corrupt her, but it could become corrupt and still command the allegiance of one who was wedded to the revolution.

Concerning Sources

This book is based mainly on materials published in Russian in the Soviet Union. The complete list of books, articles, and documentary publications that were read in the preparation of the present work would be long and of interest only to the specialist. Fortunately, this need not be provided because there is a substantial Soviet bibliographical work: *Nadezhda Konstantinovna Krupskaya. Bibliografiia trudov i literatury o zhizni i deiatel'nosti (Bibliography of Works and Literature concerning Her Life and Activities)* (Moscow, 1969). The 528 pages, and 5,117 numbered entries in this guide include most of the Soviet works consulted in the preparation of the present work, excepting various items in the huge corpus of Leniniana. Only one important Soviet work on Krupskaya has appeared subsequent to the publication of the bibliography: *Riadom s Leninym (Beside Lenin)* (Moscow, 1969), a useful collection of memoirs about Krupskaya. The bibliography itself is not quite perfect concerning the period that it covers. For example, the rather important article by Krupskaya, *"Blizhe k rabochei masse"* ("Closer to the Working Masses") , which appeared in *Pravda,* January 31,

1924, is omitted, but no systematic suppression of inconvenient writings characterizes the bibliography with respect to Krupskaya's own works.

This is not quite the case with respect to works about her. None of Trotsky's writings can be mentioned in the Soviet Union to this day. His *My Life* (New York, 1930) is the most valuable of his books with respect to material on Krupskaya. Also useful is his short obituary article for her: "Umerla Krupskaya" ("Krupskaya Died"), which appeared in his periodical *Biulleten' Oppozitsii*, no. 75-76, 1939. A survey of the materials in the Trotsky archive at Harvard University turned up only one document that is principally concerned with Krupskaya, Trotsky's letter to her on May 17, 1927.

Another Russian language source that was not covered by the Soviet bibliography was the archive of the Paris office of the *okhrana*, or secret police of imperial Russia, which is the property of the Hoover Institution at Stanford University. Most of the pertinent documents found there are cited in chapter V, but some Krupskaya letters not known in the USSR and not used in this book exist in the *okhrana* archive. Some Krupskaya letters from Swiss archives were published in Leonhard Haas (ed.), *Lenin. Unbekannte Briefe 1912-1914* (Zurich, 1967).

Writing by and about Krupskaya in the languages of western Europe or in English is very sparse. Her own *Memories of Lenin* (New York, 1930), reissued with modifications as *Reminiscences of Lenin* (Moscow, 1959), is the best-known of Krupskaya's works that have been translated into English. A number of her letters appear in translation in Lenin, *Collected Works*, vol. 37 (Moscow, 1967), but there is no substantial biography of her in any language except Russian. She appears to a modest extent in the biographies of Lenin by western writers, as well as works of broader scope, such as E. H. Carr's *A History of Soviet Russia* (New York, 1951-1964), Robert V. Daniels' *The Conscience of the Revolution* (Cambridge, Mass., 1960), Oskar Anweiler's *Geschichte der Schule und Pädagogik in*

Russland vom Ende des Zarenreiches bis zum Beginn der Stalin-Ära (Berlin, 1964), and Sheila Fitzpatrick's *The Commissariat of Enlightenment. Soviet Organization of Education and the Arts under Lunacharsky* (Cambridge, 1970).

Two scholarly articles published in the West deal principally with Krupskaya: Leonhard Haas, "Lenins Frau als Patientin bei Schweizer Ärzten," *Jahrbücher für Geschichte Osteuropas*, NF Band 17, 1969, 420-436; and Bertram D. Wolfe, "Krupskaya Purges the People's Libraries," *Survey*, summer 1969, 142-155. Wolfe is also the principal writer on Inessa Armand in *Slavic Review*, 1963, no. 1, 96-114.

The researcher who wishes to track down the sources used in the writing of this book, in addition to reliance on the Soviet bibliography cited, can refer to the footnotes on the following pages. To avoid carrying a cumbersome baggage of this sort, these notes have been reduced to the bare essentials, utilizing the following abbreviations:

("M." throughout the following stands for "Moscow")

Dridzo	Vera Dridzo, *Nadezhda Konstantinovna Krupskaya* (M., 1958)
Ist. Arkh.	*Istoricheskii Arkhiv*
Kras. Arkh.	*Krasnyi Arkhiv*
Lenin i partiia	N. K. Krupskaya, *Lenin i partiia* (M., 1963)
Len. Sbor.	*Leninskii Sbornik*
Levidova	S. M. Levidova and S. A. Pavlotskaya, *Nadezhda Konstantinovna Krupskaya* (Leningrad, 1962)
Mikhailutina	D. K. Mikhailutina, *Propagandistskaia i revoliutsionnaia deiatel'nost' N. K. Krupskoi v period 1890-1900 gg.* (M., 1959)
Okhrana	Okhrana archives, Hoover Institution, Stanford University

O Lenine	N. K. Krupskaya, *O. Lenine. Sbornik Statei* (M., 1960)
Ped. soch.	N. K. Krupskaya, *Pedagogicheskie sochineniia v desiati tomakh* (M., 1960-1963)
Pol. sob. soch.	V. I. Lenin, *Polnoe sobranie sochineniia* (M., 1958-1970) (The fifth edition of Lenin's works)
Prol. Rev.	*Proletarskaia Revoliutsiia*
Riadom	*Riadom s Leninym. Vospominaniia o N. K. Krupskoi* (M., 1969)
Vop. Ist. KPSS	*Voprosy Istorii Kommunisticheskoi Partii Sovetskogo Soiuza*
Vosp. o Lenine	N. K. Krupskaya, *Vospominaniia o Lenine* (second ed., M., 1968)
Vosp. o NKK	*Vospominaniia o N. K. Krupskoi* (M., 1966)

Notes

CHAPTER I

Nadezhda Means Hope

1. For a fuller discussion of Russian women and radicalism, see R. McNeal, "Women and the Russian Revolutionary Movement," *Journal of Social History*, December 1971.
2. *Ist. Arkh.*, 1960, no. 2, 249-250.
3. *Pravda*, 21 May 1937.
4. Walentyna Najdus, *Lenin i Krupska w Krakowskim Ziazku Pomcy-dla Wiezniow Politycznych* (Krakow, 1965), 112.
5. *Ped. soch.*, I, 10; Mikhailutina, 9.
6. *Pravda*, 21, May 1937; *Riadom*, 242.
7. Najdus, *op. cit.*, 112-113.
8. *Vosp. o NKK*, 10.
9. *Ped. soch.*, I, 9.
10. *Ibid.*, 16, 23-27.
11. *Ibid.*, I, 11; XI, 528-529.
12. *Ibid.*, I, 29.
13. *Ibid.*, III, 200-201. Krupskaya identifies the young blasphemer as the son of "Princess Dolgoruky," hence a prince himself and a scion of one of Russia's most aristocratic families, which boasted the founder of Moscow and even Rurik, the legendary founder of the first Russian state. Just how Krupskaya came to know him and how he came to be in her bedroom is a minor, but not very scandalous, mystery. It certainly seems to show that the Krupsky

family, despite its reduced circumstances, was able to meet the right people on occasion.

14. *Sovetskaya Literatura,* 1961, no. 2, 168.
15. A. Tyrkova-Vil'iams, *To, chego bol'she ne budet* (Paris, 1954), 140.
16. *Vosp. o NKK,* 32-37.
17. *Novyi Mir,* 1959, no. 9, 292.
18. *Ped. soch.,* I, 32.
19. Krupskaya's inability to cope with the economic side of Marxism is painfully conspicuous in the first two pages of her famous *Memories of Lenin.* She recalls that "the question of markets interested all of us young Marxists very much at that time [1894]," and "had a close bearing on the general question of the understanding of Marxism." But what this bearing was, she was quite unable to say, although it was clear that the people who disagreed with Lenin about this were completely mistaken and had a "mechanistic" idea about markets. This is about as far as she ever ventured into economic writing.
20. *Ped. soch.,* I, 18.
21. In general, this episode is described in *Ped. soch.,* I, 38-55. Surely the friend who introduced her to the school was Olga Grigor'ev, whom Nadezhda had known at her gymnasium. Olga soon married one Boris Witmer, who was a lecturer at the evening school.
22. *Uchenye Zapiski, Moskovskii oblastnoi pedagogicheskii institut imeni N. K. Krupskoi,* t. 158, 7.
23. *Pravda,* 28, Feb. 1939.

CHAPTER II

The Copper Ring

1. *Vosp. o Lenine,* 12.
   In English translation the words "evil and arid" (*zlo i sukho*) have been moderated by such renditions as "laconic." Her treatment of this first meeting is inadvertently confusing. In the first chapter she says that she learned about Lenin's hanged brother while "we" were returning from the evening at Klasson's. This naturally suggested to some readers that she and Lenin quickly struck up a close relationship. In a later writing, however, Krupskaya makes it clear that this "we" included other comrades rather than Lenin, who did not walk her home at that time. This fits in with other evidence that they saw each other rarely until about ten months later, and it also fits in with Lenin's well established reticence concerning his martyred brother. See *Vosp. o Lenine,* 13 and 382 respectively.

2. Quoted in R. Pipes, *Social Democracy and the St. Petersburg Labor Movement 1885-1897* (Cambridge, Mass., 1963), 53.

3. Mikhailutina, 40; *Vosp. o Lenine,* 23.

4. *Vosp. o Lenine,* 33-34.

5. *Ibid.,* 18.

6. Lenin, *Pol. sob. soch.,* LV, 172.

7. Pipes, *op. cit.,* 85.

8. *Vosp. o Lenine,* 22; Mikhailutina, 42.

9. Krupskaya in *Slavnye Bolshevichki* (M., 1968), 178.

10. *Vosp. o Lenine,* 20.

11. Reid was a prolific writer of thrillers in the late nineteenth century, not the sort of writer whose works would have interested the adult Lenin. Probably his sister Anna was supposed to understand the allusion through some kind of inside family lore among the Ulyanov siblings, who read Reid as children.

12. *Prol. Rev.,* 1924, no. 3, 108-109.

13. *Slavnye Bol'shevichki,* 181.

14. Mikhailutina, 50-52.

15. *Ibid.,* 46.

16. *Ibid.,* 54-55.

17. R. A. Kazakevich, *Mister Paips fal'sifitsiruet istoriiu* (Leningrad, 1966), 172.

18. Mikhailutina, 56-58.

19. The first version is set down by N. V. Vol'sky (Valentinov), who knew Lenin and Krupskaya fairly well in 1904, and heard it from her then. See *Encounters with Lenin* (New York, 1968), 55-58. This corresponds perfectly with a memoir written by Nadezhda in 1938, *Detstvo i ranaia iunost' Il'icha,* reprinted in *O Lenine,* 34. In view of the ordinary frailty of memory and reportage, such consistency is quite remarkable.

20. *Prol. Rev.,* 1924, no. 3, 109-110.

21. The official Soviet biography of Lenin states that she visited him regularly in jail, but offers no evidence. Against this and Stasova's story (both belated and hagiographic), one has not only Anna's memoir of 1924 but also Krupskaya's own recollections, which do not mention visiting Lenin as a fiancée. It is hard to believe that Nadezhda would have overlooked such evidence of her closeness to Lenin, which she stressed to the hilt in all her writings. Moreover, the police did not question Krupskaya about any visits to Lenin. They had a record of her visits to Lidya Knipovich in jail, and Krupskaya attempted to maintain the fiction that Lidya was her cousin, but the question of being anyone's fiancée was not involved. See Mikhailutina, 53-55.

What Krupskaya does relate is a wistful story about Lenin,

feeling depressed in jail, asking that she *and* Apollinarya Yaku-bova stand outside on the street at 2:15 p.m., so that he could catch a glimpse of them through a window on the way to the exercise-yard. This did not work, though Nadezhda was on the spot three times. See *Vosp. o Lenine,* 24. In short, Krupskaya her-self implicitly supports the interpretation offered here: Lenin did not tell her of his feelings for her until after he left the jail.

22. Dridzo, 22.

23. *Prol. Rev.,* 1924, no. 3, 119. There is implicit but convincing evi-dence in Lenin's letters to his mother and sisters in December 1897, that there was such an understanding. See below, fn. 27.

24. *Prol. Rev.,* 1924, no. 3, 119. Robert Payne in *The Life and Death of Lenin,* 205, says that Lenin proposed to Apollinarya before he was arrested. This would not be incompatible with the present interpretation, but no evidence is offered by Payne.

25. *Pol. sob. soch.,* LV, 33.

26. There was one minor exception. Krupskaya may have subscribed in her own name to the newspaper *Financial News,* because she could do so at a reduced rate as an employee of the state rail-road office, a division of the ministry that published this paper. She had no interest in it, but Lenin's idea was that she would forward it to him, probably as an economy measure for him. This could be done without using a return address that might prove incriminating. See *Pol. sob. soch.,* LV, 45.

27. *Pol sob. soch.,* LV, 59; 65; 67.

28. *Kras. Arkh.,* 1934, no. 1, 123. The letter from Krupskaya to Lenin agreeing to come as his fiancée, which must have arrived between January 4 and 7, has not been found — or at least has not been published.

29. *Ibid.,* 123.

30. A. G. Ivankov, *Lenin v sibirskoi ssylke (1897-1900)* (M., 1962) 129; Ts. S. Bobrovskaya, *Lenin and Krupskaya* (New York, 1940), 14-15.

31. Dridzo, 16, who attributes this casual reply to Nadezhda's "shy-ness, embarrassment, and fear of high-flown phrases." This is not incompatible with the present interpretation of the courtship. Dridzo and other Soviet writers are inhibited from frank dis-cussion of all this because it is no longer proper in the Soviet Union to be less than reverent toward legal marriage.

32. *Pol. sob. soch.,* LV, 67, 72, 84.

33. *Pol. sob. soch.,* LV, 388. Lenin's letters on the project are in *Pol. sob. soch.,* LV, 70, 77, 81, 82, 87.

34. *Pol. sob. soch.,* LV, 391-392. The collected letters of Lenin's rela-tives (other than Krupskaya) form a whole book, in which Nade-

zhda's name appears rarely. Although the evidence is negative, it points to the conclusion that Krupskaya was never really accepted by her mother-in-law. See *Perepiska sem'i Ul'yanovykh, 1883-1917* (M., 1969).

35. *Pol. sob. soch.*, LV, 69. The separate room was waiting for Nadezhda and her mother when they arrived. See *Vosp. o Lenine*, 28.
36. *Ibid.*, LV, 73.
37. *Ibid.*, 89.
38. Ivankov, *op. cit.*, 129, 140.
39. *Ibid.*, 140.
40. Dridzo, 18.
41. S. Beliaevsky, *Lenin v Shushenskom* (Krasnoyarsk, 1960), 19.

CHAPTER III

Siberian Honeymoon

1. Lenin was born with the family name Ulyanov, and he had not yet assumed his famous pseudonym at the time of his marriage. Upon marrying, Krupskaya therefore became "Ulyanova," and according to Russian practice should have dropped her maiden name entirely. This is what she did in various formal legal signatures, both before and after 1917. For conspiratorial purposes in the prerevolutionary years she also adopted the name Sablina, which she signed to her first literary effort. Unlike the name Lenin, her pseudonym did not become her customary name, nor did her legal name Ulyanova. Instead, she remained Krupskaya to her comrades and posterity. It is not clear how this came about. Feminism does not account for it, considering that such contemporary Russian Marxist women as Kollontai, Armand, and Krizhanovskaya went by their legal, married names.
2. *Vosp. o Lenine*, 32.
3. Dridzo, 20.
4. *Pol. sob. soch.*, LV, 391-392, 400-402, 394-395.
5. *Ibid.*, 561.
6. *Ibid.*, 94, 104, 105.
7. *Ibid.*, 145, 147.
8. *Ibid.*, 409-410.
9. *Ibid.*, 101.
10. *Ibid.*, 409-410.
11. *Ibid.*, 401.
12. *Ped. soch.*, I, 71-102.
13. *O Lenine*, 163.
14. *Pol. sob. soch.*, LV, 416.

15. *Ibid.*, 419.
16. *Ibid.*, 422-424.
17. *Pol. sob. soch.*, XLVI, 34-37. The letter was not encoded, but was written in a clear hand on lined paper, exposing Krupskaya to the maximum risk, which was not very considerate.
18. *Vosp. o Lenine*, 43-44.

CHAPTER IV

First Secretary of the Bolshevik Party

1. *O Lenine*, 21.
2. L. Fotieva, *Iz zhizni Lenina* (M., 1967), 10-11.
3. *Pol. sob. soch.*, LV, 433.
4. *Vosp. o Lenine*, 61.
5. Lidya Dan, quoted in I. Getzler, *Martov. A Political Biography of a Russian Social Democrat* (Cambridge, 1967), 64.
6. Valentinov, *op. cit.*, 79.
7. *Ist. Arkh.*, 1958, no. 2, 10.
8. *Vosp. o Lenine*, 50.
9. *Ibid.*, 64.
10. *Kras. Arkh.*, LXII, 147 ff.
11. *Okhrana*, XVIIA, folder B.
12. *Pol. sob. soch.*, XLVI, 199.
13. E. G. Mikhailutina; Levidova.
14. *Ist. Arkh.*, 1959, no. 1, 11-35. An example of her precious address-books appears in *Ist. Arkh.*, 1958, no. 1, 11-35.
15. *Vtoroi s'ezd RSDRP. Protokoly* (M., 1959), 569-570.
16. *Ibid.*, 582.
17. *Ibid.*, 566-583.
18. *Protokoly 2-go ocherednogo s'ezda Zagranichnoi Ligi Russkoi Revoliutsionnnoi Sots.-demokratii* (Geneva, 1904), 34.
19. The clash between Krupskaya and the Menshevik editors of *Iskra* is covered in *Len. Sbor.*, X, 31-34, 101-104.
20. Mikhailutina, N. K. *"Krupskaya — Sekretar' leninskoi 'Iskry',"* *Vestnik Moskovskogo Universiteta. Istorikofilologicheskaia seriia,* 1959, no. 4, 37; it is implied in several letters by Krupskaya, such as *Len. Sbor*, X, 102.
21. *Len. Sbor.*, X. 38-40, 59-60.
22. *Ibid.*, XV, 178, 212, 226.
23. *Ibid.*, X, 347-348.
24. *Pol. sob. soch.*, LV, 235.
25. *Len. Sbor.*, XV, 208, 210, 214.
26. *Ist. Arkh.*, 1955, no. 1, 21. For other examples, see 18, 20.

27. *Prol. Rev.*, 1925, no. 6, 51.
28. *Tretyi s'ezd RSDRP. Protokoly* (M., 1959), 153.
29. Dridzo, 30.
30. The very place that had provided her with her pseudonym "Sablina," for she had known it as a girl.
31. *Revoliutsiia 1905-1907 gg. v Rossii. Dokumenty i materialy. Vtoroi period revoliutsii 1906-1907 gody, kniga pervaya* (M., 1955), 116.
32. *Pol. sob. soch.*, LV, 240.
33. *Ist. Arkh.*, 1959, no. 1, 36; concerning evidence on her financial responsibility in 1912-1914, see *Vop. Ist. KPSS*, 1969, no. 2, 77.
34. *Okhrana*, XVIIIA, folder B.
35. Although the index of the minutes of the congress, as published in 1963, shows Krupskaya as a delegate with a consultative vote, the actual proceedings simply record the rejection of her claim to be a delegate.
36. *Okhrana*, XVIIIA, folder B. According to an annex to this letter, the party had just come into 60,000 rubles from an insurance policy on the life of the industrialist Savva Morozov, a wealthy sympathizer who committed suicide. Gorky's consort, Maria Andreeva, received the full value of this policy, 100,000 rubles, and passed 60,000 to the party. The accounting shows this amount at the disposal of the "commission," while almost 40,000 were paid to a mysterious "Mr. K" and an "agent" called "P. N." The whole affair was malodorous and payoffs were necessary, but the reasons for them are not clear in detail.

CHAPTER V

Comrade Inessa

1. *Len. Sbor.*, XIII, 165.
2. *Okhrana*, XVIIA, folder 1a.
3. *Ist. Arkh.*, 1959, no. 1, 36-49.
4. *Vosp. o Lenine*, 1966. Zhitomirsky, who offered Lenin advice at this time, was the police agent.
5. *Ibid.*, 173.
6. The first serious account of the Lenin-Inessa affair was Valentinov's *Encounters with Lenin* (original Russian language edition, New York, 1953), 59-62. The major essay, substantially extending the investigation, is Bertram D. Wolfe's "Lenin and Inessa Armand," *Slavic Review*, 1963, no. 1, 96-114, amplified in his book *Strange Communists I Have Known* (New York, 1965), 138-164. Concerning another alleged rival of Krupskaya, see R. H. McNeal, "Lenin and 'Lise de K . . . ': A Fabrication," *Slavic Review*, 1969, no. 3, 471-474.

7. Jean Fréville, *Lénine à Paris* (Paris, 1968), 108.
8. Jean Fréville, *Inessa Armand* (Paris, 1957) and P. Podliashuk, *Tovarishch Inessa* (M., 1965).
9. In a memorial essay on Inessa, written in 1926, Krupskaya places Inessa's arrival in Paris in 1909, but this contradicts Krupskaya's own memoirs as well as biographies by Fréville and Podliashuk.
10. *Okhrana*, XVIIA, folder B.
11. L. Fotieva, *Iz zhizni Lenina, op. cit.*, 10; *Vospominaniia o V. I. Lenine*, 72.
12. These excerpts are from a letter to Inessa from Lenin, discussing the book that she hoped to write on love. The first two quotations are Inessa's own words, according to Lenin, while the third quotation may be his paraphrase of her ideas. Inessa's letter and draft on love have not been published. *Pol. sob. soch.*, XLIX, 56.
13. *Okhrana*, XVIIA, folder B; *Ist. Arkh.*, 1961, no. 2, 112-114.
14. *Prol. Rev.*, 1925, no. 110-143.
15. There were some efforts to revive it, especially with a view to providing Lenin with loyal delegates for a conference that he convened in Prague in January 1912, but it appears from surviving correspondence that Krupskaya's role in this was modest. Probably because Lenin realized that the police could now intercept many party letters, he preferred to rely on agents, such as Sergo Ordzhonikidze, for vital communications. In an intercepted "chemical" letter of March 19, 1913, Krupskaya shows she was well aware that her communications were insecure. *Okhrana*, XVIIA, folder B.
16. *Vosp. o Lenine*, 230.
17. Krupskaya (ed.). *Pamiati Inessy Armand* (M., 1926), 8.
18. *Vosp. o Lenine*, 230.
19. *Preuves*, April, 1952, 17.
20. Alexandra Kollontai, *Bol'shaia Liubov* (M., 1927); in English: *The Great Love* (New York, 1929). This curious work had been completely forgotten until an enterprising young American scholar turned it up: Kendall Bailes in "Alexandra Kollontai," *Cahiers du Monde Russe et Soviétique*, 1965, no. 4, 471-496. Since he wrote, the Russian edition of the work has been located at the Harvard Library.
21. *Okhrana*, XVIIA, folder 1a.
22. *Pol. sob. soch.*, LV, 322.
23. *Ibid.*, XXI, 658.
24. *Vop. Ist. KPSS*, 1969, no. 2, 77.
25. *Vosp. o NKK*, 82.
26. *Narodnoe Prosveshchenie*, 1963, no. 7, 17-20.
27. *Ist. Arkh.*, 1957, no. 1, 26.

28. *Prol. Rev.*, 1925, no. 8, 124. Evidence that Stalin was using "Salin" as a pseudonym at this time appears in his *Sochineniia*, II, 233. He was also using the similar "Solin" — see 236, 243, 247. A meticulously researched essay by Ralph Carter Elwood, "Lenin and *Pravda*, 1912-1914," which will appear in *Slavic Review*, shows that there was no other editor of *Pravda* with a similar name and that Lenin was just as displeased with the editors of the paper as Krupskaya's remark indicates. His principal annoyance was the "conciliationism" of the paper's editors, that is, their moderation toward socialist sects other than his. In this context it may be that the puzzling association of Stalin and the Bund simply means Menshevism in general. In August 1912 Trotsky had convened a largely Menshevik conference in Vienna as a counterweight to Lenin's Prague conference earlier that year. Among the un-Leninist acts of the Vienna conference was a reconciliation with the Bund. Given the Bolshevik tendency to lump all heresies into one, it is possible that Krupskaya's reference to the Bund is a careless shorthand for "soft on Menshevism."

29. The most extended discussion of Stalin as a police agent is Edward Ellis Smith, *The Young Stalin* (London, 1968).

30. *Vospominaniia o V. I. Lenine*, 444.

31. *Pol. sob. soch.*, LV, 337-338, 511-512; *Prol. Rev.*, 1925, no. 8, 127.

32. *Pol. sob. soch.*, XLVIII, 179.

33. *Ibid.*, 191, 201.

34. *Ibid.*, LV, 343-344.

35. The meticulous and authoritative account of Krupskaya's medical problems and their treatment in this period is Leonhard Haas, "Lenins Frau als Patientin bei Schweizer Ärzten," *Jahrbücher für Geschichte Osteuropas*, 1969, no. 3, 420-436. Dr. Haas had access to medical archives in Switzerland.

36. *Pol. sob. soch.*, LV, 346.

37. *Vosp. o Lenine*, 230-231.

38. *Pol. sob. soch.*, XLVIII, 299. The most detailed analysis of Lenin's letters to Inessa appears in Bertram Wolfe's works, cited above.

39. *Ibid.*, XXIV, 552. The chronological entry here makes it pretty clear that Soviet archivists have this letter, which is undated but had to be written before January 9, the date of the speech. But the letter does not appear in vol. XL as it should.

40. *Ibid.*, LV, 351.

41. *Okhrana*, XVIIA, folder 1a.

42. Documentation of this whole affair is found in *Ist. Arkh.*, 1955, no. 4, 25-53. See also *Pol. sob. soch.*, LV, 446-449. *Rabotnitsa* did publish an article by Krupskaya, but not the one referred to above. See *Ped. soch.*, I, 219-222.

43. *Len. Sbor.* II, 179.
44. *Vosp. o Lenine,* 250.
45. *Ibid.,* 263.
46. *Okhrana,* XVIIA, folder 5. The identification *"maîtresse de Lénine"* occurs in two reports of the *sûreté* to the *okhrana,* one dated 19 April 1916, another 31 May 1916.
47. *Pol. sob. soch.,* XLIX, 174.
48. *Ist. Arkh.,* 1960, no. 3, 106-125.
49. *Ibid.,* 1961, no. 2, 115-118.
50. *Len. Sbor.,* X, documents 11-113 *(passim)* ; *Prol. Rev.,* 1925, no. 8, 130-137.
51. *Ist. Arkh.,* 1961, no. 5, 100-106.
52. Alfred E. Senn, "Russian Emigré Funds in Switzerland, 1916," *International Review of Social History,* 1968, no. 1, 76-84.
53. *Narodnoe Obrazovanie,* 1959, no. 2, 84-93.
54. *Ped. soch.,* I, 161-177.
55. *Ibid.,* XI, 170, 172-174.
56. *Ibid.,* I, 249-350.
57. *Pol. sob. soch.,* XLIX, 182-183; *Ped. soch.,* vol. 11, 167.
58. *Pol. sob. soch.,* LV, 454; 369-370; *Ped soch.,* XI, 351-354.
59. *Pravda,* 27 February 1929.

A Quiet Revolution

1. Leonhard Haas (ed.), *Lenin. Unbekannte Briefe 1912-1914* (Zurich, 1967) , 60.
2. *Pol. sob. soch.,* XLVIII, 245, 260-261.
3. *Vosp. o Lenine,* 289.
4. Quoted in Michael Futrell, *Northern Underground. Episodes of Russian Revolutionary Transport and Communication through Scandinavia and Finland 1863-1917* (New York, 1963) , 154.
5. *Riadom,* 99.
6. *Vosp. o Lenine,* 297.
7. *Ibid.,* 301.
8. Stasova, *Stranitsy zhizni i bor'by* (M., 1957) , 84.
9. "Memoirs of George Denicke" (Mimeographed, Harvard Russian Research Center) , 41.
10. *Vosp. o Lenine,* 296.
11. *Velikaia Okt'iabrskaia Sotsialisticheskaia Revoliutsiia. Dokumenty i materialy. Iiunskaia demonstratsiia* (M., 1959) , 486.
12. *Ped. soch.,* I, 403.
13. *Vosp. o Lenine,* 299.

14. Zhdanovskaya, "*N.K. Krupskaya v period Velikogo Oktiabria*," *v bor'be za pobedy Oktiabria* (M., 1957), 233, confirmed by Stasova in *Riadom,* 17.

15. *Vop. Ist. KPSS,* 1959, no. 9, 196.

16. *Ped. soch.,* I, 427-429.

17. Levidova, 124, 125, 127.

18. *Ped. soch.,* I, 436.

19. *Vosp. o NKK,* 101.

20. *Vosp. o Lenine,* 309-310.

21. *Soldatskaya Pravda,* 26 May 1917; *Lenin i partiia,* 18.

22. *Vosp. o Lenine,* 314.

23. *Ibid.,* 314-315.

24. *Ibid.,* 317-319.

25. Recent Soviet historical study, while respectful of Krupskaya, tends to favor the earlier date of arrival. See *Istoriia KPSS v shesti tomakh* (M., 1967), III, part 1, 301. The picture is clouded by the recollections of Fofanova in recent years. In a memoir of 1969 (*Riadom,* 98-108) she states that Krupskaya accompanied Lenin to Fofanova's apartment and stayed with him for two days. This is most unlikely. Krupskaya's famous memoirs, which miss no opportunity to show her close association with Lenin, do not confirm Fofanova's story, and in a comment on another writer's work Krupskaya once stated that nobody except Fofanova lived in the apartment while Lenin was there. (*Ist. Arkh.,* 1957, no. 2, 35-36). Fofanova also wrote an article on the date of Lenin's return, in which she attempts respectfully to explain how Krupskaya and she compared recollections while Krupskaya was writing her memoirs (after Lenin's death), and in this case Fofanova does not refer to Nadezhda as a house-guest during Lenin's stay. (*Ist. Arkh.,* 1958, no. 2, 166-169). Very likely a sense of propriety is involved in this confusion. At the time Krupskaya was writing this portion of her memoirs she was more or less under threat of the revelation (real or concocted) of Lenin's interest in other women, and her choice of the later date of his arrival at Fofanova's minimized the period he spent as her house-guest. Much later, when Fofanova wrote, Soviet official historians felt some straitlaced need to defend Lenin's supposedly unblemished monogamy, which Bertram Wolfe's writings on Inessa Armand had called into question. Thus, Fofanova's belated "recollection" that Krupskaya had been present with herself and Lenin may be read as an attempt to introduce a chaperone to the conspiratorial apartment.

26. Zhdanovskaya, *op. cit.,* 245.

27. There is some minor disagreement among the various recollections that Krupskaya set down concerning her activities at this time.

The above account corresponds to the earliest of her memories on the matter (*Vop. Ist. KPSS*, 1960, no. 2, 185). See also *Vosp. o Lenine*, 332; *Riadom*, 107.

28. *Riadom*, 107.

CHAPTER VII

First Lady

1. In February 1918, the Soviet government adopted the calendar in use in the modern world, replacing the traditional Orthodox calendar, which in 1917 ran thirteen days behind. Thus far, this book has used the old Russian calendar for matters pertaining to Russia; henceforth dates will be given in "new style."

2. Dridzo, 53.

3. *Ped. soch.*, XI, 180. This is not surprising in view of the confusion and crisis at Smolny.

4. The Bryant interview is in *The Liberator*, November 1921; the Eyre piece in the *New York World*, February 21-22, 1920.

5. At one point, it was intended that she run in the Bolshevik stronghold of Petrograd, where she was already known in local politics and probably would have been elected. See *Velikaia Okt'iabrskaia Sotsialisticheskaia Revolutiustsiia. Dokumenty i materialy. Revoliutsionnoe dvizhenie v Rossii v sent. 1917 i obshchenatsional'nyi krizis* (M., 1959), 106. However, *Riadom*, 407, shows that she was actually nominated in Viatka and wired her acceptance, a change that is not explained.

6. *Pravda*, 11 April 1919; *Ezhedel'nik Pravdy*, 1920, no. 14, 30-32; *Pravda*, 10 November 1920; *Izvestiia*, 17 July 1918.

7. *Ped. soch.*, XI, 187.

8. *Ibid.*, XI, 179-180. "Adult education" is the nearest American form to the Soviet "*vneshkolnoe obrazovanie*," literally "outside school education."

9. Sheila Fitzpatrick, *The Commissariat of Enlightenment. Soviet Organization of Education and the Arts under Lunacharsky* (Cambridge, 1970), 34. This work, based on extensive use of Soviet archives, is the most valuable study of educational administration in the early Soviet years and provides the foundation for the present treatment of Krupskaya's role in education.

10. *Pol. sob. soch.*, LIII, 134; *Moskva*, 1964, no. 4, 22-24; *Pol. sob. soch.*, LI, 278; *Ped. soch.*, XI, 245, 260.

11. *Pol. sob. soch.*, LV, 374.

12. *Izvestiia*, 1 December 1917.

13. *Ped. soch.*, I, 48, 36, 24.

14. *Ibid.*, XI, 190. Krupskaya's emphasis.

15. *Ibid.*, 203.

16. *Pravda*, 23 February 1921.

17. *Sovetskaia Pedagogika*, 1958, no. 4, 49.

18. *Pol. sob. soch.*, LIV, 52-54.

19. *Ped. soch.*, VII, 58-97.

20. *Ibid.*, XI, 212.

21. *Ibid.*, VII, 164. This figure must have been inflated by counting many part-time volunteers. It suggests that Krupskaya had already developed a sound bureaucratic taste for statistical ostentation.

22. *Pol. sob soch.*, LII, 112. Technically, Krupskaya may have headed Glavpolitprosvet as early as November 1920, but illness prevented her active exercise of this power at the end of that year, and there were alternative candidates for the post. Her definitive title to this job was established only in March 1921. The intricacies of this whole period are discussed in Fitzpatrick.

23. She attended party congresses in 1917, 1918, 1922, and 1923, but played no role as a speaker. She was not present at congresses in 1919 and 1920.

24. *Desiatyi s'ezd RKP (b)*. *Stenograficheskii otchet* (M., 1963), 164-167.

25. *Ped. soch.*, VII, 164-168.

26. Both illustrations are based on Soviet archival material in the possession of Sheila Fitzpatrick, who generously made it available to the present writer. The documents are dated 23 May 1918 and 22 August 1918, respectively.

27. *Pravda*, 6 February 1919.

28. Another archival document discovered by Sheila Fitzpatrick.

29. *Ped. soch.*, XI, 744.

30. *Ibid.*, VII, 58-62.

31. The most complete account of this episode is Bertram D. Wolfe, "Krupskaya Purges the People's Libraries," *Survey*, 1969, no. 72, 141-155. Anna M. Bourgina generously provided the present writer with a copy of the second of these directives from the Boris I. Nicolaevsky Collection of the Hoover Institution.

32. *Ped. soch.*, XI, 184-185.

33. *Pravda*, 9 April 1924; *Ped soch.*, VIII, 78-80.

34. *Ped. soch.*, VIII, 79.

35. *Krasnyi Bibliotekar'*, 1924, no. 1, 135-137.

36. *Ped. soch.*, II, 117.

37. *Ibid.*, III, 24-33.

38. V. N. Shul'gin, *Pamiatnie vstrechi* (M., 1958), 47-48.

39. The confused state of Soviet schools in this period is best described in Oskar Anweiler, *Geschichte der Schule und Pädagogik in Russ-*

land vom Ende des Zarenreiches bis zum Beginn der Stalin-Ära (Berlin, 1964).

40. *Ped. soch.,* IV, 31. See pp. 31-37 for the complete drafts of the theses.
41. *Ibid.,* 586-588.
42. *Pravda,* 23 February 1921.
43. *Pol. sob. soch.,* LV, 377.
44. *Moskva,* 1964, no. 4, 23.
45. Vladimir Bonch-Bruevich, *Izbrannye sochineniia* (M., 1959), II, 298.
46. Angelica Balabanoff, *Impressions of Lenin* (Ann Arbor, 1968), 12-13. The execution of Kaplan is confirmed in the memoirs of the officer who was in charge of the Kremlin guard at that time. P. Mal'kov, *Zapiski Komendanta Moskovskogo Kremlia* (M., 1961), 162.
47. *Novyi Mir,* 1967, no. 4, 198.
48. *Pol. sob. soch.,* L, 301.
49. Podliashuk, *op. cit.,* 119.
50. *Pol. sob. soch.,* LI, 261-262, 265.
51. *Prol. Rev.,* 1921, no. 2, 115-119.
52. *Preuves,* April 1952, 17.
53. *Pol. sob. soch.,* LII, 166; LIII, 21-22.
54. *The Liberator,* November 1921.
55. *Novyi Mir,* 1964, no. 12, 220-222. It is true that Krupskaya did have a niece, a daughter of Lenin's brother Dmitri, but she would have been younger at this time and was never close to Krupskaya.
56. *Ped. soch.,* XI, 247.
57. *Ibid.,* 247.
58. *Ibid.,* 276.
59. *Ibid.,* 349.
60. Dridzo, 81.
61. *Pamiati Inessy Armand. Sbornik* (M., 1926).
62. *Pol. sob. soch.,* LIV, 229-231, 241.

CHAPTER VIII

Widow-Designate

1. *Ped. soch.,* IX, 87-92; V, 86-92; VII, 156-163.
2. *Izvestiia,* 1 March 1939.
3. *Pol. sob. soch.,* XLV, 473.
4. *Ibid.,* 710.
5. *Ibid.,* 477. The inverted commas around "conspiratorial" were supplied by Fotieva. Lenin meant the word literally.
6. *Ibid.,* 608.
7. *Ibid.,* LIV, 674-675, with cuts. For full version, see Bertram D. Wolfe, *Khrushchev and Stalin's Ghost* (New York, 1957), 98.

8. *Pol. sob. soch.,* XLV, 591.
9. *Ibid.,* 710.
10. *Ibid.,* 343-346.
11. See below, p. 245.
12. *Pol. sob. soch.,* XLV, 592.
13. *Ibid.,* 593.
14. She read over part of Lenin's critical article "Better Less but Better" in ms. See *Pol. sob. soch.,* XLV, 712.
15. Trotsky, *My Life* (New York, 1930), 484.
16. *Pol. sob soch.,* LIV, 329-330.
17. *Ibid.,* XLV, 486.
18. Trotsky, *My Life,* 484.
19. *Pol. sob. soch.,* XLV, 486, 608.
20. Wolfe, *Khrushchev and Stalin's Ghost,* 277-278.
21. *Pol. sob. soch.,* XLV, 592.
22. *Novyi Mir,* 1967, no. 4, 199.
23. Klara Zetkin, *Erinnerungen an Lenin* (Berlin, 1957), 109. It appears that the grand old woman of German Communism had offered some kind of amateur medical advice.
24. *Ist. Arkh.,* 1958, no. 2, 161.
25. *Vosp. o Lenine,* 463.
26. *Ibid.,* 463-464. The belatedly published version of this memoir contains an ellipsis in the sentence describing what Lenin took from the Kremlin, but it is not clear whether this is merely a literary flourish or an indication of an omission.
27. *Ibid.,* 462. Lenin presumably could see Martov's picture inside black rules, not the print.
28. *Pol. sob. soch.,* XLV, 716-717; Dridzo, 62.
29. *Pol. sob. soch.,* XLV, 717.
30. *Ibid.,* 717.

CHAPTER IX

The Widow and the Legacy

1. Max Eastman, *Love and Revolution* (New York, 1964), 399.
2. I. Stalin, *Sochineniia,* VI, 46-51.
3. *O Lenine,* 11-12. No precise date has been assigned to this document, but its form makes it all but certain that it was intended as a funeral oration. The Soviet editors of the volume in which it first appeared concur in this judgment, placing it *before* the speech that Krupskaya actually did deliver.
4. *Ibid.,* 19-20.
5. Dridzo, 62. Emphasis added.

6. Boris Souvarine and Bertram Wolfe confirm that they heard through Comintern contacts not long afterwards that Krupskaya had strongly opposed the mausoleum and embalming in high party circles — in vain.

7. *Ped. soch.,* XI, 246.

8. Trotsky, *My Life,* 510.

9. In *My Life,* 509-510, Trotsky admits that he had not sent Krupskaya any note of condolence before receiving her letter, and does not mention making any reply to it. His archives contain the Russian text of Krupskaya's letter and would almost certainly contain his reply, had he made one.

10. See below, p. 261.

11. *O Lenine,* 373-378. The occasion was a meeting to mobilize party members for the "Lenin recruitment," a rapid expansion of party membership in the name of the deceased leader. This is generally held to have worked in the interest of Stalin, but Krupskaya supported it. See also *Pravda,* 10 February 1924.

12. Stalin, *Sochineniia,* VI, 69-188.

13. Wolfe, *Khrushchev and Stalin's Ghost,* 258-259.

14. *Ibid.,* 259.

15. E. H. Carr, *A History of Soviet Russia. The Interregnum* (New York, 1954), 359-361. This definitely was not a meeting of the Central Committee as such. A careful study of Central Committee documents shows that it did not meet between January 1924 and the opening of the congress in May. Trotsky calls the meeting of May 22 a *"senoren convent"* (a "meeting of elders"), which had been a practice in the Imperial Duma of Russia but had no repetition beyond this instance in the Soviet regime. In short, it was a body without legitimate status.

16. Trotsky, *The Suppressed Testament of Lenin* (New York, 1935), 13, 30.

17. *Trinadtsatyi s'ezd RKP (b). Stenograficheskii otchet* (M., 1963), 452-465.

18. *Ibid.,* 224-225.

19. *Ibid.,* 229.

20. *Novyi Mir,* 1967, no. 4, 200.

21. *Ibid.,* 202.

22. *Pravda,* 25 January 1925.

23. Carr, *op. cit.,* 285-286.

24. *Bol'shevik,* 1925, no. 16, 71-73.

25. Carr, *Socialism in One Country* (New York, 1959), II, 66. York, 1959), II, 66.

26. *Pravda,* 13 December 1925.

27. *XIV S'ezd VKP (b). Stenograficheskii otchet* (M., 1926), 158-166.

28. Stalin, *Sochineniia,* VII, 364-365.
29. *Ibid.,* 382-383. Emphasis added.
30. *XIV S'ezd VKP (b) , op. cit.,* 299.
31. *Ibid.,* 571-575.
32. Trotsky Archives, Harvard University, T880.
33. *Ibid.,* T881.
34. *Riadom,* 273.
35. *Ibid.,* 273-274; *Novyi Mir,* 1967, no. 4, 202-203.
36. Trotsky, *My Life,* 481.
37. *Khrushchev Remembers* (Boston, 1970) , 46, states that a name was mentioned, which Edward Crankshaw believes might be Stasova or Zemlyachka. Boris Souvarine, who had excellent Soviet contacts in this period, told the present writer that Artiukhina's name was the one mentioned in current gossip.
38. *Biulleten' Oppozitsii,* 1939, no. 75/76.
39. *Pamiati Inessy Armand* (M., 1926) .
40. Stalin, *Sochineniia,* VIII, 355.
41. Trotsky Archives, T950. The full text of this important document is scheduled for publication in *International Review of Social History* in 1973.
42. *Pravda,* 3 August 1927.
43. *Ped. soch.,* III, 285-290.
44. *Pravda,* 5 November 1927.
45. *Vosp. o Lenine,* 191.
46. *Pravda,* 28 October 1936.
47. This affair was first brought to light by Michael Katkov in *The Trial of Bukharin* (New York, 1969) , 48-49.

CHAPTER X

Mother of Her People

1. *Pravda,* 23 May 1925.
2. *Vosp. o Lenine,* 52-53.
3. *Riadom,* 226.
4. *Ist. Arkh.,* 1957, no. 2, 29-31, 37.
5. *Ibid.,* 38 (cf. other documents in the same article) .
6. *Leninskie obstanovki v oblasti kultury* (M., 1934) , 43.
7. *Narodnoe Obrazovanie,* 1959, no. 4, 77.
8. *Ist Arkh.,* 1957, no. 4, 77.
9. *Pravda,* 9 February 1928.
10. Dridzo, 68.
11. Memoirs of L. L. Sabaneev in Columbia University Russian Archive, 29.

12. *Ist. Arkh.*, 1958, no. 4, 69, 76.
13. Dridzo, 69.
14. *Ped. soch.*, V, 141.
15. Dridzo, 95.
16. *Ped. soch.*, V, 415.
17. *Izbrannie pedagogicheskie sochineniia* (M., 1955), 808.
18. *Ped. soch.*, V, 601.
19. *Ibid.*, VI, 318-325.
20. *Zhenshchina strany sovetov — ravnopravnyi grazhdanin. Sbornik* (M., 1938).
21. *Ped. soch.*, XI, 403. See also vol. 7, 534-557, 666-693.
22. *Narodnoe Obrazovanie*, 1959, no. 2, 77.
23. *Ped. soch.*, IV, 182.
24. The information on Krupskaya's attempted resignation is based on an interview with Sheila Fitzpatrick, who learned this from reliable Soviet sources.
25. *Ped. soch.*, IV, 269ff.; 296-298; 340-341, 346-349.
26. *Direktivy KPSS i postanovleniia sovetskogo pravitel'stva o narod-nom obrazovanii* (M., 1947), 151-159.
27. *Riadom*, 324-325. Sheila Fitzpatrick was told in the Soviet Union that there were numerous instances of rudeness by Bubnov toward Krupskaya.
28. *Ped. soch.*, IV, 574-576, 611. This appeal was also addressed to Andreev, a party leader with whom Krupskaya had little acquaint-ance, but who was regarded as a moderate among the Stalinists.
29. *Ist Arkh.*, 1960, no. 2, 184; *Ped. soch.*, XI, 628-630.
30. *Vosp. o NKK*, 165. The article eventually appeared in 1960 in *O Lenine*, 106.
31. *Ist. Arkh.*, 1960, no. 2, 185.
32. *Pravda*, 20 January 1929.
33. *Pravda*, 8 June 1929.
34. *Chto govoril Lenin o kolkhozakh i o mel'kom krest'ianskom khoziaistve* (M., 1930). A similar, shorter piece is *"Lenin i kolkhoznom i sovkhoznom stroitel'stve"*, in Krupskaya, *Lenin i partiia* (M., 1933). The distinct "right deviation" in these works is clear enough that they have never been reprinted in the post-Stalin period, despite the publication of many volumes of re-issued Krupskaya writings.
35. *Ped. soch.*, XI, 402. See also *Ped. soch.*, II, 369-383; XI, 316; *Narodnoe Obrazovanie*, 1959, no. 2, 77.
36. *Khrushchev Remembers*, 45. This is confirmed in general by R. Medvedev, *Let History Judge* (N.Y., 1971), 88-89, 198, and *Pravda*, 23 May 1930. Medvedev's informants, who allegedly were present at the meeting, seem to have suffered minor lapses of

memory. They recalled that the meeting occurred in the "summer," whereas *Pravda* reports it as May, and they think that Kaganovich led the attack on Krupskaya. According to *Pravda,* which provided a list of the important persons who attended, he was not there. Quite likely the witnesses confused him with Kuibyshev, who delivered the major speech at the meeting.

37. *XVI S'ezd VKP (b)* . *Stenograficheskii otchet* (M., 1931) , 210-214.

38. *Komsomolskaia Pravda,* 8 March 1937. Examples can easily be multiplied. One might single out Krupskaya's accolade to Stalin's *Short Course* on party history *(Ped. soch.,* XI, 737) and a statement in her eulogy (1937) to Maria Ulyanova: "Maria Ilyinicha always bore a special love for Comrade Stalin, understanding his role in the realization of Lenin's behests." *(Pravda,* 5 December 1937) .

39. Cf. *Izbrannie pedagogicheskie sochineniia* (1955) , 708, and *Ped. soch.,* V, 606.

40. *XVII S'ezd VKP (b)* . *Stenograficheskii otchet* (M., 1934) , 73-76. At one point she said: "Everyone knows what an enormous role in this victory [the building of socialism] Comrade Stalin played. . . ."

41. *O bibliotechnom dele. Sbornik* (M., 1957) , 556-562.

42. She did, however, refer to this mythical "center" in a minor piece in 1932 *(Pravda,* 21 October 1932) , which did not form a part of her memoirs. This indicates the pressure that she must have been under to contribute to the Stalin myth.

43. The concept of cleansing the party membership of unworthy persons goes back to Lenin, and Krupskaya undoubtedly accepted this concept, which is not necessarily connected with police action. In 1933 she produced two short sermons in support of the party purge that was then being prepared, but this seemed then to be in keeping with the non-violent purge. See *Rabochaia Moskva,* 3 June 1933, and *Za Kommunisticheskoe Prosveshchenie,* 8 June 1933. The reference of 1931 concerning the "Promparty" — alleged ex-Menshevik "wreckers" in the Soviet economic system — is another matter. Did Krupskaya really believe that these people were foreign agents? They had been Lenin's opponents, but she was scrupulous in her memoirs to give credit to the good intentions of people like Martov and Axelrod. Most likely she was under pressure to conform on this, too. See *O Lenine,* 236.

44. Levidova, 280.

45. *Le complôt contre la revolution russe* (Paris, 1937) , including works by Dimitrov, Ercoli (Togliatti) , Fischer, and Ponomarev as well as Krupskaya. I have not had access to the Russian edition, which was probably the same. Krupskaya also supported the

trials in her preface to the Lenin anthology *Women and Society* (New York, 1938) (there probably was a Russian edition as well, but this embarrassing writing by Krupskaya is not listed in her principal bibliography) and also in a speech to the electors of the Serpukhov district, quoted in *N. K. Krupskaya i politicheskoe prosveshchenie trudiashchikov* (M., 1939), 11.

46. *Biulleten' Oppozitsii*, 1939, no. 75-76.

47. Elizabeth K. Poretsky, *Our Own People* (London, 1969), 172.

48. *Report of Court Proceedings in the Case of the Anti-Soviet "Bloc of Rights and Trotskyites"* (Moscow, 1938), 777.

49. Dridzo, 90; *Vosp. o NKK*, 317. In 1930 she was averaging 30 to 40 letters per day, close to the early 1934 figure (*Vop. Ist. KPSS*, 1969, no. 2, 74.)

50. Dridzo, 90-91. This legend seems to have affected the memory of Khrushchev, who says that Krupskaya was in charge of dealing with citizens' complaints in Moscow in the early thirties (*Khrushchev Remembers*, 45). No doubt she did receive complaints and did badger him about acting on them, but it is almost surely mistaken to say that she held any formal post in this line. In the post-Stalin era Soviet researchers, using archives of many sorts, were careful to record all her official positions, and no doubt would have cited any job in the complaints department if there had been such a thing.

51. Levidova, 275; Medvedev, *op. cit.*, 199, 201.

52. *Vop Ist. KPSS*, 1964, no. 4, 149, which also adds the corroborating detail that the last session of the body that Krupskaya attended was on January 31, 1939.

53. Krupskaya's reaction to the interview is found in V. Shul'gin, *Pamiatnie vstrechi*, 34. Shaw's impression of Krupskaya is mentioned in *The Rationalization of Russia* (Bloomington, 1964), 30.

54. *Oktiabr'*, 1941, no. 6, 20-27; Wolfe, "Krupskaya Purges the People's Libraries," *Survey*, 1969, no. 72, 141.

55. Compare the 1926 ed. of *Vospominaniia*, 80-82, 94, 97 with the 1932 ed. of *Vospominaniia o Lenine*, 66, 75, 77. It is essentially the same book despite the rewording of the title.

56. *Riadom*, 242; *Ist. Arkh.*, 1958, no. 4, 78; *Pravda* 21 May 1937. The autobiographical work mentioned was not the brief sketch that she had already published in 1925 (*Ped. soch.*, I, 9-22). It was a more ambitious project. Part of the draft was shown to a Soviet editor (see *Ist. Arkh.* citation above), but none of it has been published to this day.

57. *Spravochnik Partiinogo Rabotnika* (M., 1957), 364.

58. Vague references to her heart problem in the thirties appear in *Novyi Mir*, 1957, no. 2, 173; *Vosp. o NKK*, 173.

59. Dridzo, 101-102; Levidova, 284; *Pravda*, 27-28 February 1939. The New York newspaper *Novoye Russkoye Slovo*, 14 June 1961, carried an article signed "U. Ton," which suggests that she was poisoned on Stalin's orders to prevent her from delivering an attack on him at a teachers' conference. It is quite incredible that she should have chosen that kind of forum if indeed she had decided to change her stance of the previous decade and make an open attack on Stalin. In addition the writer is ill-informed on various details. He alleges that Krupskaya was the "director of the library section of Narkompros," that her original private secretary was her *sister* but that Dridzo replaced this person *after* Stalin came to power, that she had been ordered to write a school text on Lenin and Stalin in the hopes that she would be insulted at having to write a tract for children and would break party discipline (as if Krupskaya had any reluctance to write tracts for children). According to this tale, Krupskaya appeared to be in good health shortly before her death (despite considerable photographic evidence to the contrary) and died after Dridzo poisoned her coffee.

CHAPTER XI

Epitaphs

1. *Izvestiia*, 28 February-1 March 1939; *Pravda*, 28 February-3 March 1939.
2. *Vsesoiuznoe soveshchanie istorikov* (M., 1964), 260.
3. *Vosp. o Lenine; O Lenine; Lenin i partiia.*
4. Dridzo; Levidova; *Ped. soch.*
5. *Nadezhda Konstantinovna Krupskaya. Bibliografiia trudov i literatury o zhizni i deiatel'nosti* (M., 1969).

Index

DATE DUE

6/28			
MR 18 '85			
~~MR 18 '85~~			
GAYLORD			PRINTED IN U.S.A.